BK
ANT

D1083927

St.

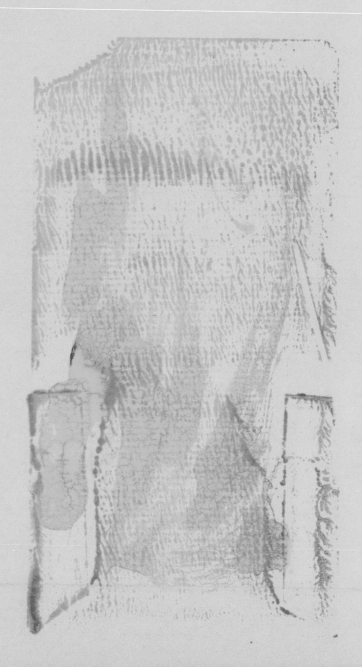

Anton Chekhov
and the Lady with the Dog

VIRGINIA LLEWELLYN SMITH

Anton Chekhov and the Lady with the Dog

Foreword by
RONALD HINGLEY

LONDON
OXFORD UNIVERSITY PRESS
NEW YORK   TORONTO
1973

Oxford University Press, Ely House, London W1

GLASGOW NEW YORK TORONTO MELBOURNE WELLINGTON
CAPE TOWN IBADAN NAIROBI DAR ES SALAAM LUSAKA ADDIS ABABA
DELPHI BOMBAY CALCUTTA MADRAS KARACHI LAHORE DACCA
KUALA LUMPUR SINGAPORE HONG KONG TOKYO

ISBN 0 19 212556 7
© Oxford University Press 1973

All rights reserved. No part of this publication may be reproduced, stored in a retrieval system, or transmitted, in any form or by any means, electronic, mechanical, photocopying, recording or otherwise, without the prior permission of Oxford University Press

Printed in Great Britain by
The Camelot Press Ltd, London and Southampton

Contents

Illustrations

All the plates with the exception of the photographs facing page 171 are reproduced by permission of the Society for Cultural Relations with the U.S.S.R

Foreword

The theme of love—important in almost all fiction—is preeminently so in the work of Chekhov, but with certain far-reaching reservations.

Avoiding 'happy endings', unwilling even to portray intermediate periods of happiness in love, Chekhov confines his evocations of amorous bliss to moments of illusory anticipation or reminiscence. His concern is neither the positive nor yet the negative relationship which man can strike up with woman, but rather the impossibility of man, of woman (of child for that matter) attaining any sort of effective rapport with another human being. 'Intimacy took place' . . . the phrase is familiar from police reports, and can no doubt be appropriate on occasion; but it is rarely so in the works of Chekhov, whose general theme is rather that intimacy did *not* take place. He returns again and again to this theme or non-theme in what, if we cannot call them love stories, we may perhaps call studies in the psychology of cohabitation. The topic is treated with his special feel for the irony of life; for drama which fizzles out as triviality; for the botched pistol shot and the mis-cued seduction.

From handling with tedious frankness the physical aspects of sexual experience Chekhov was precluded both by temperament and by the conventions of his period. Such amorous rapprochements as do occur in his writings—for example, in 'Ariadna' and 'The Artist's Story'—are unconvincing, ill-managed, embarrassing affairs serving only as a prelude to the frustration and nostalgia which he alone can delineate so movingly. No portrayer of the joys of fornication and adultery, Chekhov freed himself by such self-limitation to offer interpretations outside the range of those whose portrayal of sex is more outspoken.

Virginia Llewellyn Smith is admirably unimpressed by the various myths and legends about Chekhov the compassionate, gentle, suffering soul. She has firmly grounded her study on all the available evidence concerning his real-life erotic involvements, bringing in new archival material and fusing rigorous biographical research with a no less rigorous and sympathetic analysis of her author's imaginative writings in their totality. She shows a flair for intelligent speculation within the limits of known fact, together with a rare insight into human relationships; she has not been afraid to match Chekhov's subtlety with her own; she has even, perhaps, dug deeper into her author's psyche than he himself did or could. Her interpretation is therefore likely to shock those who comfort themselves with cosy and quaint illusions about this elusive, shy, cold, and detached artist.

To consider these matters is to marvel that the paths of art and life can diverge so widely. No sane reader would want to *model* his sex life on that of Chekhov or of a typical Chekhovian character. Nor will such a reader feel obliged to accept the Chekhovian thesis that communion between human beings is *a priori* impossible. Yet no perceptive student will fail to appreciate how rich the comments are—on love and on life in general—which Chekhov offers from his eccentric and unenviable angle. These are things which, thanks to Dr. Llewellyn Smith's researches, we can now understand more deeply than before.

Her investigation does not, of course, provide some vulgar solution to the enigma of Chekhov. Much of human personality is, in the last analysis, a mystery—and mysterious Chekhov will remain even after the appearance of this penetrating study. But he will never be the same again, for his creative and personal natures are here more clearly exposed to view than ever before.

RONALD HINGLEY

For Aida

Preface

In nearly seventy years that have elapsed since Anton Chekhov's death on 2 July 1904, there has appeared and there continues to appear an enormous volume of literature on his life and work. In the West this has largely taken the form of criticism from an independent point of view, and of full-length biographies; in the Soviet Union 'Chekhoviana' consists mainly of two types of work: firstly, of memoirs and compilations of memoirs and archive material; secondly, of works apparently motivated by the political necessity of integrating the nineteenth-century figure of Chekhov into the pattern of Soviet reality: criticisms from a Marxist point of view, and treatments of essentially uncontroversial aspects of Chekhov's existence.[1]

Nevertheless, no extensive study of women either in Chekhov's life or in his work has yet appeared. Several of the reasons for this state of affairs are obvious. Earlier in this century most of the memoir material which is a primary source of information on this subject had not been written. And later the other primary source of information—the archives—was not readily accessible to foreigners. Soviet citizens, on the other hand, who have meanwhile had access to these archives, may have had to contend with the assumption that it is frivolous to concern oneself with the private life of celebrated Russians. One elderly Soviet professor of literature drew a parallel between the subject of the present book and an article in some Soviet journal apparently entitled 'Pushkin the Gourmet' (*Pushkin kak gastronom*).[2]

The author of that article may have stooped to the trivial, but he evidently found a publisher. However, writing about matters relating to sex has its peculiar difficulties. Half a century ago those who wrote about Chekhov were conventionally reticent or euphemistic about sex, because their public expected it. And more recently in the Soviet Union writers were reticent about sex presumably because those in high places expected it.

Such an attitude on the part of Soviet Russia is not a reflection merely of prudery. Chekhov is a national asset, and the official image of national assets should not be altered or even tampered with.

Chekhov's official image is lamentably dull. His sex-life was never a part of it, as was inevitably so in the case of, for example, Tolstoy.

Why was this? One of Chekhov's biographers, Triolet, dismissed his sex-life with the comment: 'Autour de lui des femmes, beaucoup de femmes, mais il était, à ce sujet, si discret que l'on se doit de l'être autant que lui.'[3] Such forbearance will probably command sympathy, and indeed would seem admirable, had Chekhov's public image died with him. But it did not. Chekhov's image not only lives on, it has acquired in the process more than a touch of the supernatural.

Any student of Chekhov's life or work will be familiar with the hagiographical style adopted by certain of his critics: 'This star could not be dimmed even in the Russian backwoods';[4] 'Chekhov, this living phenomenon of striking depth, beauty and complexity';[5] '. . . he was a hero—more than that, *the* hero of our time . . . measured by the standards of Christian morality, Tchehov was wholly a saint.'[6]

It has in fact been known for some time that Chekhov was not as holy as that; but the details of his private life have not been helped to the light by this apotheosis—the result of chauvinism, political expedience, or simply blind enthusiasm. If Chekhov has been resurrected, he should have been resurrected in the flesh. Yet pursuing a more clear-sighted approach does present difficulties. Russian sources of information about Chekhov's relationships with women remain largely untapped by Russian critics and biographers,[7] and many writers in the West who have not worked with primary sources—even, in some cases, not with sources in Russian at all—have drawn from Chekhov's fiction and drama concepts about him which can scarcely be reconciled with the facts of his life. Consequently, many misapprehensions exist concerning both Chekhov's private life and his fictional portrayal of personal relationships—a brace of topics that cannot be disentangled one from another. The subject in itself presents a complex picture, but misinterpretation of these complexities has resulted in still greater obscurity and confusion.

A critic writes of Chekhov that he was a misogynist,[8] and Chekhov's work would seem to confirm this, for he paints a picture of womankind that is on the whole extremely unflattering: yet Chekhov himself, stating once that he disapproved of putting women on a pedestal, qualified this by the remark: 'I don't like it when realistic novelists slander women.'[9] However, this appears to be precisely Chekhov's intention. And so the comment strikes us as disingenuous. In fact we find that Chekhov could on occasion be disingenuous to the point of cynicism. Another critic writes: 'Tchehov was never cynical';[10] this is not the case, although he was perhaps more of an idealist than a cynic.

Chekhov wrote: 'In women I love beauty above all things';[11] yet he has been described as 'cet homme froid à l'égard des beautés féminines'.[12] Again, a friend of Chekhov's wrote: 'It was a rare person who could talk with women as he could, touch them, enter into spiritual intimacy with them';[13] yet Chekhov's wife, whom he dearly loved, complained to him that she as a personality was a stranger to him.

Many of Chekhov's biographers and critics have concerned themselves, to a greater or lesser extent, with the facts of Chekhov's private life, and have commented perceptively on Chekhov's relationships with women; and to these the present study is deeply indebted. Yet the contradictions that remain unelucidated would in themselves constitute sufficient justification for a separate, more detailed investigation of the topic. The principal purpose of this study, however, is to demonstrate how immensely important, indeed crucial, to an understanding of the man and the artist is the nature of Chekhov's relationships with women and the portrayal of them in his work.

In the preparation of this book much use was made of certain letters to Chekhov preserved in the *Otdel rukopisei* (Manuscript Department) of the Lenin Library in Moscow. Of those I have quoted, only the letters from L. S. Mizinova are published, and then only in part.[14] I made every effort to consult the originals of Chekhov's letters, from the published versions of which much has been omitted that is almost certainly of relevance to my topic; but I was unsuccessful. The official response to my request to see these documents was, first, that the letters were already published. When I countered that they were published with certain omissions, the answer came that the omitted material was not useful for my subject. I suggested that I was the best judge of that, and was then told that the letters were not available to scrutiny, lest they be damaged. This was not true, for later, through some fortuitous error on my order-slip or on the part of a librarian, a package of Chekhov's letters appeared on my desk; but this particular batch happened not to contain any unpublished material, and unhappily no such opportunity presented itself again. It is to be hoped that at some future date these originals will be freely available to biographers.

The system of transliteration adopted is given below on pages xix–xx. All translations from Russian into English are my own, unless otherwise indicated. In most cases, however, the titles of novels, short stories, plays, etc., are those of previous translators, in particular those used by Ronald Hingley in *The Oxford Chekhov*. With some regret I have not made wider use of his versions, because the series is not yet completed and does not at the time of writing contain many of the works referred to here; also because it has sometimes seemed desirable, in order to make a point clear, to give an exactly literal rendering of the Russian which does not read so well in English as Dr. Hingley's exemplary translation.

All proper names have been retained in their Russian forms. The Index lists non-fictional characters and few fictional ones. In the case of the latter, the reader is directed to the work in which the character appears.

All italics, exclamation marks, etc., are in the original unless otherwise stated. A series of dots in the midst of any passage cited indicates my omission of part of that passage, and three dots in parentheses, *viz.* (. . .), indicate an omission made by the editors of *Works*, 1944–51. All dates are 'old style' (i.e. twelve days behind the Gregorian calendar in the nineteenth century, and thirteen in the twentieth), unless otherwise indicated.

The titles of Chekhov's works are followed in the first instance by the Russian title and the date of publication.[15] In accordance with publishing convention the titles of novels and plays are printed in italics and titles of short stories are printed in roman type within quotation marks.

I owe a special debt of gratitude to Dr. Ronald Hingley, whose comments on Chekhov's relationships with women were the inspiration of this work, and who has given me much help and encouragement. My thanks are also due to Paul Jeffreys-Powell, Professor Edward Brown, and Professor Bram Pais for their advice on various matters; also to N. I. Gitovich for giving me the benefit of her knowledge of archive material. I am indebted above all to my husband not only for moral and financial support but for assistance with the book itself and with the mechanics of my typewriter.

VIRGINIA LLEWELLYN SMITH
STANFORD 1972

B

Systems of Reference and Transliteration

The system of reference adopted throughout this study is as follows:

(i) All quotations from Chekhov's works, including variants, manuscript fragments, and the contents of notebooks, and almost all quotations from his letters, have been taken from: *Polnoe sobranie sochinenii i pisem A. P. Chekhova* (Complete collection of the Works and Letters of A. P. Chekhov), edited by S. D. Balukhaty and others, Moscow, 1944–51 (hereinafter referred to as *Works*, 1944–51).

(ii) References to books and articles are given by citing the surname of the author or editor of the work, and a page reference. Full details of each work will be found in the bibliography. Where two or more works by the same author have been cited in the text, the title or a shortened title of the work in question is given in the footnotes on the occasion of each reference.[16] A few works—mainly *sborniki* (compilations)—which are more readily recognizable by their title than by the name of the editor have been identified throughout by abbreviations of their titles. A list of these abbreviations is given below.

(iii) Details of letters cited are given in full on the occasion of each reference, save that the abbreviations listed below and shortened titles are used when appropriate.

(iv) Archive references are to the Chekhov archive housed at the time of writing in the *Otdel rukopisei* (hereinafter: *Otd. ruk.*) of the Lenin Library, Moscow, and are given according to the system of reference employed there. Thus, the first of the three groups of figures denotes the *fond* (archive); the second the *karton* (box); and the third the *edinitsa khraneniya* ('unit of pre-servation', i.e. file).

The system of transliteration adopted is basically that used by

Soviet Studies, published by the University of Glasgow, but certain alterations to this system have been made in an attempt to strike a balance between forms sanctioned by tradition and unnecessary rigidity (without, however, sacrificing consistency within the method adopted). These alterations are as follows:

1. In the nominative singular masculine case of nouns and adjectives, the endings 'yi', 'ii', have been rendered 'y' throughout.
2. In the case of proper names of persons only:
   (a) The 'soft sign' (') has been dispensed with, in order to avoid the typographically displeasing forms Ol'ga, L'vov, etc. After a consonant and before 'e' it has seemed desirable to replace it by 'i', thus: Leontiev, Ananiev.
   (b) The nominative singular masculine adjectival ending 'oi' has been altered to 'oy', thus: Tolstoy.

Abbreviations

The following abbreviations have been used in the notes, references, and bibliography:

(i) *Titles*

Chvvs	*A. P. Chekhov v vospominaniyakh sovremennikov*, edited by S. N. Golubov and others, M., 1960
LN	*Literaturnoe nasledstvo: Chekhov* (vol. 68), edited by V. V. Vinogradov and others, M., 1960
Perepiska	*Perepiska A. P. Chekhova i O. L. Knipper*, edited by A. B. Derman, 2 vols., M., 1934 and 1936
Works, 1944–51	*Polnoe sobranie sochinenii i pisem A. P. Chekhova*, edited by S. D. Balukhaty and others, M., 1944–51

(ii) *Places of publication*
L. London
LG. Leningrad
M. Moscow
N.Y. New York
SPB. St. Petersburg

I *Introductory*

Lev Tolstoy, meeting Anton Chekhov at Gaspra at the beginning of this century, commented: 'What a nice and a fine man he is! Modest and quiet as a young lady! He even walks like a young lady. He's simply marvellous.'[1] He could not know that he was doing Chekhov's posthumous reputation a great disservice. The most trivial utterances of great men seldom go unremarked. In this instance, the unparalleled reverence accorded to the aged Tolstoy, and Chekhov's fame (soon reaching its zenith with his death in 1904) were the double assurance that Tolstoy's casual comment would be transcribed into numberless biographies and reminiscences.

Not, it might appear, a matter of great importance; but in Russia memoirs of the literary milieu have always been more abundant, and, in recent decades, generally more interesting, than biography and criticism. It has happened therefore that the impressions Chekhov's acquaintances received of him—however superficial and fleeting these might be—have contributed more to posterity's views of Chekhov than has any more fundamental investigation of his life and personality—and such investigations have, in Russia, been few. Judgements like Tolstoy's—and there were many of them—thus attained a currency out of proportion to their significance.

'Modest and quiet as a young lady': Tolstoy's remark, however, was particularly striking and memorable. For Tolstoy's own life and vast *œuvre* were both above all vigorous and colourful in character. They spoke of passionate feelings, of strong sympathies and antipathies: of a down-to-earth, if distorted, view of the world.

And what of Chekhov? He is crystallized *in aeternum* as a gentle, diffident and—to be frank—rather colourless creature. Even the photographs taken of the two writers at Gaspra seem to confirm this image of him. Chekhov's expression is distracted, mild, and pleasant: Tolstoy's, an alert glare. Bad luck on Chekhov, who probably was modest and quiet on that particular occasion, as were, no doubt, many natures more extrovert than his, showing the domineering old man the deference he expected.

There was nothing frail whatsoever in Chekhov's personality. But the effect of superficial observation has been, in his case, incalculably great, and the result is that posterity's view of Chekhov remains essentially unaltered since the decade following his death.

It was in a sense Chekhov's misfortune to be a witness to the disintegration of the Tsarist state. For on one side of the ideological fence he was labelled 'the voice of dying Russia', or something of the kind, and acquired the reputation of a gloomy pessimist, or worse—of a wistful melancholic; on the other side, he was proclaimed a prophet of the glorious Soviet future, and became a wooden figure-head of the new regime. Neither viewpoint has helped to project a more engaging image of the man.

Happily, certain relatively recent works on Chekhov have taken a realistic attitude and gone some way towards dispelling the hazy cloud of nonsense which serves as Chekhov's halo.

'Chekhov was no angel nor a person of exceptional virtue,' asserted one of his closer acquaintances, 'but a man in the full meaning of the word.'[2] It is the present writer's purpose to demonstrate how little indeed Chekhov, as man and artist, resembled the Chekhov of still-prevalent conceptions.

Although an investigation of his life and work reveals quite clearly the main traits of his personality, Chekhov does present his biographers with a formidable barrier in the shape of his extreme reticence. There are indeed arguments for respecting this reticence: undeniably, Chekhov appreciated personal privacy and disliked any invasion of it. But equally certainly, he would have disliked the thought of the misrepresentation that his image has suffered. 'Don't describe me in your memoirs,' he once told a friend, 'as a man of "attractive talents" and "as pure as crystal".'[3]

Chekhov's was a nature which resists comprehension, because it was composed of two fundamental qualities that would seem incompatible were the human personality less complex than it is. The first of these was a certain coldness, an apparent indifference, that did much to conceal the second aspect of his nature. The second was a capacity for passionate feeling.

This crucial contradiction in Chekhov's personality has received far too little attention, probably as a result of emphasis laid—in the present author's view, mistakenly—on 'sociological' themes in Chekhov's fiction. For it is only in the context of heterosexual relationships—as experienced by Chekhov and as described by him in fiction—that Chekhov can be seen in the round.

R. D. Charques, referring to three women in Chekhov's life —all of whom bore the same Christian name—described them as 'the Lydias of his evasive devotions'.[4] It is an aim of the present study to extend the meaning of Charques's eloquent phrase, showing first what Chekhov was really devoted to, and secondly, how he sought to evade that to which he was devoted.

The 'whys' of his situation beg many questions, which psychologists might perhaps consider only themselves qualified to answer. Yet it is possible, despite the dearth of available evidence concerning Chekhov's private life, to make certain deductions about the latter without reading too much between the lines.

One can also, in the case of nearly every creative writer, make certain broad assumptions on the evidence of his fiction. Of course no critic can ever be on very firm ground when attempting to relate events in an author's life to events in that author's fiction. But where attitudes, not events, are concerned, the case is somewhat altered. Here, it would seem, the essential is to show clearly when and—more important—why a collation can be made, and when and why it cannot. It should seem patently obvious, but it is none the less desirable to emphasize, that in the present study no opinion is assumed to have been Chekhov's simply because a single character expresses it. No apology is made therefore for claiming that, in the particular case of Chekhov, the fiction is even more revealing than the facts. But that is not the main reason for turning to Chekhov's fiction first. If Chekhov's were nothing but a case-history he now would be of interest solely to psychologists. It is his personality as expressed in his art that has a claim on the world's attention. And thus it is a further aim of this study to show that the ambivalence of Chekhov's nature affected his art no less than his life.

Chekhov, by general acclaim one of the giants of the nineteenth-century Russian literary scene, achieved his popularity as a master of the short story. Even the plays which brought him international fame were to some extent extensions of or derivations from the short-story form. Any preliminary understanding of Chekhov requires an understanding of how he made this genre his particular province and triumph.

Some of the reasons for this are fairly obvious. Chekhov differed from the other great prose writers of his country and era in certain fundamental ways. Firstly, although the vicissitudes of his creative life were less striking than those of, say, Dostoevsky, or even of Turgenev, Chekhov's writing was profoundly affected by certain circumstances. Unlike Turgenev, Gogol, or Tolstoy, Chekhov was born a poor man, the grandson of a serf. Writing was for Chekhov not a gentleman's pastime: it was an occupation that must above all prove lucrative. Dostoevsky knew similar financial straits; but whereas Dostoevsky's situation was such that he expanded his already immense novels purely for the kopecks that each additional page assured him, Chekhov at the time of his greatest need worked for low-quality journals where brevity was considered a prime virtue.

Simultaneously engaged in medical studies (and later medical duties), and living in a house full of dependent relatives and noisy friends, Chekhov preserved his talent by learning to write fast, to rely on snap endings and on the inspiration of the moment. Once in 1886 Chekhov told another author, Korolenko, how he wrote. He picked up an ashtray from the table: 'Tomorrow, if you like, there'll be a story—title, "The Ashtray".'[5]

Compare Tolstoy or Turgenev. Both were initially unquestionably dilettante writers, whose literary careers began when they were in their mid-twenties. They developed the habits of leisurely composition: Turgenev once described how he would lie on his sofa thinking about some character for three or four hours at a stretch.[6] Chekhov on the other hand virtually assumed financial responsibility for his family before he was twenty, at which age his literary career had its humble beginnings. This prosaic fact moulded Chekhov's gifts from the start—and criticism of his work must take into account the hurried, *ad hoc* nature of much of his writing.

One circumstance of course interfered with Chekhov's career

for the greater part of his life. This was his tuberculosis, the first symptoms of which manifested themselves in 1884. The effects of illness on his life were very far-reaching. But there is nothing to indicate that his talents would have developed along different lines had he been a fit man. Tuberculosis interfered from time to time with the pace of Chekhov's writing, but not with its style, and cannot be held responsible for that which most markedly differentiates Chekhov from the other great Russian writers of his epoch—namely, that he never proceeded from the forms of the *rasskaz* (short-story) and the *povest'* (short novel, *Novelle*) to write a novel or any extensive piece of fictional prose.

His inability, or unwillingness, to write novels rather than short stories presumably depended to some extent on the mysterious idiosyncrasies of his talent. It is known, however, that Chekhov did attempt to write a novel, when for the first time his situation as regards contracts and finance was favourable. The projected work might, it seems, have had a framework like that of Gogol's *Dead Souls*, or Lermontov's *Hero of our Time*: a series of episodes linked by a connection with a central character. But the attempt never came to anything, and no one will ever be able to state precisely why this was so.

Hypotheses have been put forward none the less, and while they cannot be taken as anything more than conjecture, they do serve to emphasize the basic difference in outlook between Chekhov and the majority of his literary peers; and this difference is of immense importance.

The narrator of Chekhov's 'Dreary History' (*Skuchnaya istoriya*, 1889) bitterly regrets his lack of a 'general idea'. It is the lack of such an idea in Chekhov himself which is sometimes supposed to have been the obstacle to his completion of a novel.

The great Russian novels of the nineteenth century were all built on a foundation of ideas. The specialist in this was Dostoevsky, for whom the idea was the essence of the novel: *Crime and Punishment* derived from the concept of man as superman, *The Devils* from the concept of Westernism as a destroyer of Russia's virtues. The actual plots, often adapted by Dostoevsky from newspaper stories, would have made interesting anecdotes of the *tranche de vie* variety; the ideas broadened the implications of Dostoevsky's novels, and gave them their quasi-metaphysical quality. Even Gogol's fantastic *magnum opus* was regarded by its author as a vehicle for ideas. Turgenev came closer to portraying realistically ordinary, albeit mainly upper-class, life: but Turgenev's characters, excellently delineated, were nevertheless fitted into a schematic framework ultimately derived from Turgenev's political standpoint. Elena, in *On the Eve*, was the girl whose lover had to be a Bulgar (dedicated to saving his country from the Turks): there were no men in Russia worthy of her—an absurd situation, it would seem, but justifiable according to the terms in which Turgenev conceived his novels.

Similarly, Tolstoy's great novels are basically *romans à thèse*. The 'war' part of *War and Peace* is a polemic; the 'peace' part, less obviously subordinate to a dominating viewpoint, is nevertheless unified by a sense of history conveyed by the gradual development of the principal characters and changing family fortunes. And the keystone of the whole edifice is, as it is also in *Anna Karenina*, Tolstoy's vision of an ideal family happiness. As for Tolstoy's other works, the majority of these quite blatantly serve as the vehicle for some *idée fixe*: only Tolstoy's early works do not seem to seek to express a 'general idea'.

It is these early works of Tolstoy's which most closely resemble the Chekhovian short story. For Chekhov's fiction is not a platform for his beliefs. Indeed, it is extremely difficult to determine from Chekhov's work what were his religious and political convictions—or whether he had any at all.

In fact, Chekhov had no religion; and he was not a 'political' writer by the standard of the many acutely politically conscious Russian intellectuals of his age—although he did, of course, evince in his work several common ethical attitudes, such as a hatred of tyranny. That he sought to propound no philosophical beliefs is less certain, for many of his characters indulge in the intellectual's predilection for 'talking philosophy', and some of the more sympathetic of them tend towards a particular brand of thought. Yet what they claim to believe in—the future happiness of mankind, for example—seems rather nebulous, and Chekhov could no more be imagined constructing a novel on the basis of this thought than on a religious or a political basis.

Chekhov never imposed a large-scale pattern on his vision of the Russian scene. Frequently he assigned to his characters a role on the contemporary sociological stage—as a 'progressive' girl, say, or as a 'superfluous' man—but the stage *is* a stage. Although they are often depicted with great subtlety, characters are seldom required to develop, because in Chekhov's work situations are described, not seen as part of a process in evolution. Chekhov gives the reader no sense of a historical past, and, save for the hazy concepts mentioned above, little idea of what the future may hold. His Russia has a static quality.

This is of course not to suggest that Chekhov's fiction is without interest for the student of Russian nineteenth-century politics or philosophy. It is simply to say that, whereas other great Russian writers of the time tended to embrace certain political and religious attitudes, Chekhov's way was to reflect the attitudes of others.

To read Chekhov's work after reading Tolstoy or Dostoevsky is like examining the details of some colossal rhetorical painting: standing so close to the canvas, one is not moved by the vision that inspired the whole, nor aware of its pattern. But it is clear that, to the artist who painted them, these fragmented vignettes were an end in themselves, and that as a recorder of detail, he brought to his work such mastery that the trivial was depicted with an emotion and subtlety worthy of the whole. That is how Chekhov's fiction stands in relation to the other great achievements of the Russian realistic school.

A combination of circumstances and his peculiar talent procured for Chekhov the undeniable mastery of his own field— and this in a country where the short story was an art form practised by many. Undoubtedly, his lack of any 'general idea' was an advantage, in that it freed him from restraint and enabled him to run the gamut of humour and tragedy, touching on both the significant and the trivial, while attempting to give the impression of an uninvolved observer of human mores.

Yet Chekhov was not simply a *détailliste* or a social documentarian. There is emotion in his art, and this cannot be ignored: to do so is to lose something vital to any understanding of Chekhov. It is the intention of this study to indicate how profound a part emotion played in his work—and how profound a part it played in his life.

'The Lady with the Dog' (*Dama s sobachkoi*, 1899) is, in the context of Chekhov's emotional life, a work of peculiar significance—but this will become apparent later. It may however be adduced in passing as a notable example of Chekhov's emotional vein transmuted into literary form. It is also probably one of the best known of Chekhov's stories outside Russia, thanks in part to Heifitz's celebrated film of the same name. There is no doubt in the present writer's mind as to which version stands better on its own merits, but one feature of the film has stuck in the memory. In the last scene Anna Sergeevna, the 'lady with the dog', weeps and gesticulates inaudibly behind a window as she watches her lover Gurov walk away. The blatantly tear-jerking quality of this scene is alien to Chekhov; but the pane of glass separating us from the lady is, however crudely, symbolically accurate.

2

Chekhov did have some firm convictions, notably on the subject of literature; and one of the most passionate of these was his belief in the writer's duty to observe and depict what he saw objectively. This seems to have been the cornerstone of his artistic credo. 'The aim [of literature],' he once wrote, 'is absolute and honest truth . . .';[7] and elsewhere: 'The artist must not be the judge of his characters and of what they say, but an impartial witness only.'[8] Again: 'Subjectivity is a terrible thing. It is bad in that it exposes the poor author entirely.'[9] Similar remarks are scattered throughout Chekhov's correspondence.

Perhaps because Chekhov himself took so seriously his function of dispassionately observing the contemporary scene, posterity has almost without exception appeared to take for granted that he actually did so. We have noted the enthusiasm which Chekhov the man could inspire in those who scarcely knew him —or did not know him at all. But no less remarkable are the claims which reputable critics have made about Chekhov the writer. It has for example been asserted that 'never was a writer in world literature more honest, more guided by conscience, more truthful than he';[10] that he 'had no judgement to pass, through either humour or tragedy, on the most ridiculous or the most depraved of his fellow-men';[11] that he 'paints all saints and sinners with an equally sympathetic brush'.[12] One critic even talks of Chekhov's 'great tolerance' only to continue to describe his depiction of 'the natural, the customary, the everyday' as being like 'a series of repulsive grimaces'.[13]

Some of these misleading comments can only derive from the 'Chekhov legend' and the associated idea that Chekhov ('quiet as a young lady') would not have hurt a fly; others, perhaps, from a preoccupation with the political issues reflected in his work, since it is true that Chekhov had no particular political axe to grind. But such a preoccupation can in itself be misleading, since socio-political problems do not constitute the main themes of Chekhov's mature work. The main themes are provided by the subject of relationships between the sexes. For all their merits, those of Chekhov's works which owe their inspiration to other aspects of existence are significantly fewer in number, and in connection with one of them Chekhov made the jocular claim that he could not bear stories which lacked 'a woman and the love-element'.[14]

To say that Chekhov was objective in his depiction of these relationships is clearly nonsense. For few authors, and certainly no other Russian 'realist' of his time, give such a one-sided picture of heterosexual relationships.

To put it briefly, the situation is that in the world of Chekhov's fiction no happy relationship between the sexes is permitted to exist. Love is sought, and not to find it appears to be a tragedy: but when it is found, love becomes a travesty of itself. Chekhov's gloomy view of heterosexual relationships is at once the most immediately striking and the most revealing aspect of his fiction.

2 *Misogyny*

As anyone can testify who has ever read the agony column of a woman's magazine, marriage makes the best copy when its difficulties are greatest. A stable relationship is seldom provocative of comment, whereas, as Tolstoy put it, 'every unhappy family is unhappy in its own way',[1] and therefore interesting. For a novelist, however, it is relatively easy to depict a happy relationship effectively. To begin with, he can use space to chronicle the mundane events that are supposed to lay the basis of family happiness—the birth of children, professional and social successes, and so forth. Also, having the leisure to show how characters develop, he can show how they become fitted for, and perhaps even grow like, one another. (Tolstoy did this admirably with Nikolai Rostov and Princess Marya.)

But the short-story writer must make a bold, brisk bid for the reader's attention. He has to excite interest and arouse a sense of participation as directly as possible. So of course he relies much more on the dramatic: elopements, quarrels, highly charged emotional situations—all the concomitants of relationships in disintegration.

It is therefore not to be wondered at that the theme of discord between the sexes figures prominently in Chekhov's work. What is surprising is the degree of prominence this theme attains. Amongst all those of his works that have the slightest claim to be taken seriously, the instances of flourishing love constitute a mathematically negligible proportion. Chekhov scarcely ever gives us even a peripheral view of a satisfactory relationship. Love-affairs grow stale, marriages sooner or later come to grief. How does this come about?

Notwithstanding the obviousness of the answer, remarkably few critics have seen fit to make a point of it. Toumanova has perhaps been most explicit, although her phraseology is character-istically delicate: 'In general Chekhov has not very much patience with women, and severely criticizes them for the mischief and disorder they create in the lives of their husbands or lovers.'[2] Another critic, Laffitte, takes the bull by the horns: 'Il ne faut pas . . . oublier,' she states bluntly, 'que Tchékov était misogyne . . . ';[3] but nevertheless she leaves largely unexplored the avenues of inquiry that this statement opens up.

And yet the topic is a fascinating one, and the questions it provokes innumerable. How much truth is there in it? Did Chekhov really have little patience with women? What, precisely, are the features of his work that support this view, and why have they received so little attention?

2

The main argument for Chekhov's having been a misogynist is plain. If we ask, what is the prime cause of unhappy love in Chekhov's fiction?—the answer is so obvious as to resolve itself into a cliché: *cherchez la femme*.

This stated, inevitably certain important qualifications must be made. Firstly, it is of great significance that much of the material which suggests that Chekhov was a misogynist is to be found in the earliest part of his work. When he wrote for *Oskolki* ('Fragments'), *Strekoza* ('The Dragonfly') and similar unsophisticated journals during the 1880s, Chekhov was even less scrupulous about the content than about the form of his pot-boilers. Bearing in mind the nature of the public he was working for, he was aiming at cheap laughs, and he obtained them by the more or less indiscriminate use of what passed for satire and ridicule, but was really pure slapstick. Inevitably the 'battle of the sexes' constituted a rich source of humorous themes for Chekhov; however, at this low level the female as distinct from the male of the species is not singled out for ridicule. The point is that someone—or everyone —should look foolish. M. Nevedomsky has correctly remarked that the humour in Chekhov's early stories serves no god except perhaps the god of youth:[4] it is a fresh, unsophisticated brand of mockery, and bias does not enter into it; it can be assumed that the phrase (describing a victim of toothache) 'like a madman, or more precisely, like a husband whose good wife has poured boiling water over him (he rushed . . . , etc.)'⁵—a simile Chekhov used more than once—is there purely for artistic effect, and one feels Chekhov himself might not have recalled his facetious use of the words when he has his brainchild Aksinya (the 'good wife', according to the values of her family) murder a baby in this way in 'In the Ravine' (*V ovrage*, 1900), one of the most bitterly ironic of Chekhov's stories.

On a slightly more sophisticated level, comic satire replaces this sort of verbal slapstick, and it is when Chekhov is writing in this vein that one can begin to suspect feeling behind his words. Thus in 'Statistics' (*Statistika*, 1886) Chekhov refers to 'three terribly tedious letters, written in a female hand and with a female odour to them'. This is the merest thread in the complex web of derogatory reflections on female culture that spans Chekhov's work. Yet there is a sting in the words. By contrast, when such satirical sallies devolve into diatribe, they lose to comic effect at least half their sting. Take, for instance, Smirnov's outburst in *The Bear* (*Medved'*, 1888):

Black eyes, passionate eyes, crimson lips, dimpled cheeks, moonlight, whispers, hesitant breaths—I wouldn't give a fig for all that nowadays, madam! I don't speak of present company, but all women, great and small, are simpering grimacing scandalmongers, full of hatred, liars to the marrow of their bones, vain, trivial, pitiless, with an outrageous sense of logic, and as for this part here (thumps his forehead), if you'll forgive my being frank, a sparrow is ten points ahead of any philosopher in a skirt! (etc., etc.).

Although by their sheer force and vividness—not to mention length, passages such as this⁶ claim our attention, they are not consciously misogynist, but comic, in inspiration; the comic effect, of course, grows in proportion to the length and vehemence of Smirnov's rhetoric.

However, a very great amount of anti-female material in Chekhov's work is not modified in this way, nor is such material weakened, as in 'Statistics', by our being aware of Chekhov's impudence rather than of his thought. At its best Chekhov's method of attacking his victims is a great deal subtler than this, and much more deadly.

It has already been emphasized that Chekhov was not always as objective as he believed he ought to be. He does not praise or blame as bluntly or as sedulously as Tolstoy, but the difference between them is one of artistic methods rather than of degrees of tolerance. Where Tolstoy would make a frontal attack, Chekhov prefers a more indirect assault. His stories are often told by a narrator, and in some cases Chekhov may be suspected of using the narrator to convey his own thoughts. Chekhov also tends to show what his characters are like through their words and deeds, or by a convenient phrase such as 'it was said that', or 'people thought that'; very rarely does he as omniscient author foist his own commentary upon the reader.

In much of Chekhov's work there is an air of restrained emotion, and it would be wrong to assume, because it *is* restrained, that the emotion is not there. Chekhov's restraint is often the most subtle way of arousing emotion. Thus, for example, he seldom describes violent physical action, especially savage action. So the mere slapping of a face shocks his reader: how much more appalling then is the murder of a baby—no one knows better than Chekhov how to appal his readers. We note that when such a murder occurs, in 'Sleepy' (*Spat' khochetsya*, 1888), the climax is achieved in two words that, grammatically speaking, lack emphasis in the sentence: *Zadushiv ego* ('Having smothered him').
. . . This back-handed style is of course a sophisticated method of obtaining the desired effect.

The fact that Chekhov wrote so many separate works makes a valuable contribution to our knowledge of his likes and dislikes: for, within the individual framework of each short story or play, the same character types and situations reappear to an extent that would be hard to find in the work of even the most prolific novelist. We become familiar with the elements of Chekhov's themes, elements from which he constructed countless variations. Thus, we come to recognize situations where Chekhov's sympathies will be pre-determined (for example, in cases involving children)—and to be on guard against having our sympathies manipulated. The rather precocious remark of an eight-year-old boy, describing his mother (of whom Chekhov disapproves): 'You see, she's a woman . . . and women always have some ache or pain'[7]—is a typical example of an attempt at manipulation.

Possibly, Chekhov's reputation for objectivity has been bolstered by readers familiar with only a small part of his literary output. For his antagonisms are perhaps only fully recognizable as such when one has read more than one of his works. Take, for instance, Chekhov's use of the adjective *tolsty*. To call a person fat, one might think, is not to damn him—until one deduces from the various contexts in which this epithet appears that it is indeed intended to be damning.

It becomes clear in fact that Chekhov has his own methods of attack which for all their obliquity are none the less damaging; and in certain cases, when confronted with some trait that he particularly disliked, Chekhov could depict with subtle savagery both men and women alike.

What then did he dislike? The evidence of his fiction is that he looked with strong disfavour on what has been accurately summed up as 'all forms of physical self-indulgence'.[8] He appeared to regard with most distaste those of his characters whose physical appetites are hearty and satisfied, and with most approval those whose appetites are small and unsatisfied. Hence the force of *tolsty*. Hence one can compare the absurd figure of Akhineev in 'Slander' (*Kleveta*, 1883) with that of Khristina Dmitrievna, the unprepossessing governess in 'A Doctor's Visit' (*Sluchai iz praktiki*, 1898): both these creatures are earmarked by their liking for sturgeon.

Chekhov furthermore seemed to dislike all the physical manifestations of physical indulgence. His protagonists have notably sensitive noses: they complain of cooking smells, but also of less unpleasant aromas: of scent, which makes a 'suffocating reek'; even of flowers (that come from a florist's) which make a room smell 'sickly-sweet'.[9]

It is also apparent that physical appearances could repel Chekhov: he has a tendency, no doubt encouraged by the example of Gogol, to describe ugly people not so much realistically as grotesquely. The shaven chin of Modest Alekseich, anti-hero of 'The Order of St. Anne' (*Anna na shee*, 1895), looks like the heel of a foot. The governor's wife in the same story has a chin 'so vast . . . that she might have had a large stone in her mouth'. Not overtly condemnatory, perhaps, but scarcely endearing.

His aversion to such physical phenomena is perhaps the most graphically expressed of Chekhov's dislikes, but the scope of his satire was by no means exhausted there. It has been frequently pointed out that Chekhov hated *poshlost'*—that peculiarly satisfying Russian conception which denotes the mediocre, the second-rate, the vulgar aspects of life. *Poshlye* people are those who are complacently content with *poshlost'*, and undoubtedly Chekhov had no time for them. Perhaps the most damning of all his 'pointer' adjectives is *solidny*—'sedate': but, as Chekhov uses it, better translated by the term 'fuddy-duddy' (or even 'square'). Chekhov's fuddy-duddies can be both male and female. Complacency in either sex, justifiable or not, irritated Chekhov. He had an aversion to people of very strong inflexible opinions. Again, where found in his fiction, this type is not confined to the female sex. There is a striking parallel of character (and to some extent of situation) between Lidiya Volchaninova in 'The Artist's Story' (*Dom s mezoninom*, 1896) and von Koren in 'The Duel' (*Duel'*, 1891).

It will be observed that there was nothing particularly strange or original about Chekhov's dislikes. Most of his targets were indeed fairly obvious ones. The point is that he did have violent dislikes, and expressed them forcefully.

3

But of course Chekhov can only be labelled a misogynist when it is clear that his malice is directed against women, unfounded, or disproportionate to the offence. His personal attitudes must be distinguished from the accepted attitudes of his time. For example, Chekhov revelled in ridiculing stupidity. Now, it cannot be denied that in his fiction he lets a great deal more emphasis fall on woman's stupidity—in the sense of ignorance—than on man's. This is so particularly in the early stories: woman is a 'pink-stocking', she enlists her mother's help to stop her husband making her read,[10] her taste in literature is execrable, and so on.

However, one cannot necessarily ascribe to misogyny this gloomy picture of woman's cultural advancement. In Chekhov's day the condition of society was such that women did not seek to compete with men, and they were encouraged in the domestic arts and in social graces rather than in intellectual advancement. And although the systematic education of women had been initiated by Ekaterina II, post-*gymnasium* education for women had scarcely been established when, in 1881, the relatively liberal Aleksandr II was succeeded by his son, whose reactionary regime threatened to stamp it out again.

The continuous attacks on women's lack of culture in Chekhov's early work would seem to accept the *status quo* with mocking good humour: but this theme, together with others similarly intended to raise a cheap laugh, disappears by about 1887. From this point Chekhov began to take writing more seriously. It has hopefully been made clear that Chekhov's early attacks on women reflected the ideas of his unsophisticated public. But—and this is what is significant—the shallow attitudes of the comic papers do not seem to have been entirely eliminated from his maturer conceptions of woman. In two late stories, and in Chekhov's last two major plays, the theme of woman's new destiny crops up again. The heroines of 'Home' (*V rodnom uglu*, 1897) and 'Betrothed' (*Nevesta*, 1903), Irina in *Three Sisters* (*Tri sestry*, 1900–1), and Anya in *The Cherry Orchard* (*Vishnevy sad*, 1903–4) are full of a spirit of restlessness and yearning for some worthwhile occupation. They are slightly reminiscent of the frustrated housewife in V. A. Sleptsov's *Hard Times* who, complaining that she 'cannot . . . pickle cucumbers', finds ploys for herself that include trying to outstare the sun.

This poor woman seems absurd to the modern reader, but one must remember that 'at the end of the 1860s and the beginning of the 1870s the problem of women's emancipation in general, and of institutions of higher education for women in particular, aroused Russian society'.[11] Yet Chekhov, one feels, in fact glosses over the issue of emancipation by shifting the difficulties which his ambitious heroines face into the vague future of their vague dreams; there is a hint of mockery of this future. Is Anya's new life really to devolve into reading books with her mother in the autumn evenings? And what of Nadya in 'Betrothed'? Chekhov originally had her leave her home town 'for ever'; but then he inserted into the final draft of the story: ' . . . as she supposed, for ever'. Vera Ivanovna, heroine of 'Home', desires passionately to escape from a life of mediocrity and stagnation, but she cannot steel herself to do so, and finally she resigns herself to the dreariest of futures. Irina in *Three Sisters* is not resigned—but she is disillusioned with the glamour of work. One does not, however, receive the impression that Chekhov is being deliberately pessimistic in the above instances; it is as if he is simply evading the task of grappling with the details of an issue that had no special interest for him.

Happily, Chekhov's fiction was not produced in a void, and when his attitude to any problem is ambiguously represented in the fiction, one can always turn to his correspondence and notebooks, the contents of which frequently clarify the situation. In the case of his views on woman's self-improvement, the evidence of Chekhov's non-fictional writing is particularly interesting. In 1883 he wrote to his brother Aleksandr: 'Here's a curious thing: in all the thirty years of their existence female doctors (first-rate doctors!) have not submitted one single serious thesis, which makes it plain that in the field of creativity they are weak.' There is a footnote: 'Remember, a perfect organism is creative. If woman is not creative, it means she is that much inferior to the perfect organism, and is therefore weaker than man, who is closer to the aforesaid organism.'[12]

This theory accords well with Chekhov's early anti-female fiction. Perhaps to this period of his life also belong a couple of jottings on a loose sheet of Chekhov's notes: 'How many idiots there are among women! People are so used to the fact that they don't notice it.' And: 'They go frequently to the theatre and read the literary journals—and all the same they're nasty and immoral.'[13] This second quotation does not, of course, necessarily refer to women, but, given its juxtaposition to the previous quotation, it seems very possible that it does.

In his mature period as a writer, also, Chekhov gave several indications that he did not have a high opinion of the female mind and spirit. 'Women,' he wrote in a letter of 1888, 'confronted with a general conception, like to pick out the glaring particular case that hits you in the eye.'* In 1900 he comments in a letter to Suvorin: The Turks 'have no religious ladies—none

---

* Letter to Suvorin, 18 October 1888. The context of Chekhov's remark was as follows: 'If Christ', Chekhov wrote, 'had been more radical, and had said, "Love thy enemy as thyself", then He would not have said what He meant. "Neighbour" is a general concept, whereas "enemy" is a particular case. The trouble after all is not that we hate our enemies, of whom we have few, but that we don't sufficiently love our neighbours, of whom we've many, we're up to our necks in them. "Love thy enemy as thyself" Christ would have said, I suppose, if He had been a woman. Women, confronted *etc., etc.* But Christ, who stood above His enemies and did not notice them, whose nature was masculine, equable, and thought in broad terms, hardly attributed any significance to the difference between particular cases of the concept "neighbour".'

of this element which diminishes religion as sand does the Volga.'[14]

One would expect Chekhov to have little patience with affected pretensions to culture such as he derides in the story 'In the Landau' (*V lando*, 1883); but in this connection a certain passage from one of his letters is perhaps surprising. Some of Chekhov's friends disapproved of his close relationship with Aleksei S. Suvorin, the publisher-cum-editor of the right-wing newspaper *Novoe vremya* ('New Times').* Among these friends was one Natalya Mikhailovna Lintvareva, an educated young woman who had attended the 'Bestuzhev Courses' of higher education in St. Petersburg. One day she took it into her head to advise Chekhov not to go and visit Suvorin, objecting to the reactionary tenor of *Novoe vremya*, and apparently also to Suvorin himself on some personal ground. Chekhov commented to Suvorin: 'She was afraid of my being influenced politically. Yes, she is a nice sincere young lady, but when I asked her how she knew about Suvorin and if she read *Novoe vremya*, she faltered, twiddled her fingers, and said, "In short, I advise you not to go." Yes, our young ladies and their cavalier-politicians are sincere, but nine-tenths of their sincerity isn't worth a damn. All this idle saintliness and sincerity of theirs is based on hazy and naïve antipathies and sympathies for people and labels, but not for facts. It's easy to be sincere when you can hate the devil you've never met and love a god you haven't the brains to doubt in.'[15]

These remarks are understandable in the light of Chekhov's strong affection for Suvorin, but they reveal a slightly astonishing intolerance of these earnest young people. It was, after all, scarcely a vice to possess political consciousness in the grimly repressive Russia of Aleksandr III.[16]

It is quite possible, in fact, that Chekhov did not display his much-vaunted tolerance when the talk turned on woman's cultural backwardness. Of Suvorin's wife, Anna Ivanovna, he wrote: 'Of all the women I know, she is the only one who has her own independent view of things.'[17] Elsewhere, in the same year, 1888, he wrote of her: 'She is as original as her husband, and doesn't think like a woman.'[18]

Later Chekhov was to become acquainted with other women who probably could, when they wished, talk 'intelligently and

* Suvorin's letters to Chekhov are not extant. The loss to Chekhov's biographers is incalculable.

take an independent line',[19] as he claimed Suvorina did. Among his female friends and correspondents—and they were numerous —there were several whom he clearly appreciated for their minds rather than for their feminine charm. They included the writer Elena M. Shavrova; the headmistress of the Yalta girls' *gymnasium*, V. K. Kharkeevich; and the blind doctor Zinaida M. Lintvareva (sister of the above-mentioned Natalya).

None the less, the image of woman as a frivolous creature finds a significant place in Chekhov's work. Thomas Winner points out that Chekhov's narrow-minded, or, as he terms them, 'narcissistic' characters include Laevsky's mistress in 'The Duel', and Kitten in 'Ionych' (1898).[20] They also include Kitten's supremely silly mother, and Winner's principal example of the type, Olga Ivanovna, the 'butterfly' in the story of that name (*Poprygun'ya*, 1892).

Olga Ivanovna is an amateur painter, a favourite of fashionable 'arty' society. The theme of the story is her inability to appreciate either the pretentiousness of this society or the true worth of her husband, Dymov, a doctor; which factors render her easily susceptible to the charm of a slick, unscrupulous young artist who seduces and subsequently deceives her. She is shallow, affected, and absurd: her house is decorated in the most ridiculous fashion, with bast shoes and sickles hanging in the dining-room, and a draped Arabian Nights-style bedroom. She refers to her husband's 'honest' hands and describes his face to her friends as 'that of a Bengal tiger', but with an expression as 'gentle and sweet as a deer's'; when Dymov, learning of her affair, remains silent, she takes pleasure in repeating the phrase: 'That man's magnanimity oppresses me!'

It is, incidentally, surely open to doubt that Dymov is, as Winner describes him, 'idealized'.[21] There are indications that Chekhov meant not to make of him a heroic figure, although the action whereby Dymov meets his death (he contracts diphtheria after sucking the infected membrane out of a child's throat) is certainly heroic. Few characters could live down the 'Bengal tiger' description, and Dymov is not one of them. The impression he makes with his perpetual 'meek smile' in the face of Olga Ivanovna's condescending treatment; his 'guilty' demeanour when she fails to appreciate an important step in his career; his announcement of dinner to his wife's guests, 'rubbing his hands' like an obsequious domestic; the adoring 'Mamma' with which he addresses his wife: all this is rather sickening, and one feels that a woman of more character would never have married Dymov, but would have left him in peace to pursue his worthy career.*

Despite all this, however, 'The Butterfly' remains a damning indictment of woman's triviality. But it is not this triviality that Toumanova has in mind when she speaks of the 'mischief and disorder' that Chekhov's women create in the lives of their menfolk.

4

Toumanova asserts that in Chekhov's fiction 'women suffer only because they are idle and selfish', but that Chekhov is still 'just' and 'tender' in his treatment of them; he implies—so Toumanova claims—that a better upbringing would have made all the difference to them.[22] This theory is probably based on the evidence of the story 'Ariadna' (1895). Several jottings in Chekhov's notebooks which reflect his poor opinion of woman's education bear directly upon this story. Thus, for example: 'Ariadna speaks three languages beautifully. A woman picks up languages quickly because there's a lot of empty space in her head.' 'A woman must be brought up to recognize her mistakes, otherwise, in her opinion, she's always in the right.'[23] A variant to the text of the story states of Ariadna that 'her ignorance and barbarity were astounding'.

In the story a young man, Shamokhin by name, relates how

* It was realized by his contemporaries that Chekhov had drawn Olga Ivanovna from life, using as his model Sofya Petrovna Kuvshinnikova, the wife of a doctor, whose liaison with Chekhov's friend the artits Levitan caused much gossip. Sofya Petrovna was over forty; ugly, with a swarthy 'mulatto' face; and with curly dark hair and a 'magnificent' figure: this according to Tanya Shchepkina-Kupernik ('V yunye gody', pp. 64–6), who also said that Chekhov 'naïvely' made the fictional character of Olga Ivanovna into a young blonde; 'naïvely' because it was none the less obvious who was his model, notwithstanding Chekhov's somewhat half-hearted assertions to the contrary (see, e.g., letter to L. A. Avilova, 29 April 1892). Levitan was deeply offended. The incident shows that Chekhov had no scruples about using other people's characteristics and lives as subject-matter for his fiction.

the vices of a girl whom he once loved have made his life a misery. Shamokhin believes that:

'Nowadays it's only in the villages that woman isn't more backward than man . . . there she thinks, and feels, and fights zealously against nature in the name of civilization, just as a man does. But your urban woman, your bourgeoise, your woman of the intellectual classes has been backward for years and is reverting to her primeval state, already she's almost half-beast, and thanks to her a great deal that human genius has achieved has been lost; woman is gradually disappearing and her place is being taken by the primeval female. This backwardness of the woman in the intellectual classes is a serious threat to civilization; she is trying to drag man after her in her regression and is impeding his advancement. There's no doubt about it.'

Now of course this passage cannot be regarded as conclusive evidence of Chekhov's misogyny: even Shamokhin, whose words they are, believes man is partly to blame for the situation, in that he refuses to treat woman as his equal, and consequently inculcates selfishness in her.

However, Chekhov depicted many women of a similar type to Ariadna without offering any such excuse for their faults. Although he claimed that the artist must be only an impartial witness, he puts his victims on trial without any counsel for the defence. Is it ever explained, or any attempt ever made to explain, why Nyuta in 'Volodya' (1887) behaves as she does? Or Arkadina in *The Seagull* (*Chaika*, 1896)? Or Natasha in *Three Sisters*, or Olga Dmitrievna in 'His Wife' (*Supruga*, 1895)? The answer is no. Yet these women—among the most impressive of Chekhov's characters, and for whom there are scarcely any male parallels, in respect of sheer unpleasantness, in all his fiction—are subjected to the full force of the author's disapproval.

How does Chekhov show this disapproval? What he makes them do—that is, their function in the plot—is alone bad enough (two of the four women referred to above are to a considerable extent responsible for the deaths of two young men), but their actions are not left to speak for themselves. Chekhov is clearly striving to have them appear as nasty as possible. For instance, Nyuta's first speech consists of a stream of uncalled-for abuse, which risks making the reader feel that his sympathies are being too harshly manipulated. Natasha is criticized by the three sisters before she has made one appearance on the stage. In 'His Wife'

Olga Dmitrievna is criticized as by an omniscient author (a method of characterization remarkably rare in Chekhov when its purpose is unequivocal criticism): 'She never believed anyone, and no matter how noble a person's intentions were, she always suspected that person of having petty or base motives, and selfish aims.'

Something has been seen of such condemnatory language in the citations from 'Ariadna' above. Vilification of the central female character forms the very crux of this story, which is why Ariadna is probably the most 'obvious' villain of all Chekhov's women. In 'Ariadna', as one critic puts it, Chekhov 'venomously destroys the charms of a beautiful woman'.[24]

Let us take a closer look at the story. The narrator, on the steamer from Odessa to Sevastopol', meets a 'rather good-looking man', Shamokhin, who beguiles him with a monologue on the Russian attitude to women: 'We idealize women too much and make demands out of all proportion to what we're likely to get.' This is the prelude to his own history of how Ariadna led him astray.

The outline of the tale is simple. Shamokhin is romantically and physically in love with Ariadna, the young unmarried sister of a neighbouring landowner. Ariadna is aware of his love but cannot return it. Another friend of her brother's, Lubkov, comes to stay. He is older, and married, but this does not prevent him from going abroad with Ariadna. The moral and high-minded Shamokhin is horror-stricken and departs for Abbazia to see what the couple are up to. There he is welcomed by an especially charming Ariadna: he cannot approve however of her un-chaperoned state, the airs she puts on in society, the mess in her hotel room, or of the amount she eats (which encourages himself and Lubkov to overeat also). When he discovers for certain that Lubkov and Ariadna are lovers, he returns to Russia feeling worse than ever.

Then Ariadna writes to him and begs him to come back. Still unable to resist her, he rejoins her in Rome, finds that Lubkov is no longer on the scene, and yielding to her persuasion becomes her lover. There follows a month of undiluted happiness. And then there follows a gradual sobering-up period at the end of which Shamokhin comes to be more than ever revolted by Ariadna's heartless sensuality, by her posing, by her talent for wasting money. Finally, here they are on board ship, returning to Russia to visit the resorts there. Shamokhin feels obliged to marry Ariadna, but when the story ends he has hopes that she will find a new admirer, and that he will regain his freedom.

The most interesting feature of this story is the extreme difficulty of denying Ariadna any sympathy, as Shamokhin does and—more significant—as Chekhov would seem to wish the reader to do. To begin with, it is impossible not to see that she has been—as one critic puts it—'served up with three of the most ineffective and exasperating men that can ever have crossed a woman's path'.[25] Then, despite Shamokhin's ominous prologue on the depths of his disillusionment, during the first part of the story it is hard to see much wrong with Ariadna. Shamokhin actually tells us that Ariadna as he first knew her was 'affectionate, talkative, gay, and natural'.

Having told us this, he plunges forthwith into details of a glaring fault—her irresponsibility in money matters. But the reader scarcely has time to shake his head over this before we are back to Ariadna behaving both naturally and likeably, at least as far as her treatment of Shamokhin is concerned. Ariadna has tasted some excitement and romance during time spent in Moscow with a rich aunt. Now, aged twenty-two, she is back in the provinces with her tedious brother. Shamokhin tells us that she was 'moved' by his love for her and 'longed' to love him in return. This comes as no surprise to the reader, since it must have been a dull life for Ariadna. Shamokhin actually witnesses her weeping from distress because she cannot love him.

Then one day she impulsively embraces and kisses him: Ariadna is trying to kindle a spark of sexuality in the only eligible man for miles around—a perfectly understandable thing to do under the circumstances, even if unwise. Shamokhin's reaction is one of pious horror, and this not unnaturally causes Ariadna irritation: he is not only wanting in ardour, but a prude, and a feeble one to boot.

The rake Lubkov is not prepossessing in our eyes, and certainly not in Shamokhin's. But when Ariadna takes the opportunity of this juxtaposition of libertine and milksop to point out a few facts of life to Shamokhin ('A woman will forgive you if you're rude and impudent, but she'll never forgive you for being so stuffy') she seems the embodiment of honesty and truth in comparison with the platitudinizing, insufferably staid Shamokhin.

In fact, up to the moment of Shamokhin's arrival in Abbazia to join the errant couple, one is hard put to it to decide whom it is that the story is really meant to attack. Ariadna is openly criticized, but Shamokhin is surely the real object of the satire?

However, as soon as Shamokhin turns up in Abbazia, the entire tenor of the narrative changes. Shamokhin is still the plaintiff, of course, but now it is apparent that Shamokhin's creator has decisively thrown his own weight behind Shamokhin's onslaught. From this moment on Ariadna is damned. She is now burdened not only with conventional faults but with the entire bundle of faults that Chekhov found particularly offensive—affectation, frivolity, petty dishonesty, indolence, sluttishness, and greed. Later, when Shamokhin becomes her lover, the list is extended to include even more shortcomings. Ariadna displays superstition, 'fabulous' cunning, savage vulgarity, and a streak of sadism. 'Even when she was in a good mood she thought nothing of insulting a servant or killing an insect. She liked bullfights and reading about murders and was cross if the accused person in a trial was acquitted.'

In fact, by the time that Shamokhin has concluded his tale, the affectionate natural Ariadna of the opening part has been entirely obliterated. Shamokhin reverts to a more sober philosophical tone and, as we know, suggests that the blame lies with women's education which, emphasizing her inferiority, turns her into a human animal. But this cannot mitigate the impression of Ariadna that he has already given us.

If, however, Shamokhin is to be found making excuses for Ariadna's behaviour, it would seem natural to look for some for him. But he does not possess the merest trace of genuine guilt *vis-à-vis* Ariadna: his desire to marry her is prompted solely by a desire to make his mistake seem less senseless. Chekhov's reader might feel less kindly disposed towards Ariadna, less sceptical of the heap of crimes Chekhov burdens her with, if Shamokhin himself felt that he had behaved at all badly in encouraging her wayward habits. As it is, even Lubkov is a relatively likeable mediocrity. Poor Ariadna!

It has already been pointed out that this story cannot be considered evidence of anti-female feeling in Chekhov solely because it consists largely of Shamokhin's tirade against Ariadna in particular and 'urban women' in general. Chekhov's artistic sense precludes him from dispensing with the narrator, who breaks the flow of what would otherwise be uninterrupted diatribe, and represents ordinary man as opposed to Shamokhin, whom he describes as a 'fanatical convinced misogynist'. But the narrator's interruptions are of a perfunctory nature and do little to muffle the reverberations of Shamokhin's outburst. Moreover, the narrator's personal observation of Ariadna at the end of the story only serves to confirm the unpleasant image of her that Shamokhin has propagated.[26]

The importance of 'Ariadna' in the pattern of the present study does not however depend upon an affirmative answer to the question: is Shamokhin Chekhov's mouthpiece? 'Ariadna' is important because it is the only full exposition of a conception concerning woman which dominates a large part of Chekhov's work: that *through her sexual power*, woman represents a potential threat to man's happiness.

Shamokhin writes of Ariadna: 'She had me in subjection from the first day of our acquaintance—nor could it have been otherwise.'

'Nor could it have been otherwise.' There is a fatalistic ring to the words: man is helpless in the tyrant's grip. The situation where man is weak and woman strong occurs very frequently in Chekhov's work. 'Volodya' is the story of an adolescent boy's physical obsession with an older woman who tempts him. Taking a realistic view, one could ascribe the strangeness of his sensations and inability to resist the woman simply to the effects of nascent sexual desire (it is to a certain extent one of Chekhov's 'clinical studies')—but still Nyuta retains the air of an enchantress: it is as if she has bewitched Volodya. A similar situation crops up in 'The Consequences of Leisure' (*Ot nechego delat'*, 1886) in which a husband tries to shake the family tutor out of the spell cast on him by the seductive mistress of the house. In 'Champagne' (*Shampanskoe*, 1887) the narrator's wife's aunt, to whom the narrator is instantly attracted, reminds him of the refrain from a popular song:

> Black eyes, passionate eyes,
> Ardent and beautiful eyes,
> How I love you!
> *How I fear you!*[27]

Needless to say, she is the bearer of misfortune. The narrator declines to say precisely what happens between them, but simply refers to a terrible raging whirlwind which 'wiped off the face of the earth wife and aunt and [his] strength', leaving him alone in a dark street. The story is in fact a sort of fairy-tale, with the aunt playing the part of a wicked enchantress.

'A Story without a Title' (*Bez zaglaviya*, 1888) relates how an old monk returns to his community from a visit to the outside world and tells the other monks about the evils that exist there, notably about a certain underdressed whore. Next morning the monk discovers that all the others have rushed away to the town, as if drawn by a spell. The element of comedy in this does not detract from its cynicism, which is what gives the story (and the otherwise banal image of the whore) its impact.

Chekhov appears to detect this sort of power in women even in his most balanced moments, that is, at times when his writing seems quite devoid of emotion. The relationship in *Uncle Vanya* (*Dyadya Vanya*, 1897) between Astrov and Elena, which is based on his sexual attraction to her, is depicted with delicacy and without over-statement, so that Astrov's description of Elena as a 'vampire' comes almost as a shock, although it is particularly apt and illuminating.

Some of Chekhov's women who ensnare men are not merely egocentric like Elena, or ill-natured like Nyuta, but seem to have no soul at all, to the extent that they cease to be people and appear more like vessels of some monstrous power. Such a woman is Susanna Moisevna, the Jewish temptress in 'Slime' (*Tina*, 1886), which describes how two men are held in the thrall of this sort of superior prostitute. Her remoteness from everyday life is emphasized by her alien race, her seclusion, even by the unfamiliar scent that surrounds her. There is a similar element of strangeness in the central character of 'The Witch' (*Ved'ma*, 1886), a young girl, Raisa, with a handsome expressionless face, whose husband believes her to be a diabolical enchantress.

It is, predictably, in 'Ariadna' that the ultimate dictum on woman's soulless charm is found. Of Ariadna Shamokhin says: 'When she spoke to me of love, it seemed as though I heard the song of a toy nightingale.'

Men in the toils of such women are enthralled by the woman's sexuality. This is emphasized by the fact that Chekhov's temptresses are not necessarily beautiful. Sometimes it is explicitly stated that they are not, as in 'Volodya': 'Nyuta was plain and not young'. Their advantage is that their attractions are sexual; and these the reader is made aware of. When Nyuta first appears, it is with the top button of her blouse undone. Of Strelkova— 'Milady' (*Barynya*, 1882)—who makes one of her serfs become her gigolo—Chekhov writes: 'She was not beautiful, but she could appear attractive. She had a full, pleasant, healthy-looking countenance, while her neck . . . and bust were magnificent.' Again, emphasis on the 'bust' (*byust*), and particularly noticeable is the phrase 'she could appear attractive' (*nravit'sya mogla*). One recalls the Ariadna of whom the disillusioned Shamokhin says: 'She woke each day with but one thought: how to appear attractive!' (*'nravit'sya!'*).

In Chekhov's fiction, the awareness of their charms which women demonstrate by behaving coquettishly is inseparable from vice. Here is how the narrator of 'Champagne' describes the first impression made on him by his wife's aunt: 'It seemed as though everything right down to the smallest speck of dust grew younger and more cheerful in the presence of this fresh young being who exuded a strange sort of perfume of beauty and corruption. And that our guest was corrupt I could tell by her smile, by her perfume, by the special way she glanced and fluttered her eyelashes, by the tone in which she spoke to my wife—a decent woman.' The key phrase here is that which links the woman's sensuous beauty with corruption. It is not just that Chekhov's temptresses have a vaguely alarming air of evil about them: they are in most cases explicitly shown to be sexually immoral. If, lacking a husband, they cannot go in for adultery, they are, like Ariadna, promiscuous. This is one specific, obvious way in which they harm men. (For Chekhov's typical promiscuous female never makes a man happy for long.)

Cruelty is another form in which the abstract evil they represent is as it were crystallized. This has already been observed in Ariadna (who is described in a variant to the final text as 'as cruel as a savage'). In 'Superfluous Men' (*Lishnie lyudi*, 1886) the reader is confronted with a crowd of *dachnitsy*—middle-class wives sojourning in their country villas, with husbands visiting only at the weekends. Chekhov was doubtless not the only person to envisage immoral goings-on in this context: but so that it may

D

be plain what he thinks of the ladies in question, he has one of them teach a small boy to pin live insects to a board.

More often than not the actions of these temptresses speak for themselves. It is not necessary for the author to comment on Nyuta's cruelty when, having encouraged Volodya to embrace her, she rejects him and calls him an 'ugly duckling'; nor on Arkadina's, when she taunts her son with his socially inferior origins. It is quite apparent that each is to some extent responsible for the suicide of the youth concerned. Arkadina is of course partially redeemed by the fact that her attitude to her son is based on love as well as hatred. Most of Chekhov's enchantresses are distinguished by their inability to love.

This trait is also reflected in two important comic female characters. In *The Bear* the heroine is in deep mourning for her husband. It later transpires that he deceived her and that she was not happy with him. Then why the exaggerated mourning? Underlying the obvious humour of the situation, could there not be a reflection of the idea that for women love is something assumed rather than felt, a kind of acquisition prompted by custom, like a new article of clothing? The obvious instance of a woman's love appearing in this light is of course in 'The Darling' (*Dushechka*, 1898), in which the heroine's tastes and interests change with each new husband, to whom her affections are wholeheartedly transferred. One forms a similar conception of Olga Ivanovna's love in 'The Butterfly', especially at the beginning of the story, when she is seen showing off her new husband, Dymov, to her friends.

Although 'The Butterfly' is in some respects a sombre story, Olga Ivanovna does not belong to what might be called Chekhov's rogues' gallery of faithless wives. Her infidelity does not mean that she can feel only sensual passion and not love. It means that she does not understand what love is, confusing it with emotional thrills and (misplaced) admiration. And there develops in her the 'right' attitude to her infidelity: as her husband lies on his death-bed she broods on the past, on her affair, and: 'She no longer thought of the moonlit night on the Volga, nor the protestations of love, nor of their poetic life in the hut, all she could think of was how, as the result of her idle whim, her silliness, she had become soiled from head to foot in a filthy, sticky mess which would never wash off.' Similarly, Sofya Lvovna's affair with 'little' Volodya in 'Big Volodya and Little Volodya' (*Volodya bol'shoi i Volodya malenk'y*, 1893) is a bitter, humiliating experience. But at least Sofya realizes this: when she visits her foster-sister, a nun (who provides an effective parallel to the sinner), Sofya feels that together with her 'something impure, wretched, and shabby' enters the cell.

This recognition of impurity is all-important. Unabashed sensuality is the cardinal sin in Chekhov's women. Once again Shamokhin's words come to mind: Ariadna 'was sensual, as all cold people generally are'.

That their crime is connected with sex seems to be the chief reason for the particularly harsh treatment Chekhov metes out to the majority of those women in his work who commit adultery. In the stories which will now be discussed there is a quality of vehemence that is rare in Chekhov's writing. 'Autumn' (*Osen'yu*, 1883) describes how a sober, good-hearted landowner has become a hopeless alcoholic because his wife has left him. Before the wedding, a serf recalls, the bride would return every kiss with two kisses: but very soon after this 'the snake', as the servant describes her with loathing, ran away to her lover, and the gloom of the story devolves into maudlin pathos, the last lines being: 'Spring, where art thou?' The wife in 'The Consequences of Leisure' is called 'Nothing more than a good-for-nothing, nasty little slut!' In 'Enemies' (*Vragi*, 1887), although the guilty woman never appears, the situation brought about by her activities is calculated to set our sympathies against her. Feigning illness, she sends her husband for the doctor and in the meantime escapes to join her lover. The husband, when they arrive to find the patient gone, is beside himself with rage. 'Why this filthy rascally trick? Why this diabolic reptilian (*zmeiny*) game?' he cries. (The word *zmeya*—'snake'—and its derivatives are frequently used by Chekhov in describing women of whom he disapproves.) The 'filthy trick' is the worse in that it affects the doctor too: his only son has just died, he has left his wife alone with the body, and now he finds he was called out for nothing. Again, we notice, Chekhov brings in a child when he wishes to enlist our sympathy on a particular side.

Even a figure incidental to the narrative, such as Vlasich's wife in the story 'Neighbours' (*Sosedi*, 1892), can be stamped on our minds as a monster of depravity: in this instance, by Vlasich's calm exposé to Petr Mikhailich Ivashin of the facts of his married life: 'Of all my neighbours you alone were not her lover.'

As for Olga Dmitrievna, 'His Wife' can scarcely have been bettered as a miniature portrait of an unpleasant female. Chekhov here uses the device of putting abusive language into her mouth, a method of denigrating a woman's image which he employed particularly well. One is not surprised that the specific crime of which such a woman should be accused is infidelity. Similarly with Natasha in *Three Sisters*: it seems almost inevitable that adultery should be added to the sum-total of her iniquities.

Few writers of Chekhov's calibre have been so uncompromising in their attitude to erring womankind. Confronted with these soulless temptresses, grimly wielding their disconcerting power, one would give a great deal to encounter just one good-natured, happy and unrepentant hussy. Furthermore, one misses the element of compassion: nowhere in Chekhov's work is there room for an exposé of the adulteress's feelings, helping the reader to understand her *while at the same time her fault is condemned*. Chekhov gives us no Anna Karenina, no Madame Bovary.

How rightly Erenburg observed that Chekhov could never have said, as Flaubert did, 'Madame Bovary, c'est moi.'[28] Flaubert was able to reveal Emma's mind and situation in all their mediocrity, and yet, without sentimentalizing her, to retain her hold on the reader's sympathy.

Nor did Flaubert require in order to do so the scope of the entire novel format. He could do it in a few lines. Here is Emma, back from the ball which marks the point at which corruption begins to leave its impression on her. 'Elle serra pieusement dans la commode sa belle toilette et jusqu'à ses souliers de satin, dont la semelle s'était jaunie à la cire glissante du parquet. Son cœur était comme eux. Au frottement de la richesse, il s'était placé dessus quelque chose qui ne s'effacerait pas.' The ominous significance of the moment is clearly underlined: but how complete, how tender an understanding of his heroine Flaubert compels in these few words. Chekhov too was skilled at evoking sympathy with a telling phrase: yet he never granted Ariadna and her fellow-sinners a fraction of such insight or compassion.

While not exonerating Emma, Flaubert, it will be remembered, left us with no delusions concerning the ungentlemanly behaviour of her various lovers. In Chekhov's fiction, however, although roughly a third of straying partners are male, nowhere is there a single man in whom this fault is condemned as harshly and deliberately as it is in the case of those women mentioned above.

5

If one discounts the large number of early stories dealing with the subject of adultery in which, because of their farcical nature, the concept of 'blame' is irrelevant, then there is scarcely one man left in the whole of Chekhov's imaginary world who is clearly depicted to be guilty of sexual infidelity without what one might call mitigating circumstances. There is Panaurov in 'Three Years' (*Tri goda*, 1895); while he is intended to be seen in this light, he is perhaps too clearly seen to be condemned: for unlike most of Chekhov's adulteresses, Panaurov is seen in the round. The errors of his ways are obvious: he has two families, neither of which he has made happy, he is improvident, weak, and thoughtless: but he is depicted as a person in his own right, with some views of his own and some good points. Moreover, his wife Nina loves him, and Laptev (the principal character) can understand why. Panaurov's sins are not diminished, but we come half-way to understanding, and thus half-way to forgiving him.

Panaurov is not the only adulterer for whom no excuse can be inferred, but in certain other cases the edge is taken off the moral by the satirical treatment of a situation, in stories which are distinguishable from the purely farcical anecdotes by a more savage note in the underlying irony. Thus in 'Bad Weather' (*Nenast'e*, 1887): a young wife thinks that she has discovered that her husband is deceiving her. He is; but he lies his way out of a tight spot with ridiculous ease, because his wife is pathetically anxious to believe him innocent. The point is that the story is a parody of a tragic situation, so that the husband's misdemeanours cannot be taken seriously.

A similarly satirical treatment of a potentially tragic situation is found in 'Ninochka' (1885), an even more ironic tale than 'Bad Weather'. The narrator is approached by his friend Vikhlenev to mediate in a marital quarrel. The outcome of the narrator's efforts with Ninochka, the wife, is that he moves into Vikhlenev's house and Vikhlenev is banished from his bedroom to a store-room. If the concept of guilt is at all applicable to characters treated so satirically, one might note that Ninochka is partly responsible for what happens: does she not immediately tell the narrator that the cause of her quarrelsomeness is boredom? The inference to be drawn by the narrator is plain: women should be provided with some diversion.

In 'Slime' and 'Ariadna' there are three obviously immoral men—but the responsibility for their infidelity lies equally with the women involved, with the almost literally enchanting Susanna Moisevna and with the unprincipled Ariadna, who agrees to go abroad with Lubkov without a chaperone. Also guilty, albeit to a lesser extent, are Sofya Lvovna, and Sofya Petrovna in 'Misfortune' (*Neschast'e*, 1887)—a wretched pair—because it takes such a short time for their admirers, 'little' Volodya and Ilin, to seduce them. Both stories, 'Big Volodya and Little Volodya' and 'Misfortune', revolve around the weakness of the pursued, not the wickedness of the pursuer.

It is interesting to observe how in other cases where a man is guilty of sexual immorality the weight of Chekhov's censure is not merely distributed, but shifted right off the man and on to the woman. This can happen when he is in the thrall of a corrupt woman, as in 'Champagne' or 'The Consequences of Leisure', and in 'Milady', in which last, however, though the woman's desire for the man is sexual, her power over him is not, but is based on the fact of his serfdom.

In 'The Black Monk' (*Cherny monakh*, 1894) the guilt must be imputed to neither the man nor the woman, but to the hallucination which, driving Kovrin to madness, causes him to leave his wife and live with another woman.

However, Chekhov did not always present sexual infidelity in such simple terms as the above examples demonstrate. A more complex problem of guilt in man–woman relationships is expounded in 'The Examining Magistrate' (*Sledovatel'*, 1887). The examining magistrate tells how an intelligent, non-superstitious young woman (he later turns out to be speaking of his wife) predicted that she would die soon after giving birth to the child she was carrying. Having harped on the subject incessantly up till the day of her confinement, she does in fact mysteriously die half an hour after being safely delivered of the child. The examining magistrate's companion extracts from him an admission: 'One day she found her husband with a certain lady.' Although she had appeared to forgive him, her husband is now led to the realization that her death was suicide, and that his infidelity, which he regarded as meaningless, was the reason for it.

Yet the point of this tale is not to show the damage that marital infidelity can do; the examining magistrate is no villain, because the point of the story lies in the exaggeratedly spectacular nature of the wife's revenge, and the epigraph to the tale may be found in the words of the wounded and genuinely bewildered husband: 'Well, it was my fault, I was the guilty party, but imagine finding it easier to die than to forgive! That's precisely female logic for you—a cruel, ruthless logic.' It is impossible to imagine this story being told from the point of view of the woman. She is simply a rather unconvincing symbol of this 'female logic'. ('Female' translates the Russian adjective *bab'ya*, which derives from the word for 'peasant woman', and in this quotation has a derogatory sense.)

Thus again in a case of male infidelity the issue of the man's moral guilt is side-stepped. In other instances Chekhov goes further and depicts a man who is guilty but yet more admirable than not. Doctor Blagovo in 'My Life' (*Moya zhizn'*, 1896) and Vlasich in 'Neighbours' are among the most sympathetically depicted of Chekhov's male characters, and each, while married, lives with another woman. We know, however, that Vlasich's wife is worthless, and as for Madame Blagovo, since she is not living with her husband and in the absence of information to the contrary, it is tempting to make a similar assumption in her case.

What seems clear is that Chekhov was capable of regarding unfaithful husbands with equanimity, and that this was not in general the case when he was dealing with unfaithful wives. This attitude was of course common. But it is interesting that Chekhov, or more particularly, the wise and compassionate Chekhov of popular legend, should hold it. The larger vision of most great writers failed him here.

Even more interesting, perhaps, is the fact that such an attitude is not discernible in the stories that deal with peasant life. In 'Peasants' (*Muzhiki*, 1897) a young girl, Fekla, is unfaithful to her absent husband. She is wayward and depraved, but she appears as no Ariadna: when she gets her deserts at the hands of some village louts, she inspires nothing but pity.

Similarly, Chekhov invites compassion for the unfaithful and potentially treacherous 'peasant women' in the story of that name (*Baby*, 1891); and moreover, compassion for Mashenka, the heroine of the tale within this tale, who is found guilty of murdering her young and blameless husband, which she did rather than leave her lover. Chekhov was capable of making even an incidental character a monster—but Mashenka is not a monster: if anyone is, it is her lover. One of the men in 'Peasant Women' utters what one might expect to be Chekhov's own verdict on the affair: 'the female sex causes a deal of evil and harm of all kinds in this world'. But Chekhov's sympathy is clearly with the women in this story. It is they who demand understanding. Again, Agafya, the peasant girl married to a 'fine young man', but committing adultery with another, is to be pitied, not condemned (*Agafya*, 1886).

The basis for Chekhov's difference in attitude to peasant women lies in the fact that his view of the peasant world is detached almost to the point of condescension. His peasant characters generally resemble animals—some attractive, some bestial and repulsive. His stories about them have a pastoral charm, or are fraught with sociological significance: however, in Chekhov's work psychological interest really only enters the picture with the *meshchanin*, or lower-middle class, and the same is true for any suggestion of moralizing.

The most obvious explanation for this would seem to be that Chekhov, concerned as he undoubtedly was for the well-being of the peasants, felt no sense of personal involvement in their lives. But when he describes the lives of the sort of people whom he mixed with socially, his emotions are engaged.

Not however every emotion that we might expect to encounter. Despite his pillorying of unfaithful wives, in Chekhov's fiction the passions of male jealousy are curiously muted. The typical Chekhovian cuckold meekly pushes a perambulator containing what is presumably his rival's offspring (*Three Sisters*), or, even more self-effacing, he simply departs from the scene, as in 'Terror' (*Strakh*, 1886). There are of course exceptions: in 'Enemies' Abogin flies into a violent rage when he discovers that his wife has run off with another man. But it is the expression only of wounded pride: Abogin explicitly states that it is not a question of regretting her preference for someone else. A very similar situation is found in 'His Wife'. The deceived husband's reaction to his wife's misdemeanours is not one of grief: it is his 'plebeian fastidiousness' (*plebeiskaya brezglivost'*) that is offended. The point is that neither of these men loves his wife anyway.

Love does play its part in 'The Story of an Unidentified Person' (*Rasskaz neizvestnogo cheloveka*, 1893). The narrator, an intellectual who has taken a job as a servant, adores from afar his master's mistress. But there is no jealousy theme. Why is this? Because the young man's love for Zinaida Fedorovna is compounded out of pity and his own desire for prosaic married comfort—'a garden with paths, and a little house'. The destructive and corroding passion of sexual jealousy—at the basis of Tolstoy's *Kreutzer Sonata*, of Dostoevsky's *Idiot*, of Strindberg's *The Father*, nowhere in Chekhov attains anything approaching the atavistic intensity with which those authors portrayed it. Only in 'The Examining Magistrate' do we glimpse such a feeling—but it is in a woman, and her emotions remain an unknown factor.

This is not simply because she is a woman—though Chekhov certainly did not have Tolstoy's gift of complete identification with the opposite sex. Chekhov could not under any circumstances have portrayed this woman's emotions vividly. If the agony of sexual jealousy is absent from his work, this is because the pleasure of sexual fulfilment is also absent.

And yet there is, as we have seen, emotion in his portrayal of sexual relationships: indeed, if Chekhov is to be described as a misogynist, it is on the basis of the vehemence with which he depicted woman in her sexual role. If we now turn our closer attention to Chekhov's views on sexual relationships, we could do worse than bear in mind the expression '*plebeiskaya brezglivost'* ', suggesting as it does an outlook totally unreceptive to any conception of the 'noble' *crime passionel*. For to Chekhov sex was one thing, and nobility quite another.

3   *Sexual Relationships*

In Chekhov's serious fiction, when a marriage breaks down because of the man's shortcomings—which happens much less frequently than vice versa—this is almost always because the man in question is in some way a mediocre creature, a *poshlyak*. The husband of the 'lady with the dog' is a 'lackey'; Modest Alekseich in 'The Order of St. Anne' is a pompous fuddy-duddy; Aleksei Alekseich, the fiancé of Nadya in 'Betrothed', is also pompous, besides being idle and fat (a characteristic which always implies Chekhov's disapproval). But the harm women do to men almost always stems from the woman's sexuality.

When he writes about sex Chekhov is not at ease. He treats the subject most successfully in the comic-anecdote form, and it is in this form that he most openly recognizes the fact of sex. In 'He Quarrelled with his Wife' (*S zhenoi possorilsya*, 1884) an irate husband is mollified by the 'touch of a little hand' in bed to the extent that he 'put out his hand behind him and encircled the warm body'—which turns out to be that of his dog. This is probably the nearest Chekhov ever came in his work to describing a sexual advance.

This anecdote was entirely appropriate to the low-quality journal for which it was intended. It appeals to a simple bawdy sense of humour. So does 'A Romance with a Double Bass' (*Roman s kontrabasom*, 1886). A musician, Smychkov, and a beautiful princess—strangers to one another—have their clothes stolen while they are bathing in a river, in her case while she detaches from her fishing-line the bouquet which he has tied to it. He offers to take her home when night falls if she will in the meantime take refuge in his double-bass case. On his way, however, he sees what he thinks are the thieves, and pursuing them abandons the case. It is picked up by his friends and taken to the party—in the princess's house—where Smychkov was due to play that evening. The *dénouement* can readily be imagined; meanwhile Smychkov, appalled at losing case and contents, vows never to give up the search and remains in nothing but his top-hat under the bridge, becoming a local legend.

Here the comedy of the situation is enhanced by a pseudo-delicacy of style and sentiment: 'the eccentric young woman cast off her ethereal clothing and her splendid body plunged into the billows right up to the marble shoulders'. And: the 'gallant Smychkov', offering her the case, 'felt for a moment that in yielding the case he was profaning sacred art'.

Extremely reminiscent of Gogol's treatment of sex, and possibly derived from his style, is the coyness with which Chekhov will often skirt the subject. The landowner in 'A Daughter of Albion' (*Doch' Al'biona*, 1883) does not simply undress: he 'finds himself in the garb of Adam'; similarly, an actress's naked body is referred to elsewhere as 'Eve's raiment' (*odeyanie Evy*).[1] In 'A Work of Art' (*Proizvedenie iskusstva*, 1886) the bronze candelabra is described as being formed of: 'two female figures in the costume of Eve, and in poses which I lack both the courage and the temperament to describe!'

The fact of sexual desire is put in the most delicate phraseology: 'Papa thought the schoolmaster's wife very good-looking, and that if she were completely clothed she would not be so delightful' ('Papa'—*Papasha*, 1880).[2] 'Grokholsky liked to kiss Liza every minute. Without these honeyed kisses he could not live . . .'.[3]

However, unlike Gogol, whose entire outlook was so divorced from reality that concepts such as 'taste' have little relevance to his style, Chekhov was capable of writing in a tasteless tone. 'In Spring' (*Vesnoi*, 1887) is the monologue of a tom-cat mainly on the subject of its sex-life: 'Oh, when I am dead and they take me by the tail and fling me into a sewer, not even then . . . shall I forget the gaze of her slit eyes, her velvety fluffy tail! For one movement of that graceful unearthly tail I'd sacrifice the whole world! . . . Our she-cats, particularly those from tea-shops, are virtuous. However much they may love you, they never give in without protest. You have to be possessed of perseverance and will-power to achieve success. . . . There's a frightful fuss, so that the sweet moment comes usually not earlier than 4–5 a.m.'

There is no artistic merit in this, which indeed is probably why

Chekhov excluded it from his collected works. There is an even less pleasant salacity in 'A Woman's Vengeance' (*Mest' zhenshchiny*, 1884): a doctor pays a call and finds that his patient, Chelobitiev, has gone to consult the dentist without waiting for him. The doctor demands payment for his trouble from the patient's wife: the husband, however, has all their money on him. The doctor rages until the wife falls swooning into his arms: 'An hour later the doctor left the Chelobitievs' flat. He felt irritated, and guilty, and pleased . . .'.

Of course Chekhov was churning out this trash with little in mind save a public whose literary tastes he had accurately divined. Therefore, he cannot meaningfully be criticized for writing it. Yet it should be borne in mind that, unlike his peers who never worked for the penny-dreadfuls, Chekhov must inevitably have acquired—although perhaps to a lesser extent than others in the same position—a facile vulgarity of style and even of outlook which was thereafter not easily eradicated. The persistent habit of playing for cheap laughs surely must in part account for the fact that Chekhov, who was in other respects anything but vulgar, could not even in later years write about sexual relationships without a faint but distasteful undertone of uneasy salacity.

Typical of this style is the use of dots (as above, in the last-cited passage) to show that the rest is to be left to the reader's imagination. 'Misfortune' ends as follows: Sofya Petrovna, yielding to Ilin's campaign of seduction, 'pressed on, conscious neither of the wind nor of the darkness . . . an irresistible force drove her forward, and she felt that if she stopped, it would push her from behind. "You immoral woman!" she muttered mechanically. "You vile woman!" She gasped for breath, feeling hot with shame and numb in the legs, but that which thrust her onwards overcame her shame, her reason, and her fear . . .'. The effect of this coy innuendo is particularly unfortunate here. Although Sofya Petrovna's situation is commonplace enough—the pressure from an admirer for whom she cares little threatening her sense of duty to the husband whom she does not love—there is a subtlety, rare in Chekhov's work of this period (1886) in the way he depicts Sofya Petrovna's reaction to it. It is clear that her rejection of Ilin is indeed a case of playing hard-to-get, but on the other hand there is something genuinely touching in her desire to feel something for her husband (a possibility dispelled by the sight of him chewing in a scene strikingly reminiscent of that where Anna Karenina is repelled by her husband's ears); we note that Sofya Petrovna asks her husband if they may go away on a trip together—and that she is touched by her own virtue and resolution in doing so. She gives Ilin the opportunity of making advances to her, and then gives her husband the opportunity of preventing the rendezvous that Ilin has arranged by telling him that she is in love.

Sofya Petrovna's conflicting impulses give the story the ring of truth and also impress on us that there is a certain degree of genuine pathos in the situation. And yet the end of the story is reminiscent of a woman's magazine romance. Why not simply say that passion thrust her onward—Chekhov uses the word *strast'* in exactly this sense of passion, lust, in 'The Lady with the Dog' —or if that were too strong a word for the readers of *Novoe vremya*, why not omit the sentence altogether? 'Misfortune' is not the sort of pseudo-vaudeville stuff where this brand of pseudo-delicacy is in place.

However, although it is out of key with the balanced tone of the rest of the story, the rather hysterical note on which 'Misfortune' ends is less surprising when one considers the part played by sexual relations in many of Chekhov's stories: when a man and woman start to sleep together, the trump of doom sounds for their relationship. It is not for nothing that Sofya Petrovna's story is called 'Misfortune', and there is little doubt as to who is unfortunate—certainly not the phlegmatic husband. We know that Sofya Petrovna is not going to enjoy her affair, just as no good comes to Sofya Lvovna from her affair with 'little Volodya', or to Olga Ivanovna from her affair with Ryabinovsky.

Involvement in a sexual relationship frequently leads to the woman's humiliation. One factor which may contribute to this is the egocentricity of the man—a theme that reappears throughout Chekhov's work, and which will be discussed later; but very often the degradation of the woman is clearly connected with the fact that her relationship is illicit, whether she be a prostitute, like the embarrassed girl with a drunken lover in 'A Stroll in Sokolniki' (*Na gulyan'e v Sokolnikakh*, 1885), or a ladylike adulteress like Zinaida Fedorovna, or like Anyuta, the pathetic artist's model who is about to be abandoned by the sixth man whom she has lived with.[4] We are sorry for Anyuta, but the degradation of her position does not prevent us from feeling that it is her own fault, because she has put herself in a slave's position.

But if the humiliation which a sexual relationship brings in its wake is for women, in the majority of cases, the wages of sin, in two important stories which deal most specifically with the effect of sexual experience on a man, the man's suffering is imposed on him by the woman. In both 'Volodya' and 'Ariadna' a man's first sexual relationship is described. 'You live like a monk,' Lubkov tells Shamokhin, before the latter falls—literally—into Ariadna's clutches. 'Volodya' was originally called 'His First Love'; this title was dropped, either because it is misleading or else rather too obviously ironic: the factor common to both stories is that they deal with sex without love.

The most memorable feature of Volodya's encounter with Nyuta is his acute shame. He experiences this sensation even before he makes advances to her: 'he felt a strong urge to see Nyuta . . . to hear her laughter, the rustle of her dress—this desire was not like that pure poetic love which he knew about from novels and dreamed about every evening as he went to bed; it was strange, unintelligible, he was ashamed of it and feared it as something very bad and impure, which it pained him to acknowledge in himself . . .'. Nyuta makes an appearance, and Volodya, confused by her coquetry, blurts out that he loves her, and manages to embrace her awkwardly. The embarrassment he feels when she departs is excellently, succinctly conveyed: 'Volodya was left alone. He smoothed his hair, smiled, and paced up and down two or three times, then sat down on the garden seat and smiled again . . .'. But there is a note of artificiality in the continuation of the paragraph: 'He felt so intolerably ashamed of himself that he was amazed that a human being could experience shame so acutely and so violently. He gave a shame-faced smile, muttered some disconnected words, and gesticulated.' Significantly, he feels this shame even before he hears Nyuta describing the incident to the other women in the house. However, he later sees the occurrence in perspective, and abandoning his intention of returning to town for an important examination, he forms a resolution to make advances to Nyuta again.

In this he is eventually successful: 'Then it seemed to Volodya that the room, Nyuta, the dawn and he himself—all merged into a single sensation of acute, extraordinary, unprecedented happiness, worth giving his life for and going to eternal torment . . . .' Immediately, however, retribution follows:

. . . but half a minute passed and all this suddenly vanished. Volodya saw only a fat, ugly face, distorted by an expression of distaste, and he himself suddenly felt disgust for what had occurred.

'Well, I must be off,' said Nyuta, surveying Volodya with aversion. 'What a plain, pathetic creature you are . . . ugh, you ugly duckling!'

How hideous her long hair, voluminous blouse, her footsteps, her voice now appeared to Volodya!

'Ugly duckling,' he thought when she had gone. 'I am ugly in fact —everything's ugly.'

Volodya commits suicide. His reasons for killing himself include his failure to take the examination, and the antipathy his mother inspires in him, but his 'filthy memories' are what ultimately drive him to despair.

Bliss is followed by humiliation. Is this a microcosm of sex as Chekhov saw it? This, at any rate, is exactly what happens in 'Ariadna'. Shamokhin's love for the girl 'entered into its last phase, its last quarter' precisely at the moment when Ariadna makes advances to him. He becomes her lover, and from this time enjoys a month of pure bliss 'like someone deranged'. But then disillusionment gains the upper hand. Shamokhin is humiliated both by Ariadna's depraved behaviour and by the knowledge that she does not love him.

Nyuta and Ariadna are villains, which is why, ostensibly, these sex-relationships do not work out: while the pathos of Volodya's and Shamokhin's respective situations derives largely from the fact that it is their first experience. However, just as significant as the failure of the relationship after sex has entered into it is the attitude of the man concerned to the relationship. He is *ashamed* of his physical passion.

It is apparent that both Volodya and Shamokhin are peculiarly sensitive characters, and this to a great extent explains the almost morbid attitude of each to his first sexual experience. It is difficult to feel that Chekhov can be entirely in sympathy with a character who makes such a pale impression as Shamokhin does; and in the documentation of Volodya's feelings there is a certain, rather unpleasant, quasi-detached meticulousness, which produces the impression that the author is being superior and at the same time taking a slightly salacious pleasure in the process of description.

But a similar attitude is presented with greater sympathy in the experience of the shy, bespectacled Ryabovich, hero of 'The Kiss' (*Potselui*, 1887); who, wandering into a dark room in the course of a party, intercepts an embrace intended for somebody else. The feelings this incident arouses in Ryabovich are described as follows:

> When he returned to the ballroom, his heart was thumping and his hands trembled so noticeably that he hurriedly hid them behind his back. At first he was tormented by shame and by the fear that the whole room knew that a woman had just embraced and kissed him, and shrinking, he glanced uneasily about him, but once assured that people in the room were chatting and dancing quite calmly as before, he abandoned himself wholly to this new sensation which he had never experienced in his life before. Something strange was happening to him. His neck, so recently encircled by soft, fragrant arms, felt as if it were anointed with oil; on his left cheek near his moustache where the unknown woman had kissed him, there was a slight, trembling, agreeable chill, like the sensation of eating mint drops, and the more he rubbed the place, the more strongly the chill made itself felt, and all of him from top to toe was filled with a strange novel feeling which grew stronger and stronger. . . .

The character's mood is most effectively evoked by his actions and physical sensations. Here, more than in 'Volodya', the description of these (sounding like an almost doggedly faithful transcription of personal experience) has the ring of truth: here Chekhov is on firmer ground than when he talks of 'shame'. The use of such emotive words here, as in 'Volodya', entails the risk of being trite. Though the idea of shame is less sedulously, and thus less embarrassingly, explored in 'The Kiss' than in 'Volodya', it is there, connected with sexual experience.

Three stories constitute a minute proportion of Chekhov's work, and therefore they may seem paltry evidence of the existence of a continuing theme, until one remembers that very few indeed of Chekhov's stories come to grips with the subject of sex at all. Very rarely are we told anything about the sex-life of Chekhov's characters beyond the first kiss.

This is not unusual, given the literary conventions of the time, and neither is there any reason why Chekhov should go into details about sex: but the fact that his allusions to the bedroom are so few makes what he does say the more significant.

One of these rare references is to be found in 'One of Many' (*Odin iz mnogikh*, 1887), in which a savage attack on women is developed, starting with a husband's complaints about having too many errands to run between home and the *dacha* where his wife is living. The sketch was later adapted into a one-act farce: *A Tragedian in spite of himself* (*Tragik po nevole*, 1899), and from this version of the text, which is fairly close to that of the story, several lines were omitted: after the guests he loathes leave the *dacha* there is, as the unhappy man puts it, 'another torture: my lady wife graciously claims her marital rights to my person . . . would you believe it, I'm so scared that when she enters my room at night it puts me in a sweat and panic grips me.'

This is intended to be taken as a joke; but no such sense of fun underlies the following comment in 'Betrothed', Chekhov's last published story and one of his most earnest works. The bride-to-be, Nadya, inspects her future home with her fiancé. They enter the bedroom: 'Here in the gloom stood two beds side by side, and it looked as though when the bedroom was being furnished someone had had the idea that things were always going to go very well in here, and that anything else was out of the question.' Now the irony of this comment lies in the fact that already, before the marriage, Nadya is feeling disgust for her fiancé, Andrei Andreich, disgust for his arm around her waist. He is a typical *poshlyak*. In Chekhov's work a happy sexual relationship is constantly associated with the concept of *poshlost'*, with mediocrity and the trivial.

2

What lay at the bottom of Chekhov's disapproval of woman in her sexual role? Was it simply deference to the moral conventions of his time? Was it a strict sense of personal morality? Or was it a less cerebral feeling, a private sense of repugnance—a distaste, in fact, for sex?

The beginnings of an answer can be found in Chekhov's reaction to the various attitudes towards sex evinced in the work of the other masters of Russian prose whose work one might expect to have influenced him.

E

Of Gogol's influence on Chekhov's early prose style mention has already been made. Gogol's attitude to sex, however, was so abnormal that it can be easily discounted as an influence on Chekhov's, or indeed anyone else's, attitude in this sphere.

Actual sexual desire was perhaps most unequivocally described by Turgenev. In his *On the Eve* there is a climactic scene where the hero Insarov struggles with desire for his fiancée Elena. Turgenev's conveyance of the situation by circumlocution and by Insarov's altruistic appeals to Elena to leave are embarrassing to the modern reader, for whom the closure of the episode with Elena's 'Then take me' comes as some relief. More successful is the treatment of a similar situation in *Fathers and Sons* where Bazarov is overcome with desire for Odintsova—who, however, does not return his passion. Here Turgenev's straightforward approach and the absence of lofty sentiments are definitely more in tune with our age: nevertheless, even in *On the Eve*, given the conventions of the time, Turgenev was in advance of most of his contemporaries in dealing with the subject as frankly as he did.

Chekhov seems to have been unimpressed by Turgenev's boldness. In a letter to Suvorin of 1893 he criticized Turgenev's principal female protagonists: 'All Turgenev's women and girls are intolerably artificial, and, if you'll forgive me, fake. Liza, Elena, aren't Russian girls but sort of prophesying priestesses, stuffed with ideas beyond their station in life. Irina in *Smoke*, Odintsova in *Fathers and Sons*, all these ardent, voracious, insatiable tigresses seeking for something—it's so much rubbish. When you think of Tolstoy's Anna Karenina, all these Turgenevan ladies with their seductive shoulders can go to blazes.'[5]

Chekhov had, reasonably enough, made a summary distinction between Turgenev's lofty-minded young girls—the obvious 'heroines'—and his older, worldly temptresses, who are in a sense at once both heroine and villain. However, pure or impure, Turgenev's women, as far as Chekhov was concerned, could not win either way.

Yet it is perhaps worth remarking that neither Irina nor Odintsova fulfils the promise of her seductive shoulders adequately from the point of view of the hero, since neither is prepared to commit herself to a sexual passion. It is the mere idea of either as a sexual object that calls forth Chekhov's strong words. Why this should be so will eventually become clear.

Meanwhile, we must note that it was definitely not conventional prudery *vis-à-vis* feminine immorality which inspired his criticism of Turgenev: in conventional terms, Odintsova is not immoral at all, and besides, Chekhov's reference to Anna Karenina makes this clear. In fact, he had a particular fondness for Anna Karenina, that seductress *par excellence*, who is more highly sexed and more wayward than either Irina or Odintsova.*

But Chekhov accorded Tolstoy a general admiration and indulgence with which he did not favour Turgenev. Throughout his life he regarded Tolstoy with affection and reverence, and during the latter 1880s his creative activity was markedly influenced by Tolstoy's ideas and artistic forms: it is Tolstoy alone who can be said to have influenced Chekhov's fictional treatment of sexual relationships.

Tolstoy's influence is clearly discernible in a number of works which Chekhov produced in the years 1886-8, in stories which deal with man's fraternal relations to others, and also in others concerning sexual relationships. 'Misfortune' was written during this period,[6] and so also were several works bearing more or less directly on the theme of prostitution.

This last theme Chekhov treated with an interesting blend of reportage and emotive detail. In 'A Male Acquaintance' (*Znakomy muzhchina*, 1886) he ostensibly makes light of it. A courtesan visits a dentist whom she once knew to borrow money, but her courage fails her at the moment of asking and she submits to having a tooth extracted instead. However, this story ends happily: the girl weeps, but by the next evening she has found a new man. The implication is that her troubles are trivial and her capacity for being hurt slight.

The mood of 'The Chorus Girl' (*Khoristka*, 1886) is more sombre and its tone more strident. In this the degradation of a prostitute, Pasha, is poignantly described. The wife of one

* Chekhov makes his affection for Tolstoy's heroine clear in a letter to M. P. Chekhov of 10 March 1887. 'Dear sweet Anna,' he writes, was his 'only consolation' during the train-journey from Moscow to St. Petersburg. The Soviet editors of *Works*, 1944–51, have appended a note to the foot of this letter: 'he refers to Anna Karenina'; and there is no reason to disbelieve it. However, one may observe a particular anxiety on the part of the editors to assure the reader that it was no other Anna, since they have here defied their usual practice of siting notes at the back of the volume, where they might possibly be overlooked.

Kolpakov, one of her clients, comes to her claiming that Kolpakov's children are starving, and demanding that Pasha hand over the presents which he has given her. The prostitute is overawed by the other's presence: 'Pasha felt that the lady in black with the angry eyes and white slender fingers must find her disgusting and hideous, and she began to feel ashamed of her podgy red cheeks, her pockmarked nose and the lock of hair on her forehead which refused to be combed back. And she felt that if she were thin, wore no powder and did not have that lock of hair, she could conceal that she was a loose woman and it would not be so frightening and humiliating to confront the unknown, mysterious lady.' Finally, browbeaten and compelled through a sense of her own guilt and pity for the children, she hands over all her jewellery, not merely the oddments she has received from Kolpakov, who preferred to give her cakes. He, hiding next door, has overheard all, and when his wife leaves Pasha turns to him in an access of indignation; but he is concerned only with the degradation of his wife, and shouts at the girl: 'Get away from me—you scum!' It is obviously impossible not to feel revulsion both for him and for his bullying wife, and pity for the prostitute, who is shown to have a natural goodness lacking in her accusers.

Although in these two stories Chekhov is clearly attempting to strike a balance between showing sympathy for the girl and revealing the sordidness of prostitution he has not found the right touch to bring off either aim, artistically. 'A Male Acquaintance' is too fanciful to bear the weight of its sarcastic moralizing overtones, as revealed, for example, in the second paragraph: 'but . . . what could you buy for a rouble? For that amount of money you couldn't buy a smart short jacket, nor a tall hat, nor bronze-coloured shoes, and without these things she felt she might as well be naked.' 'The Chorus Girl', on the other hand, suffers from a rather heavy-handed laying-on of pathos. Pasha's anger and humiliation are telling enough without the story closing on the following unnecessary, tear-jerking sentence: 'She recalled that three years ago a merchant had beaten her for no reason at all, and burst into even noisier sobbing.'

Much more successful is Chekhov's treatment of prostitution when he simply touches on the theme (as he does in 'The Kiss'), or when he treats it quite straightforwardly. In 'Words, Words,

Words' (*Slova, slova, slova,* 1883) a young man interrogates a prostitute, demanding to know the cause of her fall. She suddenly sees him as her saviour—but his next remark shows that his interest has been merely casual. Jejune and sentimental as the story is, it is more successful than 'The Chorus Girl' and 'A Male Acquaintance' because in this fragment Chekhov is not afraid of taking an unequivocally solemn and restrained approach to what he certainly regarded as a serious theme; the uneasy tone apparent in 'A Male Acquaintance' and 'The Chorus Girl' would seem to result from the author's determination to sit on the fence.

For the same reason 'Nervous Breakdown' (*Pripadok,* 1888) is successful, although the moralizing element in it is strong. It is Chekhov's most significant attack on prostitution. The hero of the story, Vasiliev, visits a brothel with some friends, hoping to find the inmates eager for salvation. He finds instead that the girls regard their occupation with complacent *sang-froid*: one, who is weeping and whom he believes and hopes to be in despair, turns out to be simply drunk. His horror leads the young man to a nervous breakdown.

But although he was merciless in depicting their moral degradation, Chekhov did not make villains of fallen women where these found themselves on the lowest rung of the social ladder; and in this attitude to prostitution he was clearly affected by the sense of social guilt which influenced him, Tolstoy, Dostoevsky, and many other Russian writers of the time: notably, V. M. Garshin, whose pessimism drove him in 1888 to despair and suicide, and for whom Chekhov in fact wrote 'Nervous Breakdown'. (It was his contribution to a memorial volume for Garshin.) He wrote to Suvorin apropos of this: 'In this story I've stated my opinion, for what it's worth, of rare people like Garshin. . . . I say a lot about prostitution, but solve no problems. Why doesn't your paper write about prostitution? It's the most dreadful evil, after all. Our Sobolev alley is a slave-owners' market.'[7]

These words bear witness both to Chekhov's social conscience and to an aspect of his view of prostitution which is significant. One of Chekhov's most cherished tenets was a belief in the importance of human dignity and self-respect in personal relations. At the age of nineteen he had written in answer to a self-deprecating letter from his younger brother Misha: 'You know where you should admit you're worthless? Before God, perhaps, in the face of intelligence, beauty, nature, but not before men. Before men you must acknowledge your own worth.'[8] And in a letter to his loose-living eldest brother Nikolai in March 1886 Chekhov made it clear that he considered thoughtfulness and mutual respect in human relationships more important than the observation of conventional morality. ('Cultured people,' he declared, *inter alia*, 'when living with someone . . . are tolerant of noise and cold and burnt meat and witticisms and the presence of outsiders in their home.')[9]

The prostitute, then, could arouse Chekhov's sympathy and receive unusually generous treatment at his hands, since she represented for him the victim of a debasing social evil. Yet she did not—and it is important to realize this—represent for him anything more deserving of sympathy than this. This is a significant difference between Chekhov and many authors, including several of his contemporaries, who made a heroine of the prostitute—or a prostitute of the heroine. They regarded her not only as a pitiable victim of her environment, but as a creature in no way intrinsically corrupt—as a creature totally pure in the sight of God. In *Resurrection* Tolstoy created an archetypal figure of this stamp in Maslova. But it was really Dostoevsky who made a speciality of the 'pure prostitute' and elevated her to a metaphysical status. His Nastasya Filippovna in *The Idiot* and Sonya Marmeladova in *Crime and Punishment* are much less 'real' than Turgenev's virtuous young ladies; they are symbols of the Dostoevskian concept of purity, which is to be found in the heart, not in deeds.

It may be that Chekhov, who had but a qualified admiration for Dostoevsky, was in his own fiction making a conscious attempt to reintroduce into literature a realistic image of the prostitute. Evincing sympathy for her did not prevent him from showing up the seamy side of her life for what it was.

His doing this was however not entirely promoted by the feeling that prostitution was a blot on society's escutcheon, nor by his desire to depict reality objectively. There is strong evidence that on a personal level also Chekhov felt deep distaste for not only prostitution but casual sexual relationships in general. In the letter to Nikolai quoted above there are some most significant lines. Defining further his idea of a cultured (*vospitanny*) person, Chekhov states that such people: 'try as far as possible to subdue and ennoble the sexual instinct (. . .) . . . What they need in a woman isn't bed, horse-sweat (. . .), not the sort of intelligence that manifests itself in the ability to deceive people with fake pregnancies and tell incessant lies. . . . What they—especially artists—need is freshness, refinement, humanity, the ability to be not a (. . .) but a mother.'[10]

It is not only the righteous tone of this letter that is reminiscent of Tolstoy: the sentiments expressed—this disgust for the animal nature of sex—were also extremely Tolstoyan. Tolstoy apparently, 'stood beside the bed and wept'[11] after his first experience with a prostitute. With Tolstoy, however, sentiment was apt to be one thing and action another. 'Did you go whoring a lot in your young days?' the old man was once heard to ask Chekhov, adding reflectively, 'I was an indefatigable ——' (he concluded the statement apparently with a 'coarse peasant expression')[12].

Chekhov's reply to this was an inaudible murmur, accompanied by an embarrassed tug of the beard. It was not his way to make what amounted to public pronouncements on such a topic. Certainly there is, as we have seen, considerable emotion in his story 'Volodya', in which the hero suffers spiritually much as Tolstoy claimed to have suffered: this could be said to argue that Chekhov was repelled by the idea of youth being seduced by an immoral woman. But it is not to say that Chekhov also stood beside the bed and wept after his own first casual sexual experience. Actually, the more one learns about Chekhov, the less probable does it seem that this was the case.

In attempting to assess Tolstoy's influence on Chekhov's personal life, one must not overrate the importance of the undoubted literary influence. Tolstoy's thought did at one time influence Chekhov's attitude to sex: this was when Tolstoy published *The Kreutzer Sonata* (1889), that extraordinary plea for total chastity in heterosexual relations made by a hero-villain whose misfortune is to have murdered his wife because he believed her unfaithful: which by its very novelty, not to say absurdity, made an impression on the entire Russian intelligentsia, including (by his own admission) Chekhov. This is not to be wondered at, as his own predilection for moralizing—the propensity that compelled him to lecture his elder brothers on the subject of their personal lives—seemed to be strongest in the last years of the 1880s.

The effects of Tolstoy's newest propaganda were however in Chekhov's case short-lived. After his return from Sakhalin Island in 1890 he wrote to Suvorin: 'Before my trip *The Kreutzer Sonata* struck me as an event, but now I find it ridiculous and senseless. I've grown up as a result of the trip, or something, or else I've gone out of my mind—God only knows.'[13] There is probably some truth in the first of Chekhov's assumptions, that his Sakhalin experiences had hastened his maturity; but in any case, in the matter of personal credos and commitments, as in politics, extremism was always alien to Chekhov's nature, and this fact is in itself the most potent argument against any supposition that Tolstoy effectively influenced Chekhov in the course of his personal life. A puritanical element sometimes discernible in the young Chekhov's epistolary injunctions and in his fiction cannot be considered the result of Tolstoy's influence. Rather, Tolstoy's ideas appealed to Chekhov precisely because there was already something of the puritan in him—a chord that was struck by Tolstoy's first tentative gropings after a new moral code. But when Tolstoy went further, Chekhov was not to be one of the fanatic disciples who would follow him into eccentricity.

Chekhov summed up Tolstoy's influence on himself with a clarity and honesty that demand credence: 'Tolstoy's philosophy,' he wrote to Suvorin in 1894, 'affected me deeply and had hold of me for 6 or 7 years. It was not his basic attitudes that impressed me, I'd always been familiar with them, but the Tolstoyan way of putting things, the rationalism, and, probably, its brand of hypnotism. But now something in me protests; sense and fair-mindedness tell me that there's more love for mankind in electricity and steam than in chastity and vegetarianism. . . . But it's not a question of that, of *pro* and *contra*, it's that somehow or other Tolstoy has sailed away from me, is no longer in my heart and has left me, saying: behold I leave this thy house empty.'[14]

These cool phrases, so uncompromising in their rejection of the philosophy that meant everything to Tolstoy, serve to emphasize how very great in fact was the gulf between the two men as far as attitudes to sex were concerned. And this dis-similarity is yet further emphasized by what we know of Chekhov's personal sex-life.

3

Unfortunately, there exists a minimum of documentary evidence concerning these most private of Chekhov's affairs. However, it is clear that Chekhov's sex-life was very different from Tolstoy's. Whereas Tolstoy's disgust for the pleasures of the flesh was in part engendered by the strain of repressing his strong, and to him shameful, sexual desires, neither driving passion nor any distressing sense of guilt were a feature of Chekhov's sex-life. This at any rate is the conclusion to be drawn from the sources of knowledge available to us.

Chekhov claimed to have 'discovered the secret of love at the age of thirteen'.[15] This however need not be taken as seriously as it has been by certain critics. The assertion, made to a friend, Tikhonov, formed part of a potted autobiography ostensibly intended to be printed under a portrait of Chekhov in a newspaper. The tone of the entire piece suggests that Chekhov wrote it with his tongue in his cheek.

Nevertheless there are indications that his sexual interest in women started at a relatively early age, and was not impeded by youthful diffidence. Misha Chekhov describes in his reminiscences of Anton how on one occasion the latter, meeting a beautiful young girl at a well, suddenly embraced her.[16] Little is known about further amorous exploits at this period of Chekhov's life, but his correspondence of the early 1880s is peppered with references to 'maidens' (*devitsy*), women, and various specific but unidentifiable females. Aleksandr Chekhov in his letters to Anton mentions a brothel in Taganrog in a way which, although sadly unilluminating, suggests that Anton had some knowledge of the place.[17] Similar references to women occur throughout the period of Tolstoy's literary influence. In 1886 Chekhov comments in a letter to a friend: 'Re the pretty women you inquire about, I make haste to "assertain" that there are many of them in Moscow. Just now a whole bevy of them were with my sister and I melted, like a Jew confronted with a gold coin.'[18] In June of the same year he writes to Leikin, the editor of *Oskolki*, from Babkino, a country estate where he was taking a holiday: 'You ask what I spend my money on? On women!!!!'[19] In 1887 in a letter to

F. O. Shekhtel he states, somewhat mysteriously: 'I'm just going to a certain little lady's. I shall do some "writing" at her house.'[20] Here Chekhov's inverted commas suggest that he was referring to some less-than-proper activity, as do also the editors' omissions in cases like the following, where Chekhov, back at Babkino, appeared to find the resources of the place diminished: 'The weather here is filthy: it pours with rain every five minutes. Life's dull and sad,' he wrote, paraphrasing Lermontov's verse, 'and there's no one to (. . .).'[21]

Hoping, perhaps, for better things, he informed Leontiev in the following January: 'In March I'm going to the Kuban'. There: "*Amare et non morire*" . . .'.[22]

Chekhov clearly encouraged his men friends to see in him, if not exactly a womanizer, then at least a gay dog. That he could successfully convey this impression is shown by the reminiscences of certain of his contemporaries. Nemirovich-Danchenko, for instance, writes of him that 'he was apparently very successful with women'.[23]

It should be noted however that Nemirovich-Danchenko admitted his source for this conjecture to be rumour; and in general one must be cautious of ascribing too great a significance to the impressions of Chekhov's contemporaries. There is some reason to suppose that Chekhov let people think what he felt they might like to think about his attitude to the opposite sex. While he was giving it out to his men friends that he was no great respecter of morality, we find him describing Yalta to his straight-laced sister Masha in a highly prudish tone, referring to women in 'bustles which give very frank expression to something very nasty'.[24] Again, to the society women who flirted with him he gave the impression that he returned their interest, or as Nemirovich-Danchenko put it: 'I think he knew how to be charming.'[25]

Not that there is any evidence that he did not actively enjoy such casual flirtations. Photographs show that Chekhov was good-looking rather than the reverse, and it is plain both from the enormous number of his female admirers and from the accounts of other contemporaries that he was attractive to women.[26] This would naturally make it the more likely that he was attracted to them. It is worth recalling in this context Potapenko's assertion that Chekhov 'was a man in the full meaning of the word'.[27] Another friend, Levitan, wrote in a letter to Chekhov: 'I'm no good at accomplishing feats, except amorous ones, which you're not so bad at either.'[28]

There was even an occasion when a fellow-voyager on the boat from Sevastopol' to Odessa accused Chekhov of making indecent proposals to his daughter (an accusation which, it need hardly be said, Chekhov denied).[29]

As the years passed and his contemporaries married, so that his bachelor status became more noticeable, Chekhov apparently wished his friends to think that the pursuit of girls formed an important part of a gay and dissipated life. 'In a place where there's lots of good wine and excellent horses,' he wrote to Leikin from Yalta in 1889, 'and where there's one man to every 20 girls, it's hard to economize.'[30] Several months later he told Pleshcheev with mock ruefulness: ' . . . in Petersburg I ate a great many dinners, and a great many suppers, but didn't captivate a *single* lady . . .'.[31] He talked with delight of various anonymous *devitsy*, of whom he was meeting more and more. 'They are,' he said, 'such that if I were to drive them out to my dacha, we would have a jolly muddle, pregnant (*chrevaty*) with consequences.'[32]

This, however, was the most frivolous period of Chekhov's life. It ended in 1890 with his departure to Sakhalin Island. From this year, and hence despite an increasingly sceptical attitude to Tolstoy's cult of chastity, Chekhov referred less and less frequently in his letters to amorous exploits. When he did so, it tended to be during his trips abroad. On Sakhalin Island, it is true, he was repelled by the degradation of the female population, who were exploited sexually as well as in many other ways, and his comment on an official visit to the brothels there (guided by a police officer) was: 'revolting'.[33] But in Ceylon, on the homeward journey, he claimed to have had his fill of 'bronze-skinned women (. . .)'.[34] Some years later, while staying at Biarritz, Chekhov wrote to both his friend Lika Mizinova and to Suvorin's wife about a certain Margot, a 'maiden' of nineteen years whom he had employed 'for practice in French'.[35] A month or two later while staying in Nice he told Suvorin that he was 'making sacrifices to the goddess of love (. . .)'.[36]

Several reasons spring to mind to explain our impression that Chekhov's sex-life was largely confined to his periods of residence abroad. It is quite possible that the affairs he referred to were merely elaborations of the facts: this was probably so in the case of Margot at least, for Chekhov made no significant claims about her and was very likely using her as a pretext to shock or to amuse his women friends. Or one might suppose it to be for discretion's sake that Chekhov kept his bouts of philandering for abroad. But he had no ties in Russia to prevent him from consorting with women, nor did he ever reject, so far as we can tell, a youthful assertion that 'anyone has the right to live how and with whom he pleases',[37] if this betokened the belief that there was no moral stigma necessarily attached to extra-marital sex.

It would seem much more probable that it was the tedium of leading a solitary existence in strange towns which drove Chekhov in his late thirties to 'make sacrifices to the goddess of love'. In the context of this phrase Chekhov also remarks that he is doing nothing else save eating and sleeping, that he is already bored and wants to go home. In two later letters from Yalta, Chekhov says that he has considered having an affair 'with a pock-marked peasant', and, subsequently, with 'some ugly and stupid woman'.[38] His tone is facetious, but his words point to the fact that his need for diversion was paramount at such times. Confined to Yalta in February of 1900 he said in a letter to Gorky that he was bored by, *inter alia*, the lack of women there.[39]

It is interesting to observe that the attitude to women he displayed to Gorky seems to have been altogether that of a connoisseur. After his first meeting with Gorky, Chekhov remarked in a letter to his friend Lidiya Avilova: 'I want to acquaint [Gorky] with women, since I think he could do with this, but he fights shy.'[40] A rather similar condescension is to be found in his comments on Tolstoy, recorded several years previously: Tolstoy's opinions, Chekhov wrote to Pleshcheev in 1890 (the year of disillusionment), 'on syphilis, foundling homes, on the repugnance women feel for intercourse and so on, are not merely open to question, they quite plainly show him to be an ignorant man who hasn't taken the trouble, in the course of a long life, to read 2 or 3 books written by specialists'.[41] Chekhov was of course justified in laying claim to a better medical knowledge of women, but Tolstoy, who was after all married (and, it is worth noting in the context of Chekhov's remark, to a woman who was much less highly-sexed than her husband), certainly had an immeasurably broader physical knowledge of the opposite sex. It may be that Chekhov's air of knowledge of women, in all

senses, was attributable in part to his writer's pride. He believed
in depicting things as they were—and it was perhaps unthinkable
to him that he should credit other writers with a closer experience
of reality than his own. At least, such a spirit of rivalry seems
discernible in an early criticism of his brother Aleksandr's fiction.
Of a character in the latter's sketch 'At the Lighthouse'[42] Chekhov
had this to say: 'Olya . . . is no use, like all your women. You
have no idea about women.' Now, it is true that Olga, the
lighthouse-keeper's seventeen-year-old daughter, is a peculiarly
unprepossessing mixture of child and adolescent: she divides her
time between kissing her father's moustache ('—only wipe it
first—'), executing *entrechats* and gazing pensively out to sea; but
Anton himself later fell into exactly the same trap of sentimentalizing his heroines, and to do so is not in any case proof of lack of
knowledge of women. Anton's criticism seems the more arrogant
when one considers that, as the correspondence between the
brothers clearly shows, Aleksandr was very much occupied with
the opposite sex and took a considerably greater interest in
acquiring knowledge of it than Anton seems ever to have done.

4

How great, in fact, was Chekhov's knowledge of women? To
put it more bluntly, did he actually have sexual intercourse with
any, or all, of the *devitsy* to whom he referred so suggestively?
The problem that faces Chekhov's biographers here is not
Chekhov's discretion so much as that of the present custodians of
his letters. However, one can give free rein to speculation about
the degree of Chekhov's involvement with women, knowing that
his talk of them was not at any rate entirely a façade.

It is important to ascertain this, and it is possible to do so, for
there does exist documentation concerning one at least of
Chekhov's liaisons, his affair with the actress Lidiya Borisovna
Yavorskaya.

Unfortunately, Chekhov's letters to this woman, with one
exception, are not extant; but hers to him, though few in number,
and hitherto unpublished, are an invaluable source of knowledge
about his relationship with her, and are unique among the
material that has so far come to light on Chekhov's dealings with

women, in that they constitute virtual proof that more than mere friendship was involved.*

In 1893, when she was about twenty-one, Lidiya Yavorskaya came to Moscow from Kiev and joined the Korsh Theatre Company there. She was already divorced from her first husband and she embarked on a gay *vie mondaine*. It is not clear precisely when her affair with Chekhov began; but it is clear that their intimacy developed over a period of time: that it was not, for Chekhov at least, *le coup de foudre*. Yavorskaya's letters to Chekhov of 1893 and 1894, dating from December 1893, give the impression that she was anxious to clarify Chekhov's attitude towards herself. They include a flattering request that he should write a play for her benefit night, and a coy demand that he bring her a prescription when she is ill ('I don't dare to count on your magnanimously visiting the infirm Yavorskaya, but I hope . . . '. In Russian: *Ne smeyu rasschitivat' na Vashe velikodushnoe poseshchenie nemoshchnoi Yavors., no upovayu.*⁴³ These words are typical of the grandiloquent style Yavorskaya frequently adopted in her letters to Chekhov.) In October 1894 she invites him to her room in the following terms: 'There shall await you . . . everything you want, and above all myself. *Joking apart*, I beg you, do come.'⁴⁴

In four further letters of January 1895 (three of which are dated in Chekhov's hand) the relationship is clearly on a more intimate footing. Lidiya, it seems, was now forcing the issue. A grandiose declaration on an enormous sheet of paper with a seal, dated 1 January 1895 and signed 'Lidiya the First' gives leave of absence until 3 February to 'the general of literature and knight of the order of St. Tatyana the Martyr and of Lidiya the First, and private of our own escort, Anton Pavlovich Chekhov.'⁴⁵

Any attempt to judge how intimate were Chekhov's relationships with women must take into account the use in his letters of the pronouns 'you' (*vy*) and 'thou' (*ty*). *Ty*, in general, was in the

---

* Tanya Shchepkina-Kupernik, Yavorskaya's almost inseparable companion and also a friend of Chekhov, denied that this was the case. She claimed in her memoirs that Chekhov, physically attracted to Yavorskaya and having heard the many malicious rumours in circulation concerning her accessibility, took offence when he became convinced that his flirtation with her would not go beyond flirting (i.e. that she would not have a love-affair with him). However, Tanya may have been concealing the truth—either from her undoubted loyalty to her friend, or from an obscure sense of jealousy—or possibly she did not know the truth.

nineteenth century less freely used among contemporaries than it is in present-day Russia, and was the form of address normally employed between members of one family, close friends of the same sex, and lovers. Chekhov's use of *ty* in his extant correspondence with women is minimal, being confined to letters to his sister, and to Olga Knipper, where the adoption of *ty* almost certainly marks the point at which she became his mistress. Likewise, his being addressed by women as *ty* is indicative of the nature of their relationship to him. In two of her letters of January 1895 Yavorskaya uses both *ty* and *vy* in a rather unorthodox mixture. She addresses Chekhov as 'darling' (*dusya*) and refers to her kisses, even her 'ardent' kisses. 'My darling,' she writes, 'it is terribly hard for me to part from you, just as though the very best part of my heart were torn away . . . don't forget her who loves thee alone, thy Vasentasena.'⁴⁶ 'Vasentasena', according to Tanya Shchepkina-Kupernik, was the heroine of an 'Indian drama' that Yavorskaya starred in. In the play, wearing blue lotus-blossom in her hair, she would drop to her knees before her 'chosen one' and declaim, 'Only, unattainable, wondrous one . . .'. 'And when Anton Pavlovich arrived and entered the dark-blue drawing-room, Lidiya would adopt the pose of the Indian heroine, would fall on her knees and, stretching out her hands would exclaim: "Only, unattainable, wondrous one!"'⁴⁷

It all sounds very innocent, even tame: well can it be imagined that Tanya, playing the part of spectator to such goings-on, might identify with the saintly martyr. Indeed, she referred to this period as that of the couple's 'mild flirtation',⁴⁸ but that there was more to it than that is apparent from an undated letter written by Lidiya to Chekhov which undoubtedly belongs to this same period.⁴⁹ It addresses Chekhov as 'Karudatta'—Vasentasena's counterpart in the play (as did two other letters, one dated by Chekhov January 1895). Lidiya's undated letter bears the address: 'Nizhegorod Gr. Hotel—Room 9 alas not 5' (Chekhov in January of 1895 had stayed in the Moscow Grand Hotel, room 5). In the blank verse in which it is partially written the letter declares:

> . . . and thou knowest not how thy Vasentasena
> Thy Southern flower, thy 'little sun'
> Here suffers in the lair of the Volga-folk
> Who take from her 4 r. a night

> For a hotel room so unlike,
> Alas, that room in the Moscow
> In which she with thee
> Tasted of unearthly bliss.

The meaning of this seems unambiguous, although elsewhere in the letter Yavorskaya keeps to the *vy* form of address. It is an almost inescapable conclusion that, in January of 1895 at least, in Moscow, Chekhov and Yavorskaya were lovers.

What then broke up the affair? For the relationship was clearly of relatively short duration. By March it seemed to be over. In that month Lidiya, still on tour, wrote to Chekhov that he had 'forgotten his Vasentasena'.[50] 'Remember,' she continued, 'dear Anton Pavlovich, that I love you sincerely and have missed you very much. . . . I want to regard you as my friend,' she adds. The tone of the letter, however, is light and casual: 'I stayed of course at the Moscow(!) room 6. Your Lidiya' is how it ends. It is clear that Lidiya, as always, is thinking of her career: her main request of Chekhov is that he should come to Petersburg to give her 'moral support' when she appears there.

It might well have been her preoccupation with her career and obvious ability to take love-affairs in her stride as something secondary that constituted, for Chekhov, a large part of Yavorskaya's appeal. Whatever form it took, the affair seems to have made no lasting impression on him. His rare references to Yavorskaya at the supposed height of his interest are casual: thus, to Suvorin in January 1895: 'Yesterday I went to Korsh's theatre and saw *Sans gêne* . . . the main part is played by Yavorskaya—a very sweet woman.'[51] More significant is the confidence he made to the same correspondent eleven days later: 'Fie, fie! Women take away one's youth, but not in my case. In the course of my life I've been steward, not master, and fate has hardly spoiled me. I've had few affairs and am as like Ekaterina as a nut (*orekh*) is to a battleship. Silk nightgowns only spell pleasure to me in that they are soft to the touch. Comfort has its appeal for me, but debauchery has no allure. . . .'*

---

* Letter to A. S. Suvorin, 21 January 1895. 'Ekaterina' refers to Catherine the Great, renowned for her love-affairs. In this same letter Chekhov makes the following comments, which would be of great interest if the authorities permitted examination of the original document: from the published version

The inference is clear: whatever form the 'unearthly bliss' of room 5 had taken, it had not been a prolonged sensual orgy.

Was it possible that the relationship had been a bitter experience for Chekhov which exacerbated in him a distaste for women who entered into purely sensual relationships? Such a theory seems at first reasonably plausible, because the year 1895 saw the creation of Ariadna, Olga Dmitrievna in 'His Wife', and Arkadina in *The Seagull*.

Chekhov's further comments on the girl are not however those of an embittered or disillusioned lover, but sound more like an impartial judgement on a not very close acquaintance. 'She's educated and dresses well, sometimes is intelligent,' he remarks to Suvorin. He continues to say that Yavorskaya does not deserve the harsh criticism that she receives—that minus a couple of faults, affectation and over-acting, she would be 'a real actress'. 'A curious character anyway . . .' thus Chekhov sums up what sounds like a fair appraisal.[52] He did not however seem prepared to take Yavorskaya's part against Suvorin, who knew the lady well and had a poor opinion of her. He once stated: 'Yavorskaya is entirely compounded of affectation, envy, vice, and falsehood':[53] faults which did not deter him from frequent meetings with her on the social plane. A subsequent letter from Chekhov to Suvorin[54] suggests that the latter was voicing some criticisms and suspicions of Yavorskaya: but Chekhov's reaction was mild, not at all that of an offended lover: 'Your opinion of Yavorskaya didn't strike me as harsh.'[55]

Suvorin was not alone in disliking Yavorskaya. Tanya Shchepkina-Kupernik said that the company of Korsh's theatre were jealous of her, and that 'she inspired an amazing amount of

there have been excised what are clearly two proper names. 'Come, but don't kiss "the feet of (. . .)". She's a talented girlie, but she's hardly likely to strike you as sympathetic. I'm sorry for her because I'm vexed with myself: three days in the week she repels me. She's sly as the devil, but her motives are so petty that she's more like a rat than the devil. But (. . .) is a different matter. She's a very kind woman and an actress who might come to something if she wasn't spoilt by the school. She is a little hussy, but that doesn't matter.' It seems likely that the last lines refer to Yavorskaya. D. Gillès states in his biography of Chekhov (p. 244) that the 'talented girlie' (*talant-livaya devochka*) of whom Chekhov writes in this letter was Tanya Shchepkina-Kupernik. Gillès does not give the source of his information.

F

malicious gossip'.* Yavorskaya herself in a letter to Chekhov of March 1894 had complained vehemently of vile rumours circulated by a male former friend of hers, apparently to the effect that Tanya was a Lesbian and the girls' friendship unnatural.[56]

Her unpopularity, combined with rumours of her liaison with Chekhov,[57] undoubtedly helped to give rise to various theories that Chekhov was in fact depicting Yavorskaya in Ariadna, or in Arkadina.[58] The factual grounds for such theories would seem precarious and few: really only that Arkadina is an actress who has an affair with a writer (but she is the wrong age); and that Ariadna is the right age (but her history is quite unlike Yavorskaya's as Chekhov knew her. When Chekhov met her, Yavorskaya was divorced from her first husband. Later, she married into the nobility, as we leave Ariadna on the point of doing: but Chekhov could not have known that she would do this).†

More extensive are the speculative grounds for such theories. Yavorskaya may well have been, like Ariadna and Arkadina, a woman of loose morals:‡ she also was almost certainly vain, and probably spoilt. Misha Chekhov tells a pathetic story of how he

---

* Shchepkina-Kupernik, *Dni moei zhizni*, p. 280. Suvorin's diary (pp. 95–6) offers the following example of the 'malicious gossip' that surrounded Yavorskaya—a tale told him by the actress Krestovskaya: 'In Kiev, Yavorskaya was given a part over Krestovskaya's head. She acted so badly in it that when her husband and friends presented her with flowers the audience hissed; and thereby gave Krestovskaya double cause to resent her, because Krestovskaya's name still appeared on the billboards. Yavorskaya was angry too, and spread rumours to the effect that it was stooges specially hired by Krestovskaya who had hissed her.' 'This is Yavorskaya all over,' was Suvorin's comment.

† Suvorin (p. 113) commented on Yavorskaya's marriage in August 1896: 'Received a telegram saying Yavorskaya has got herself married to Prince Baryatinsky. She is older than he is and doesn't love him. Unless she has children by him she won't put up with him long, either that or he won't put up with her.'

‡ Suvorin (p. 114) describes how Tanya Shchepkina-Kupernik came to him with a grievance soon after Yavorskaya's second marriage. In Prince Baryatinsky's presence the two women had been talking of their past and its attendant gossip. Tanya rashly remarked: 'There's no smoke without fire'. Lidiya was incensed at this indiscretion, and sent Tanya packing, despite an awkward attempt by the latter to smooth things over. Presumably the breach was not permanent, since Tanya does not mention any such thing in her memoirs. These give a somewhat governessy impression, but the above incident shows that she was less prim in real life than on paper.

was sent by brother Anton to fetch Yavorskaya from the theatre to a celebratory dinner on St. Tatyana's Day, 1894—a treat to which he, Misha, was greatly looking forward. Arriving during the performance, he was persuaded by the actress to wait and see her 'die'—she was playing the title role in *La Dame aux camélias*. After that Misha was obliged to wait until she had recovered from the emotional effect of her acting, and by the time she had then changed, the dinner was over.[59]

Bunin remembers Chekhov saying that actors and actresses were 'vulgar people, permeated through and through with conceit'.[60] But Chekhov married an actress notwithstanding, and one who was probably herself not above feelings of professional pride and jealousy. At least, some excerpts from Olga Knipper's correspondence with Chekhov would suggest that this was the case: 'Yesterday after Act I,' Olga writes on 21 February 1901, 'Yavorskaya came sneaking into my dressing-room to make my acquaintance. What for? She flattered me in such a digustingly vulgar way. After Act 4 she threw Stanislavsky a red carnation from her bosom—touching!' And on 24 February: 'Yavorskaya again came sneaking into my dressing-room, she crawls and flatters and invites everyone to come to her place. Impudent woman.' And again on 2 March: 'On the 5th I've invited Yavorskaya home, but I certainly shan't be there. I can't stand the sight of that coarse woman, and have given orders that she is not to be admitted to my dressing-room during intervals, otherwise I'd be rude to her.'

Just as Yavorskaya's professional interest in meeting Knipper was doubtless increased by the desire to see Chekhov's girl-friend, so Olga's dislike of her was possibly connected with the suspicion, or knowledge, that Yavorskaya was Chekhov's ex-mistress. Chekhov's calmly judicious reply to Olga's remarks gives nothing away: Yavorskaya visited the theatre, he said, as would Sarah Bernhardt, sincerely wanting to give pleasure by her attentions.[61]

Given Chekhov's independent character, it seems improbable that Yavorskaya's unpopularity influenced him to discontinue their relationship; it is much more likely that it was her faults *per se* which hastened the break-up of the affair. But there is no *evidence* that Yavorskaya made Chekhov suffer or indeed that she caused him disillusionment in any way. It is much more probable that Chekhov's affair with Yavorskaya, however great a degree of intimacy it involved, was entered into in a casual spirit, and broken up by the circumstance of her obligation to go on tour in the spring of 1895—and that it left neither of them with any cause for regret or recrimination.

5

If at this point Chekhov sought further such relationships, whether in the world of the theatre, or in the *demi-monde*, then his delight in them was short-lived. For towards the end of 1895 Chekhov wrote to Suvorin saying that, although he was afraid of marriage and routine: '... all the same it's better than tossing in the sea of life, bobbing about in the frail bark of profligacy. And I no longer care about mistresses, and in my relations with them am gradually becoming impotent.'[62] The reference to mistresses remains obscure, but it need not delay us. Chekhov may have been writing loosely, having only one ex-mistress, Yavorskaya, in mind, or there may have been other women. What is arresting here is the mention of impotence, and it is tempting to seize it and make a connection with Chekhov's unsympathetic depiction of sexual relationships. If Chekhov were indeed impotent, it might be argued, this could explain the violent dislike he felt for, say, Ariadna.

Such simplifications cannot however be applied here. For, throughout his career as a serious writer (and before that, whenever he was writing at all seriously) Chekhov presented a consistently gloomy view of sex. Whereas, it seems, it was in the very midst of this career that Chekhov himself fell into a state of apathy towards sexual relationships, and a period of his life began in which, we surmise, liaisons like his affair with Yavorskaya were the exception rather than the rule.

The beginning of this period of apathy can be established with some certainty, thanks to a revealing reference to the matter made by Aleksandr Chekhov in a letter to Anton of 15 April 1893: 'I read your last letter,* old chap, about your becoming

---

* The 'last letter' of Anton's to which Aleksandr refers is unfortunately not extant. 'Palogorch' and 'Alyatrimantan' (see below) were nicknames for their father Pavel, Egorovich Chekhov. The palace in which he sang was the palace of Tsar Aleksandr I in Taganrog. The mongoose was a pet Chekhov brought back from India, but which he donated to the Moscow Zoo after it had escaped several times.

indifferent. It's a great, great pity, Antosha, but it can't be helped.
Judging from my own experience, I think this has happened very
early. But we children of Palogorch seem for some reason to be
in a rush where life's concerned, against our will, and the fates
compel us to age morally sooner than we should. Uncle Mitrofan
has only now begun to submit to the decree of time and at our
age he was more of a lad than you or I. On the other hand,
however, he didn't write *Ivanov*, "Ward no. 6" and so forth. Just
compare the number of years he and Alyatrimantan had to sing
in the palace and occupy themselves with the pounds and ounces
behind the shop-counter to achieve only the slightest approxima-
tion of something equal to the brainwork that goes into one line
you write! It's these lines, as I see it, that are swallowing up our
lives prematurely. And it probably also counts for a lot (at least,
I'm inclined to think so, and if I'm mistaken, too bad) that you
live like a monk. Your prime is passing, and it will have passed
before you notice, and then all you'll have left is to go to the zoo
and talk to your mongoose about the pleasures of bachelor life.'[63]

Aleksandr's theory about his brother—that the energy which
might have been devoted to women was spent in the process of
literary creation—seems fairly plausible. Some men could of
course find time for both women and writing, and indeed Aleksandr himself was clearly one of these, despite his identification
with Anton's situation. But Anton, who was more industrious
than either of his brothers, appears to have been less easily
distracted from the serious job of making money. It is significant
in this connection that by the end of the 1890s Chekhov had
become an established and successful writer and that the grinding
pressure of the necessity to work had been largely removed from
him. Significant because it was then that Chekhov met Olga
Knipper, who was to become his wife, and with whom his sexual
relationship appears to have been normal.

There emerges here a minor but curious point, which is that
certain commentators on this relationship seem unwilling to give
Olga the credit for the renewal of Chekhov's interest in sex. The
critic Jacoby says, apropos of Chekhov's attraction to Knipper:
'C'est un problème médical, probablement l'effet à retardement de
la tuberculose, qui passe pour agir comme un aphrodisiaque.'[64]
This may have been the case, but it would seem more probable
that his double burden of work and ill-health was such that

Chekhov simply lacked the impetus to seek for a sexual relationship, waiting till one was thrust upon him.

Chekhov's biographer Rachmanowa presents Olga Knipper as an over-sexed, calculating hussy who seduced an unwilling Anton Pavlovich. While disregarding this unashamedly fictionalized account, we may concede that Olga may well have taken the initiative; but there is no reason to believe that Chekhov's response was forced. 'I look lustfully at the two beds in my room,' he wrote to Olga from a Viennese hotel a few months before their marriage. 'I shall sleep, and think!'[65] In 1902 he writes: 'I'm eating for ten men. One snag—no wife, I'm living like a monk.'[66] There are a great many more such comments in his letters to Knipper and many more deleted passages. The level of intimacy at which the editors of the 1944–51 edition of Chekhov's works and letters made cuts can be illustrated by citing the following remark of Chekhov's, omitted from that edition but published elsewhere: 'I'm sleeping excellently, but I don't call it sleep since my dear little housewife isn't beside me.'[67]

There can be no doubt that Chekhov was physically attracted to Olga Knipper. However, there can equally be no doubt that the happiness of his relationship with her depended on factors other than physical attraction.

Nearly a decade before he met his future wife, Chekhov had written to his brother Aleksandr: 'Between a woman who sleeps on a clean sheet and one who lolls on a dirty one and laughs merrily when her lover (. . .) there is the same difference as between a drawing-room and a pub.'[68] The language Chekhov uses—*drykhnet* ('lolls') and *khokhochet* ('laughs loudly') emphasizes the vulgarity of the scene envisaged. Here, admittedly, Chekhov's viewpoint seems commonplace enough, and it is arguable that he would only have considered making such a hackneyed point to a man like Aleksandr, whose letters to Anton suggest that he had a crude conception of heterosexual relationships. But the sentiment and tone are similar to those of the earlier homily addressed to Nikolai ('they need . . . the ability to be not a (. . .) but a mother'),[69] and together the two letters are as graphic an expression as could be required of that fundamental, deep distaste for certain aspects of sex which Chekhov displayed throughout his life.

Gorky testified of Chekhov that 'coarse anecdotes never

amused him'.[70] Chekhov, setting down his own anecdotes and stories, despite intended objectivity revealed everywhere an aversion for anything that could conceivably be interpreted as a debasement or vulgarization of sex—a puritanical refusal to accept its existence in the context of unadorned sensuality or commercialization. He depicted with hatred women treating men as a means to sexual gratification, and with revulsion those whom men treated likewise.

As we have seen, this attitude cannot be explained by the 'sour grapes' theory. By the time he confessed that he was 'gradually becoming impotent', Chekhov had had experience of casual sexual relations. The impotence, if it was not caused by physical exhaustion, was the result of his dislike of such relations, not the cause.

Did, then, his harsh portrayal of women like Ariadna derive from his personal experience of such women? The possibility remains that it did, but there is no factual evidence available that suggests Chekhov ever suffered so.

Women other than Yavorskaya have been put forward as prototypes for Ariadna and her fellow-villains. Sobolev in his biography of Chekhov refers to the history of Chekhov's classics master in Taganrog, who married a beautiful girl named Ariadna and whose private life was very unhappy.[71] Masha Chekhova pointed out that Arkadina was reminiscent of Mariya Andreevna Potapenko, the unpopular wife of Chekhov's friend Ignaty Potapenko.[72] Misha Chekhov claimed that 'His Wife' was 'virtually the biography' of Al. Al. Sablin.[73] Misha himself was briefly engaged to a certain countess, Klara Ivanovna Mamuna, who, to his surprise, terminated the engagement by marrying another, richer man.

The existence of these putative prototypes does not however account satisfactorily for the vehemence with which Chekhov attacked the fictional characters; for none of these women had injured him personally. Mamuna of course had injured his brother, and of her Chekhov wrote scathingly: 'Misha . . . shoved under my nose the countess's tender, loving letters, begging me to solve this psychological riddle. The hell with solving it. A woman doesn't wear out a pair of shoes before she's lied five times. Still I rather think Shakespeare said that too.'[74] Shakespeare, however, did not present one sex in so much worse a light than the other. Chekhov must have heard tales of erring husbands also. Why did he not pillory them, if he wished to appear objective?

It would seem that Chekhov's treatment of women of the Ariadna-type can only be fully explained if we recognize the strength of his attachment to his extremely personal concept of what a sexual relationship should be. It was a concept which, for all it owed to a humanitarian idea of morality, seems to have owed more to a sense of the aesthetic.

6

People who have no moral objection to the idea of, say, adultery may well be intolerant of sexual relationships in which they themselves would not indulge for aesthetic as opposed to moral considerations. It is extremely significant that Chekhov occasionally betrayed a markedly intolerant attitude towards unorthodox forms of love. In a letter to Suvorin of 1895 he made the cryptic comment: 'The weather in Moscow is good, there's no Lesbian love either'; and he continues: 'Brrr! Thinking of those persons you write me about makes me feel sick, as though I'd eaten a rotten sardine. There aren't any of them in Moscow, thank heavens.'[75] These are harsh words from a writer frequently praised for his tolerance: but already two years earlier we find Chekhov using a similarly condemnatory tone apropos of Emile Zola's novel *Le Docteur Pascal*, in which the central relationship, between a twenty-five-year-old girl and her uncle, who become lovers, is designated by Chekhov 'perversion'. It is not the blood relationship that he has in mind, however, but the difference in age between the doctor and his niece.

Chekhov's general attitude to sexual relationships between old men and young women will be discussed later in the context of his artistic treatment of young women. Meanwhile, what he has to say on the subject of *Le Docteur Pascal* reveals so much—about Chekhov, not about Zola—that his comments must be treated at some length. 'Pascal is well brought off,' he wrote, 'but there's something essentially nasty about this Pascal.' Chekhov now alludes to a Biblical story, that of Abishag, the young slave-girl who was procured to keep the ageing King David warm. (The connection is that Pascal, when he conceives a desire for his niece Clotilde, recalls this story.) 'When I have diarrhoea in the night,' Chekhov continues, 'I put the cat on my belly and it warms me like a compress. Clotilde, or Abishag, is that same cat, warming King David. Her role in life is to keep an old man warm, nothing more. What an enviable fate! I pity this Abishag, who composed no psalms, but probably was more pure and more beautiful in the sight of God than the man who ravished Uriah's wife. She's a human being, she's an individual and she's young and naturally she wants youth, and I'm afraid it takes a Frenchman to make her into a warming-pan for a hoar-headed cupid with sinewy legs like a cock's, in the name of God knows what. It is offensive to me that Clotilde should be used by Pascal, and not by someone younger and stronger: old King David fainting in the arms of a young girl is like a melon already caught by the autumn frost which still aspires to ripen, every vegetable has its day . . .'.

Already from his determined confusion of two very different relationships—for King David, unlike Pascal, 'knew not' the girl and moreover Clotilde is in love with Pascal and gives herself freely—it is apparent that Chekhov has interpreted Zola very much after his own fashion. He has remained wilfully insensible to what Zola is saying. 'From a humanitarian point of view,' Chekhov concludes his criticism of the novel, 'there's little wrong in Pascal's sleeping with a young girl (*devitsa*)—that's his own affair; but it is wrong that Zola has applauded Clotilde for sleeping with Pascal, and bad that he calls this perversion love.'[76]

This last remark is particularly interesting, for the following reason: there is no suggestion in Zola's novel that this relationship between a man of fifty-nine and a girl of twenty-five needs to be whitewashed. Nor is Zola attempting to prove that love *can* be concomitant to such circumstances. He had no need to do so, for he himself, in his late forties, fell in love with a girl of twenty, and Pascal is to a certain extent a self-portrait. Zola intends us to accept *a priori* the fact that Clotilde and Pascal are in love. What could be less equivocal than the description of them walking together: 'Ils semblaient marcher dans la gloire'?

In the face of the emotion with which Zola describes this love, Chekhov's comments on the novel seem gross and insensitive.

It is not a question of mere prudery. For Zola, as much as Chekhov, is aware of the extent to which Pascal is laying himself open to attack, and his love for Clotilde brings Pascal problems. Although in appearance he is remarkably youthful, the age-difference worries him, as an aesthetic and practical bar to the relationship: 'Il avait une horreur de son âge.' Finally, in order to secure Clotilde's future, he makes the agonizing sacrifice of sending her away against her will.

The doubts, the recriminations, the anguish, are all Pascal's—and his struggle is the heart of the novel: yet Chekhov can dismiss all this passion with the cool comment that 'there's little wrong' in it, and 'that's his own affair'; in an earlier letter to Suvorin he even described Pascal as 'invented'.[77] His feeling is all for Clotilde, whom he described in the same letter as being more successful than Pascal. 'I can feel her breasts and waist,' he wrote, but his comparison of her with the 'invented' Pascal would suggest that she has for him more than a physical reality—that she lives for him as a personality.

In fact, it is precisely Chekhov's conception of Clotilde that is pure invention, for his picture of Clotilde/Abishag as some sort of slave who 'naturally wants youth' cannot be reconciled with the circumstances of the novel as Zola presented them. Although her confession of love to Pascal (deliberately) recalls the Abishag–David relationship: 'Tu es mon maître, c'est toi que j'aime' it is Clotilde who rejects her suitor, the young doctor Ramond, whom Pascal believes to be his rival. For Clotilde, there is no difficulty in choosing between them. She quite simply loves the one and does not love the other. She sees Pascal's age as no obstacle to their love. On the contrary, she states: 'Ma joie est que tu sois âgé et que je sois jeune, parce que le cadeau de mon corps te ravit davantage.'

The doubts are Pascal's, the confidence is Clotilde's. So, if Chekhov thought their relationship was a perversion, it is hard to see how he could avoid blaming Clotilde (of whose sensual response to Pascal we are incidentally left in no doubt).

Chekhov's revulsion for the part played by Clotilde in the novel appears to be a deliberate rejection of the novelist's invitation to delight in his protagonists' happiness. His refusal to acknowledge Pascal and Clotilde's love as a fact, his mutation of it into something almost obscene ('in the name of God knows what') is reminiscent of Tolstoy's wilful blindness in the face of what displeased him.

Why should he react like this? The reason is that the idea of Clotilde represented for Chekhov something important enough to obliterate the actual Clotilde whom Zola described. For Chekhov she represented, among other things, the possibility of sex in an ideal form. Chekhov was not averse to the idea of sex as something intrinsic: 'probably my old age . . . won't be free from attempts to "draw my bow", as Apuleius puts it in *The Golden Ass*,' he commented towards the end of his criticism of Zola. And, as we have seen, the image of Clotilde attracted him sensually. But Chekhov was averse to the idea of sex as an end in itself; and hence a note of irritation enters at this point into his comment on Zola: 'And what barbarity: surely sexual potency is no sign of true life, of health? (. . .) All thinkers were impotent by the age of forty, while 90-year-old savages keep 90 wives . . .'.[78]

The physical image of Clotilde represented to Chekhov, through his own system of association, a set of personal values, aesthetic and spiritual, to which he was strongly attracted: and his criticism of *Le Docteur Pascal* shows that tendency towards withdrawal from harsh facts and even from logic which occasionally manifested itself when he defended this set of values.

In the letter to Aleksandr of January 1889 previously quoted, Chekhov rebuked his brother for the way in which the latter treated his wife: 'You regard decency and culture (*vospitannost'*) as superstitions, but one must after all protect something—if only feminine weakness and the children—protect at least the poetry of life, if the prose is already done for.'[79] The last sentence is sarcastic but it is none the less revealing. Was Chekhov so insensitive as not to realize that the keeping-up of appearances could scarcely be called 'poetry'? Perhaps not—dealing with the blustering Aleksandr no doubt gave rise to many rash and thoughtless remarks—and yet this reference of Chekhov's to 'poetry' recalls another remark, albeit made in a different context and two years later. His friend Elena Shavrova had apparently made what Chekhov interpreted as disparaging comments about bachelor gynaecologists.[80] Chekhov replied: 'We old bachelors smell like dogs? So be it, but permit me to dispute that doctors of women's diseases are at heart libertines and cynics. Gynae-cologists deal with the most brutal prose such as you couldn't imagine, and to which perhaps, if you knew anything about it, you would attribute, with the savagery characteristic of your ideas about things, a smell worse than doggy. He who ceaselessly sails on the sea loves dry land; he who is eternally absorbed in prose pines for poetry. All gynaecologists are idealists.'[81]

Chekhov himself did not specialize in gynaecology; but the rhetorical heat with which he defends gynaecologists suggests that he was very sympathetic to what he thought to be their outlook. 'Brutal prose' (*neistovaya proza*) is a strong phrase—astonishingly strong, until one realizes that Chekhov himself 'pined for poetry' in human relationships to such an extent that he was thereby made capable of neglecting verisimilitude and the demands of his art when he depicted the woman's part in a relationship.

4 *The Romantic Heroine*

Happily for the male, not every woman in the world of Chekhov's fiction is an enticing vessel of evil. In 'Beautiful Women' (*Krasavitsy*, 1888) a young boy tells of an encounter with two beautiful women and his attendant impressions. He describes how he is affected by the sight of one of them, Masha, a young girl with large dark eyes, a white neck, and undeveloped figure, the daughter of an Armenian, at whose house he and his grandfather stop in the course of a journey: 'Masha aroused in me neither desire, nor ecstasy, nor delight, but rather a heavy, albeit pleasurable sense of melancholy. It was a melancholy as vague and undefined as a dream. For some reason I felt sorry for myself and my grandfather and the Armenian and the girl herself, and I felt as though we had all four lost something important and necessary for life which we would never retrieve.'

A yearning of this sort not uncommonly takes possession of Chekhov's men. Sometimes it is defined as a longing for love, sometimes it remains undefined, but it is always a yearning for something loftier than a merely carnal relationship. Such a yearning is almost invariably stimulated by the presence or the memory of the romantic heroine.

'Romantic heroine' is intended as a simple definition of the female love-object, who is usually but not always the heroine in terms of plot. (Likewise, the word 'hero' has occasionally been used to denote her lover where the latter is not the true hero of the story.) 'Romantic' in this context is to be taken as embracing two meanings of the word: firstly, and obviously, it implies a connection with some kind of love-relationship; secondly, it implies a connection with vision and the imagination.

In many respects the most typical romantic heroine is Misyus in 'The Artist's Story'. The artist, staying with one Belokurov in the country, meets the neighbouring Volchaninov sisters, Lida, and Zhenya or 'Misyus' (so-called in imitation of her pronunciation of the name of an erstwhile governess—Miss Hughes, presumably). After some days the artist falls in love with Misyus and wants to marry her. But Lida, who disapproves of him, intervenes and sends Misyus away.

Although she is the heroine of this little tragedy Misyus does not have a large speaking part. She reads to the point of tiring her brain, gazes at the artist's work 'rapturously', and 'sorrowfully' at her elder sister when the latter orders her about. However, we are told that she tells the artist eagerly about a chimney catching fire in the servants' hall and a large fish being caught in the pond; also a conversation is reported wherein Misyus relates how a peasant has been miraculously cured by a wise-woman. But although we are told that she also spoke to the artist about God, eternal life, and miracles, we are left in ignorance of what she actually said on these subjects. Thus it is not easy for the reader to follow the artist to the conclusion that Misyus is possessed of a 'rare intellect'. Moreover, Misyus 'listened and believed and did not ask for proofs' of the philosophical platitudes trotted out by the artist (and in which he does not really believe himself), simply because she stands in awe of him; she also stands in awe of her sister, and hence cannot understand how Lida can be wrong in her opinions. These stated facts are difficult to reconcile with the 'breadth of outlook' which 'delighted' the artist. We can more readily believe that—as he himself states, explaining the sources of his outburst of feeling for Misyus—the artist loves her for her admiration of him, and because she thinks differently from his enemy Lida—plausible enough, if unromantic, reasons for love. But the other reason he gives for his love is the only one likely to make Misyus's attractiveness come alive for the reader: this reason is Misyus's looks.

'How touchingly beautiful were her pale face, slim neck, delicate hands, her weakness . . .' exclaims the artist. He has already commented more than once on the immaturity of Misyus's figure, emphasizing her weakness and fragility. In fact, this concept of Misyus as weak and frail—a defenceless creature—is not merely the only endearing quality she possesses; it is in a sense the only real thing about her, the only quality that exists outside the artist's conception of her.

Misyus is physically vivid by default of any other more striking qualities—but also, for the habitual reader of Chekhov, because she reminds him instantly of others among Chekhov's romantic heroines, with whom she has certain physical features in common. In 'Lights' (*Ogni*, 1888) Ananiev describes the schoolgirl Kisochka whom he once loved. She was: 'rather pale, fragile, delicate—as though she would float away up to the sky like thistledown if blown on—with an expression of gentle astonishment, small hands, and long soft hair down to her waist, which was as thin as a wasp's—altogether ethereal and translucent, like moonlight.'

Not all the heroines of this type are as weightless as Kisochka and Misyus, but where not actually stated to be thin (*khudoshchavy* or *toshchy*) they are at least described as *stroiny*. This is most accurately translated by the genteel 'shapely' or clinical 'well-proportioned', but although in Russia today *stroiny* may mean 'plump and shapely', the word as used by Chekhov tends to exclude plumpness. Thus the *stroinye* legs of Olenka in 'The Shooting Party' (*Drama na okhote*, 1884) are compared to needles, and the adjective is used in direct conjunction with *khudoshchavaya* to describe Tanya, heroine of 'The Black Monk'.

The sum of Tanya's physical attributes again reminds us of Misyus. In his mind's eye her husband sees her as 'small, pale, very thin, so that her collar bones showed; the eyes wide-open, dark, intelligent . . .'.

In 'My Life' the narrator is struck by the splendid dark eyes and pale face of his sister Kleopatra. The narrator of 'The Story of an Unidentified Person' describes his first meeting with Zinaida Fedorovna: 'I discerned a white face, with soft lines, a prominent chin and long dark eyelashes . . .'. It does not matter if Kleopatra's pallor is the result of illness, or Zinaida Fedorovna's the result of face-powder (there is something suspicious in that 'white' instead of the usual 'pale'), nor even if, when in 'A Dreary History' Katya appears at her guardian's window with staring eyes and a face that is 'pale, stern, and fantastic, like marble in the moonlight', this is because, as Nikolai Stepanovich comments: 'In the moonlight all women appear to have large black eyes and people seem taller and paler . . .'. The point is that Chekhov constantly reiterates these physical attributes in his heroines: eyes, pallor, fragility. Of course, his use of such stereotyped attributes must be to some extent ascribed to the demands of the short-story technique, in accordance with which the writer must compose a picture in a few bold strokes or rely on the shorthand of novelistic conventions. Thus for instance the vision of Katya in harsh chiaroscuro which appears at Nikolai Stepanovich's window gives the scene—the climax of the story in terms of action—the necessary dramatic effectiveness. Thus Kleopatra's lovely eyes—the mirror of the soul—and pallor may be roughly translated into the commonplace of spiritual beauty in a sickly frame—giving her a certain tragic status.

On the whole, however, Chekhov's variations on Misyus's appearance would seem to indicate a penchant for this type of feminine looks. With their large eyes and corporeal frailty, these heroines of Chekhov's love stories are reminiscent of some timid animal, a deer or a hare. Of course, there are variations in their size, in their degree of physical beauty (although many are 'beautiful', most at least 'pretty'), and in hair-colour (although where this is specified, it is usually blonde). But there is one attribute which is common to all Chekhov's romantic heroines: their youth. The maximum age for such a heroine is about twenty-five (Zinaida Fedorovna, Katya, Kisochka); the youngest, Anya in *The Cherry Orchard*, is seventeen; Misyus is seventeen or eighteen; most are about the age of twenty.

The emphasis on youth is closely connected with an even greater emphasis on purity. In Chekhov's fiction purity is, for the man who loves the girl in question, one of her most attractive qualities, closely associated with the happiest part of the romance. Thus Nikolai Stepanovich recalls the passionate love he felt for his wife when he married her—love for, *inter alia*, her pure soul; Trigorin in his first love-scene with Nina Zarechnaya talks of her expression of 'angelic purity'; the artist states that on his first visit to the Volchaninovs 'everything seemed young and pure' to him; even Natasha in *Three Sisters* is invested briefly with an aura of romance when Andrei Prozorov declares his love for her: 'Oh youth, wonderful splendid youth! . . . My dear, good, pure darling, marry me! I love you as I've never loved anyone.'

If he were not an idealistic, unrealistic dreamer, Andrei could never have fallen in love with the vulgar earthy Natasha. For the conception of 'purity' as applied to the romantic heroine means, essentially, that she stands for the elevation of love to a spiritual plane. Natasha makes a mock of this concept not so much by

Chekhov and Tolstoy at Gaspra, 1902

Chekhov in 1882

committing adultery, as by doing so with a creature as philistine as herself. There is no suggestion that she has fallen in love with Protopopov.

If the romantic heroine commits adultery, then the chances are that her husband will have proved himself wanting from a moral or spiritual point of view. Thus, Kisochka's husband is a philistine, and furthermore he keeps a mistress. Anna Sergeevna's husband is a 'flunkey' (*lakei*)—one of Chekhov's most damning moral indictments. The romantic heroine is not considered to have done wrong, because she seeks to exchange a relationship debased by her husband for a loftier one. Yet she does not take the step of adultery lightly. Typically, 'Anna Sergeevna, this "lady with the dog", took what had happened [i.e. her adultery with Gurov] . . . very seriously, as if she had become a fallen woman . . .'. And she says that 'sin' disgusts her.

An exception is Zinaida Fedorovna, whose husband we do not know to be at fault; but still she, as opposed to the man she adores, Orlov, represents spiritual love. Or, as Orlov puts it, talking of love: 'That which I've hitherto considered trivial nonsense she is forcing me to elevate to the level of a serious matter, I am serving an idol which I have never thought to be a god.'

In other cases the heroine's husband is not at fault, and then she remains faithful to him: Anna Alekseevna Luganovich in 'About Love' (*O lyubvi*, 1898) does not yield to her love for Alekhin, or even acknowledge its existence until it is too late for anything to come of it (thus comparing favourably on the moral scale with Sofya Lvovna in 'Misfortune'). Yuliya Sergeevna, the heroine of 'Three Years', is faithful to Laptev, without loving him. When she does eventually come to love him, it is for his spiritual qualities. Like Irina in *Three Sisters*, Yuliya decides to marry for complex reasons not including love, and like Irina she at this stage bitterly regrets the true love she had been dreaming of, where her heart would be involved. Where there is a relationship without love, there is no happiness for the romantic heroine. Katya, heroine of 'A Dreary History', when she falls in love writes a 'poetic and rapturous letter' to the professor, but the relationship devoid of love on her part that—it is implied— Mikhail Fedorovich offers her cannot make her happy.

We see that it would be wrong to assume that the concept of

'purity' connected with Chekhov's young heroines necessarily connotes sexual innocence or chastity. But what it does connote is a quality that they all have in common, and which is best summed up by the epithet 'childlike'. Whether or not she is literally chaste, the romantic heroine is untouched, in herself, by the evils and vulgarity of the world, either because of her total inexperience of the world, or because, having encountered these things, she has not as yet been driven to adopt a cynical attitude towards life.

The romantic heroine, when confronted with the realities of life, appears weak and defenceless. In 'The Black Monk', Tanya reacts to Kovrin's proposal of marriage like a rabbit before a snake: 'She was stunned, and bent forward, shrinking, seeming to age ten years in a moment, but he thought her beautiful, and expressed his delight aloud: "How lovely she is!" ' As it is for Kovrin, an apparent defencelessness is also for Gurov an attractive quality. The following passage marks the real beginning of Gurov's interest in 'the lady with the dog'. He 'recalled how recently she had been a schoolgirl . . . recalled how her manner of laughing, and of conversing with a stranger was still shy and awkward—probably it was the first time in her life that she had been on her own in a situation like this, with men following her and gazing at her and talking to her with but one unavowed purpose, which she could not fail to suspect. He recalled her slender, frail neck, her beautiful grey eyes. "There is something pathetic about her all the same," he thought . . .'. We are reminded of the attitude of another seducer towards his victim. The lover of the peasant girl Agafya watches her go with a face which is 'pale, and frowning with an expression of repelled pity such as people feel when they see animals tormented.'

Pity for the helplessness and weakness of the girl is no barrier to sexual desire; it may even increase it, which is perhaps most explicitly indicated in 'Lights'. Kisochka, in a state of hysteria, running away from her vulgar unkind husband, meets one Ananiev, whom she last saw as a schoolgirl, on the way to her mother's house. Although the thought of making love to Kisochka keeps constantly recurring to Ananiev, he strives to remember his sense of decency. But when Kisochka shows her appreciation of his sympathy by laughing, weeping, and gazing at him with 'tearful, shining eyes', Ananiev relates how: 'The childlike joy on her face, the tears, the meek smile, the soft hair escaping from under her scarf, and the scarf itself, carelessly thrown over her head, brought back to me in the light of the streetlamp the old Kisochka, whom one wanted to stroke like a cat . . . I could not restrain myself and began to stroke her hair, her shoulders, her arms . . .'. And he seduces her.

This passage indicates that the immediate, the sexual appeal of the romantic heroine lies in her defencelessness, her weakness. But it also indicates the essential childlikeness which is almost invariably a fundamental quality in the Chekhovian romantic heroine, and of which the girl's external appearance of helplessness—tears, timidity and so forth—are merely the most readily discernible aspect.

The romantic heroine is characterized by her lack of sophistication, by her sincerity, by her straightforward, ingenuous approach to life.

The pathos of Kisochka's fate lies in her absolute faith in Ananiev's honourable intentions. In 'The Story of an Unidentified Person' we find a similarly touching ingenuousness in Zinaida Fedorovna's uninhibited delight in the novelty of her position after she has moved into Orlov's apartment. This delight is what invests her illicit love-affair with romance, this, and the blind enthusiasm of her vows to love Orlov 'perpetually' and 'her naïve, almost childlike certainty that she too was steadfastly loved and would be for ever . . .': which certainty, according to the narrator, 'took five years off her age'.

Not every romantic heroine has such faith: no sooner has Gurov seduced Anna Sergeevna than she suggests that he will now no longer respect her—although without cynicism, for she is convinced that she has done wrong and that therefore Gurov is right to despise her. Yet, in spite of her conscience, Anna Sergeevna gives herself willingly, without—it is implied—the unnecessary talk and affectation that accompany Gurov's wife's love-making. Anna Sergeevna's approach to infidelity is simple and submissive, and her love for Gurov equally straightforward. She wears her heart on her sleeve, and in this respect resembles Kisochka, Misyus, or Tanya. The love of Chekhov's romantic heroines is 'that naïve, unquestioning love people feel only for those very close to them, for members of their family'—the love Kovrin senses Tanya feels for him, and a love which usually

originates in childhood, owing to the simplicity and impression-
ability of the child.

It is this sort of love which Katya feels for her guardian,
Nikolai Stepanovich—and it is his feeling for her that constitutes
the real 'love-story' in 'A Dreary History'; not her liaisons, of
which we know virtually nothing.

Katya's dependence on the professor—her need for love, which
reminds us of Kisochka—is another of her childlike qualities.
But of these, probably the most engaging is the innocence and
the optimism with which she approaches life. As a child, Nikolai
Stepanovich recalls, her most salient characteristic was the
'extraordinary trustfulness' which 'always illuminated her little
face'. When Katya grows up, she leaves home to join a theatrical
company, and Nikolai Stepanovich describes the letters he
receives from her: 'Her first letters . . . were astonishing. I . . .
was simply amazed that those small sheets of paper could en-
compass so much youthfulness, purity of heart, and saintly
naïvety . . . every line breathed trustfulness. . . .' He also notes
that although the letters contained discriminating, intelligent
opinions worthy of a 'sound masculine intellect' with all this
there were 'masses of grammatical errors and hardly any punctuation marks.' Significantly, however, when Katya falls in love,
though her letters are 'as splendid as before', Nikolai Stepanovich comments: 'now they had punctuation, the mistakes in
grammar had gone and there was a strong masculine odour about
them.' This love-affair, resulting in an illegitimate child which
later dies, means the annihilation of Katya's innocence, trust, and
hope.

The freshness and optimism of a child's outlook in a young
girl on the threshold of adult life, and the subsequent disintegration of this outlook, is a theme that recurs more than once in
Chekhov's work: in 'Three Years', where we encounter the
heroine Yuliya precisely at the moment when she is faced with
abandoning her childhood dreams of romantic love; and, notably,
in *Three Sisters*: Irina's youthful and infectious *joie de vivre* is
destroyed during the course of the play by several blows of fortune
and by the crushing weight of frustration. Her progress to disillusionment is paralleled by that of her sister Masha, accomplished
before the play opens, in the time since she married a stuffy
schoolmaster whom she admired at the age of eighteen.

However, disillusionment is not always the end of the story.
Perhaps the archetypal childlike and optimistic heroine is
Kleopatra, sister of Misail Poloznev, the narrator of 'My Life'.
Like Yuliya's, Kleopatra's childhood has been prolonged by the
way her father treats her. Then one day she drives out of town to
visit her brother with her friend Anyuta Blagovo and Anyuta's
brother, Dr. Blagovo. On this occasion Misail notices that she
seems extraordinarily cheerful, and he comments: 'In this present
gaiety of hers there was something childlike and naïve, as if the
joy which in our childhood was stamped out and stifled by our
harsh upbringing had now suddenly been aroused in her soul and
was breaking free.'

Kleopatra's happiness is partly, though perhaps unconsciously,
due to the fact that Blagovo is there, for she falls in love with him
(and later bears his illegitimate child). Blagovo does not suggest
that she should go away with him, and—ironically enough—
treats her like a child when he is attending her in her last illness.
But Kleopatra remains blissfully happy, adores him, rejoices in
the thought of the child, and if disillusionment does over-
whelm her at any point before her early death, we are not told of
it.

Kleopatra's death is infinitely less heart-rending than the
death-in-life which preceded her love-affair. But not every
romantic heroine has to die: sometimes the caged bird escapes
and finds freedom. At the end of 'My Life' Masha makes a heavily
symbolic departure for the New World; in *The Seagull* Nina
Zarechnaya soars out of the provincial quagmire. That the seagull
is shot down, that Nina is disillusioned, is less relevant than the
fact that she escaped: when in the last act she reappears in Treplev's study, it is to make this point. The image of a caged bird,
or, alternatively, that of a bird at liberty, is very frequently
associated with Chekhov's romantic heroines.

It is however a symbol as vague as it is commonplace. In the
final scene between Nina and Treplev we are moved not so much
by her lofty phrases as by the spectacle of his wretchedness.
Similarly, once Masha has blithely sailed away to America,
Chekhov does not care what becomes of her: it is with her husband's sense of loss that he is concerned. The 'new life' to which
these heroines aspire is only theoretically of more interest to him
than is the fate of, say, Misyus, who departs on some conventional

trip under her mother's aegis. The significance of the romantic heroine lies not so much in what she does as in the gap she leaves behind. For whatever intervenes between her and her lover, be it death or fateful circumstance or some flaw in the girl herself, like the *blaue Blume* of the German romantics she is always present at the edge of the hero's vision, always promising eternal bliss, never offering more than an ephemeral glimpse of happiness.

2

How successful is this type of heroine in the role that Chekhov allots her? How credible is she and to what extent does she engage our sympathy? An example from *Ivanov* (1887–9) indicates how both the credibility and the attractive qualities of a character can be forfeited. Anna Petrovna, Ivanov's dying and neglected wife, throughout the play has an adult outlook on her situation, and this makes her sympathetic. But her consistency as a personality is flawed by one of her first lines, in Act I, when she calls to her husband: 'Nikolai, let's turn somersaults in the hay!' This makes a jarring impression for two reasons: in retrospect, because it is out of character, and at the time because the obvious childishness of the remark strikes us as sentimental. Of course the risk involved in investing with a streak of childishness any character that one is intended to take seriously is precisely that the character may appear to be sentimentalized. *The Seagull* contains the following piece of dialogue:

NINA: What kind of tree is that?
TREPLEV: An elm.
NINA: What makes it look so dark?
TREPLEV: It's evening, everything's getting dark.

Now one may find this sort of ingenuousness on Nina's part touching, or one may not, but here the childishness of the heroine must be brought out, because one of the fundamentals of the play is precisely the contrast between Nina's youthful inexperience and the sober mature outlook she has acquired in Act 4, after two years have elapsed. Her artlessness at the beginning of the play is exaggerated, but this serves only to reinforce the impression of strength she makes in the last act. Moreover, her age makes her artlessness reasonably credible, and she is at least consistently artless until the last act.

However, as the extracts above indicate, the romantic heroine may be credible without being particularly engaging. How appealing one finds her depends in the last analysis upon whether or not one finds the image of the childlike heroine too sentimental and idealistic to begin with.

The sentimentalization and idealization of the romantic heroine is almost inevitable: for she belongs not in a realistic exposé of events and feelings, but to the dimension of someone's (occasionally her own) imagination or vision. Thus the romantic heroine may be said to have a 'poetic' quality.

How such a quality is acquired is best illustrated by a few examples. Nina Zarechnaya, for instance, by her reiterated comparison of herself to a gull reveals the symbolic aspect of her role: her flight from home and convention and her subsequent disillusionment in Trigorin and the outside world are symbolized by Treplev's wanton destruction of a soaring bird. Similarly, Irina in *Three Sisters* discloses a further dimension of her personality when she compares herself to a locked piano, the key to which is lost; and this disclosure gives her a tragic status, albeit for but a moment's duration. And for Chebutykhin she represents a link with the past, when he was in love with Irina's mother. Likewise, Anya in *The Cherry Orchard*—a mere esquisse of a character in a role devoid of any seriousness—is invested briefly with romance when Trofimov refers to her as his 'sun', his 'spring'. Sergei Petrovich in 'The Shooting Party', when he first sees Olenka, states: 'I was still a poet and in the ambience of the forest, of the May evening and of the evening star now beginning to glitter, I could look on a woman only with a poet's eyes—I gazed at the girl in red with the same reverence with which I was wont to gaze at the forests and the mountains and the azure sky.' Thus Olenka is elevated from the mundane, and the idea that there is something special about her is maintained to the end of what would otherwise be the rather sordid story of a depraved and abused adolescent. Olenka's fall from her state of innocence becomes singular and terrible only through Sergei Petrovich's dramatization of it: 'I was of the opinion that mud cannot help being mud, and one cannot blame gold coins which circumstances cause to fall in the mud—but previously I did not know that gold coins can dissolve in mud and mix into a single mass with it. So even gold is soluble!'

'The Shooting Party' is of course an experiment in genre, to some extent a parody. It is painted in crude colours. In later works the 'special' quality of the heroine is revealed less obviously. Katya's importance in the life of the old professor, Nikolai Stepanovich, is not fully disclosed until the last words of what has been an on the whole laconic account of his interest in her: 'Farewell, my treasure!' We can compare this recognition of what Katya has meant to him with the artist's lyrical if rather trite outburst apropos of Misyus: 'I envisaged her as my little queen, who together with me would hold sway over these trees and fields, over the mists, the dawn, this wonderful enchanting world of nature . . .'.

This quality of 'poetry' is specifically pointed out to us. Unlike the quality of goodness as we perceive it in, say, Sonya of *Uncle Vanya*, it is not an intrinsic feature of the character as she appears to the audience or to the reader; it is part of someone's *Weltanschauung*, not of the world itself.

Chekhov did not have a monopoly of poetic Russian heroines. Tolstoy's Natasha Rostova is seen by Prince Andrei almost exclusively in poetic terms: we discover a more mundane Natasha only after her marriage to Pierre. Turgenev's young heroines, so despised by Chekhov, in fact bear a strong superficial resemblance to his own heroines in that their youth, purity, and attendant virtues seem to promise the hero fulfilment of his hazy dreams.

Tolstoy's and Turgenev's heroines, however, have a solidity and an individuality generally lacking in their Chekhovian counterparts. Natalya Lasunskaya in Turgenev's *Rudin* is poeticized by the hero. She loves him too, but she is capable of making mental reservations: 'he treats me like a child'. Impossible to imagine Misyus conceiving such a thought. Chekhov never shatters as effectively as this the romantic heroine's cloying coating, nor for that matter gives us such a refreshing insight into her personality. However, the heroines of 'Lights' and 'The Lady with the Dog' are not wholly dependent for their appeal on 'poetry': Ananiev's conception of Kisochka as a sort of martyr ('A good, well-meaning creature in torment'), and Gurov's daydreams where he sees Anna Sergeevna as 'more lovely, young, and tender than she had been' are the first steps in a process of poeticization, but they are not followed up; and these two stories are surely the better for it. For as a literary device the use of 'poetry' can make a character more interesting, but the potential weakness of this method of evoking a personality lies in the necessity of the reader's understanding the thought-process or apprehending the mood of the person through whose eyes we see the heroine. Thus, if we do not happen to find the artist's evaluation of Misyus convincing, it may be hard for us to appreciate her poetic qualities. For some, of course, there may be no difficulty: one biographer of Chekhov has described her as 'an enchanting wraith of feminine loveliness'.[1]

There is at any rate certainly something in that 'wraith'. For, except in the plays, Chekhov's romantic heroine is seen exclusively through the eyes of a third, and incidentally male party (Chekhov or the narrator), and she tends to remain a rather shadowy and enigmatic figure, compared with, say, Olga Mikhailovna in 'The Party' (*Imeniny*, 1888) or the schoolmistress in 'In the Cart' (*Na podvode*, 1897). It is partly due to this quality that the romantic heroine is memorable, for the reader does not know enough about her to prevent him from envisaging and even metamorphosing her in accordance with whatever her characteristics may mean to him personally.

That merely the evocation of a beautiful young girl can set the imagination to filling in the rest of the picture *ad lib.* is demonstrated by Zaitsev's interpretation of the peasant Lipa in 'In the Ravine' as a quasi-biblical figure.[2] Lipa, though hers is not a love-story, conforms physically in most respects to the type of the romantic heroine, being thin, frail, under-developed, with a 'sad, timid smile', and big masculine hands 'like two large pincers'; and her alternating fits of uncomprehending happiness and fear may suggest to some animal rather than divine innocence. There is certainly no apotheosis of Lipa in the story as it stands, although she is of course intended to provide a striking contrast to the evil Aksinya.

The main difference between the romantic heroine and the 'Ariadna-type' of heroine—whom it would seem appropriate to designate henceforward the 'anti-heroine'—should by now be apparent. The anti-heroine drags the concept of love in the dirt by associating it with deception, self-interest, immorality, and above all with sex. The romantic heroine puts love on the spiritual plane. Her behaviour towards men is never vulgar or cruel; by comparison with the tough, domineering, strong-willed anti-heroine she is gentle and submissive.

As regards physical attributes, there is no clear dividing line between her and the anti-heroine, since there is no distinct physical type of the anti-heroine; but the following passages are interesting in this connection. From 'The Black Monk': Kovrin 'could never have fallen in love with a robust, sturdy, red-cheeked woman, but this pale, weak, unhappy Tanya attracted him.' Of Polya, Orlov's singularly unpleasant maidservant, the narrator of 'The Story of an Unidentified Person' writes: 'Probably a . . . footman (*lakei*) or a cook would have found her alluring, with her ruddy cheeks, snub nose, screwed-up eyes, and plump figure, already verging on the corpulent.' In the manuscript fragment of 'Peasants' a prostitute is described posing for a photographer as a page, astride a chair, 'with her thighs, encased in knitted stockings, lying flat across the chair like two fat boiled sausages'.

It is not astonishing that one should prefer the physical type of the romantic heroine to creatures made so unattractive by graphic description of this kind, but the very bluntness of his prose here is an indication that Chekhov personally found overweight women unsuitable candidates for poeticization. During a trip to Italy in 1891 he wrote to his sister: 'I saw the Venus de Medici and believe if she were dressed in modern clothes she would be hideous, especially about the waist.'[3] Where women of flesh and blood were concerned he was apt to be even more brutal in his judgements. Of a certain woman doctor he said: 'She's a plump fatty lump of meat. If she were stripped naked and painted green, you'd have a marsh frog.'[4]

The connection between obesity and gluttony is an obvious one. The anti-heroine who is fat is twice damned because she clearly overeats in addition to her other sins. The romantic heroine on the other hand scarcely seems capable of such a mundane act as eating. She escapes the fate of the Yalta women who, according to Chekhov's withering comment, smelt of ice-cream,[5] and of the dancers of whom he wrote to Suvorin: 'I know nothing about ballet, I only know that in the intervals the ballerinas smell like horses.'[6]

Physically as well as on the deeper spiritual plane, the romantic heroine seems immune from the ills that flesh is heir to. She is Snow-White in her glass coffin, waiting to be brought to life by the prince's kiss. Conversely, the anti-heroine is only too patently about to go to seed. A significant point about her is that she is on the average older than the romantic heroine. Thus for instance Olga Dmitrievna in 'His Wife' is twenty-seven, Susanna Moisevna is over twenty-eight, Nyuta and Strelkova are about thirty, Arkadina is about forty. In short, in Chekhov's work there is a distinct bias towards youth in the female sex.

Nowhere is this bias more marked than in Chekhov's treatment of adultery. We have seen with what severity Chekhov depicted unfaithful wives. But for one category of them he made an exception. One cannot fail to notice his tolerance towards young women who are the victims of an older man, usually, although not always, the husband. Except in a few early farcical anecdotes, Chekhov's attitude to the protagonists in such situations seems well-defined, and it appears as though for him the mere fact of youth in such circumstances were an adequate excuse for infidelity. Olenka, heroine of 'The Shooting Party', who commits adultery within ten minutes of being married, retains to the end an aura of childish innocence: although from her photograph her eyes stare out 'arrogant' in their depravity, the narrator Sergei Petrovich remembers her 'with her guileless, childish, naïve, kind little face and loving eyes'; and that this should be the case is surely connected with the fact of her marriage to an elderly man, Urbenin. The reason for Sergei Petrovich's horror at the prospect of this is vividly conveyed: 'I stared at that beautiful girl, at her young, almost childish face . . . I suddenly imagined beside her stout, elderly, red-faced Urbenin with his protruding ears and rough hands, the touch of which would only scratch a young female body that had just begun to live.' As a personality Urbenin is something of an exception in that he is treated with compassion. The only other elderly husband of a young girl for whom we feel anything approaching sympathy is Savely, the husband of Raisa in 'The Witch'; but our attitude to him is ambivalent for Raisa has two faces: on the one hand she appears as an evil temptress, justifying her husband's revulsion and fear of her; but on the other hand she appears as a normal young girl, frustrated and wretchedly unhappy.

Chekhov's sympathy for the girl in such cases is betrayed even in apparently lighthearted exposés of the situation. 'The Chemist's Wife' (*Aptekarsha*, 1886) describes how a young wife entertains —relatively innocently—two young men while her old and ugly husband is asleep. Most of the story is told with appropriately childlike gaiety, and absence of profound undercurrents, the girl's situation at the beginning of the story being viewed through her own uncomprehending vision. But at the end, when the young men have gone and the girl is brought back to reality, a note of unexpected passion and resentment is struck: ' "How unhappy I am!" said the chemist's wife, staring malevolently at her husband . . . "Oh, how unhappy I am!" she reiterated, and suddenly began to weep bitterly. "And nobody, nobody, knows." ' Similarly, the satirical tone of 'The Order of St. Anne' does not prepare us for the unequivocal judgement, as decisive as a snap of the fingers, pronounced on Modest Alekseich when Anna rounds on him with an exasperated: 'Get out, you blockhead!'

What is particularly interesting about both these stories is that the heroine is pretty, frivolous, and of dubious morals, which is basically all that is wrong with other female characters whom Chekhov did not spare: for instance, Olga Ivanovna in 'The Butterfly' and Sofya Lvovna in 'Big Volodya and Little Volodya'. Now, Sofya Lvovna's husband is elderly—but he looks young for his age and is still a ladykiller: he is not old sexually. This— that a young woman should have a husband who is too old for her in this respect—appears to be what Chekhov finds distasteful. It is significant that the theme of sexual relations between a young girl and an old man is one of the few that Chekhov treats seriously in his earliest work. In 'At Sea' (*V more*, 1883) two sailors are spying on a newly-married couple, but even the old, hard-bitten sailor is disgusted when the husband sells his young wife temporarily to an elderly banker. In 'The Image of his Grandfather' (*Ves' v dedushku*, 1883) an old man's marriage to a seventeen-year-old is put on a par with adultery. And yet—and this is significant—Chekhov does not delve into the feelings of these youthful victims, any more than he does in the case of a hardened hussy like Ariadna. They are symbols of abuse, not real people.

Why Chekhov should have written as he did of *Le Docteur*

Pascal is now clear. Clotilde is a young slim girl in a white dress: 'elle était charmante, avec ses grands yeux, son visage de lait et de rose, dans l'ombre des vastes bords (de son chapeau).' Doubtless she became identified in Chekhov's mind with his personal image of the romantic heroine; and, having 'poeticized' her into something she is not, he cannot accept her in the role that Zola has her play.

Thus from this attempt to indicate the salient features, physical and otherwise, of the romantic heroine, and comparison of her with the anti-heroine, several factors emerge which would appear to shed some light on the mind of the author. Firstly, the romantic heroine represents an outlook which is aesthetic rather than ethical, in that it is less concerned with a framework of morality than with certain arbitrarily chosen qualities. These qualities— childlike behaviour, purity, meekness, the ability to love wholeheartedly and faith in this unquestioning love—are clearly shown by Chekhov to be virtues: every one of his villains is conspicuously lacking in them. It is a commonplace enough set of values, but this need not detract from the interest of Chekhov's heroines, nor prevent us from becoming sympathetically involved in their fate. What could detract from their appeal is the danger of sentimentalization, a danger that Chekhov does not entirely avoid, just as he tends towards excess in his vituperative treatment of the anti-heroine.

A second interesting aspect of the romantic heroine is her superficial image, her youth, looks, and the characteristics that make her immediately attractive to the hero—her weakness, defencelessness, and so forth. In this respect she is more of a stereotype than is the anti-heroine.

Her essential quality—that of impermanence—is not novel either: many a fictional heroine is loved only to be lost. But in the Chekhovian romantic heroine this quality is fundamental to an original degree; it goes so far that her presence tends to be much less impressive than her absence. And this brings us to the crucial question: in what sense is the romantic heroine 'real'? To what extent is her image a projection of Chekhov's personal taste in women? Or is she simply a symbol of certain spiritual values? Or does she represent a memory of the past, based on a real woman but owing her ephemeral nature to Chekhov's own experience of lost love?

3

Any search for the original of the romantic heroine must take into account her fate, no less than her nature. In Chekhov's fiction the theme of lost love runs parallel to that of love ending in disillusionment. But each of the two themes is approached from a different angle. The foundering marriage (or liaison) tends to be viewed from without. The subject-matter in itself contains material that makes for an effective narrative: arguments, violent action, squalid detail. It need only be set down vividly and with economy. The theme is ideally suited to the writer possessed of the appropriate skills, and Chekhov was such a writer. From an artistic point of view, his treatment of this theme can only be faulted when his facility runs away with him, causing him to exaggerate and to reveal the limitations of his outlook.

To the biographer, of course, these limitations—Chekhov's puritanical and intolerant tendencies—are fascinating. But they are a feature of Chekhov's personality that is relatively easy to discern: as can be seen from his correspondence, Chekhov did not attempt to conceal from his friends, any more than from his readers, the sort of thing that made him angry.

The author's approach in the 'lost-love' stories, on the other hand, is emphatically not one of observation. The romantic heroine is a hazy creature inhabiting a dream-world. The term *nastroenie* (mood), describing the essence of this world, has become the hack-word of Chekhov criticism: the masterly evocation of *nastroenie* was Chekhov's special contribution to the short-story tradition. But the significance of this for the biographer is that, thanks to their introspective nature, in the lost-love stories we are touching upon those of Chekhov's emotions that lay deepest.

It goes without saying that every story of lost love cannot be interpreted as an expression of Chekhov's personal emotion. In the context of Chekhov's entire *oeuvre*, however, the theme acquires a more than passing significance. In 'The Mirror' (*Zerkalo*, 1885), a young girl searches for her future husband in the glass, according to a Russian custom. She dreams, and her dream is of married life, but not of happiness: life with her husband turns out to be a burden. The 'grey backdrop' of her vision tells her that: 'For personal happiness a harmonious duo is not enough. What is needed here is a harmonious trio, where the third person is life itself. But life never enters into the alliance . . .'. Chekhov omitted these lines from the second printing of the story. Perhaps he felt that they sounded a little too gloomy for the comic papers. Or perhaps he realized that he had given rather too pompous expression to a trite snippet of philosophy.

Be that as it may, the idea that 'life never enters into the alliance' might well occur spontaneously to any student of Chekhov's fiction: for few writers can have depicted so persistently the persecution of would-be lovers by inimical forces. [7]

Not surprisingly, in the earliest stories the situation tends to be purely farcical. In 'A Forced Declaration' (*Vynuzhdennoe zayavlenie*, 1889) a pair of lovers eloping in a carriage are caught because the horse dies. Sometimes the situation devolves into complete absurdity. 'On Christmas Eve' (*V rozhdestvenskuyu noch'*, 1883) is a parody of a story in the romantic style. On a wild night a young girl waits anxiously for her husband, who is returning from a sea-fishing trip. Here is the surprise: she hopes he will not return (the marriage, of course, is unhappy)—and when he does she is visibly in despair. Whereupon the offended husband jumps back into the boat and orders his deaf idiot servant to row off again. Then the wife shrieks for him to come back: and eventually he orders the servant to turn the boat. But the servant cannot hear, and the story ends with the boat approaching an ice-floe; as for the woman: 'On the night before Christmas she fell in love with her husband . . .': with which astonishing sentence the story ends.

Elsewhere, when Chekhov is in a more serious vein, fate assumes the guise of social forces. Thus, 'On Account of some Apples' (*Za yablochki*, 1880) relates how a sadistic landowner catches a peasant couple stealing fruit and forces them to thrash one another with a stick. After this degradation the girl departs to the left, the boy to the right, and they never meet again.

Quite different are the social circumstances of Misail and Masha Poloznev, as described in 'My Life', but similarly, it is these circumstances that break up their marriage rather than any initial flaw in the relationship. Strongly influenced by Tolstoyism, they attempt to lead a purifying life of manual labour; their efforts, however, are fruitless, for the lack of cooperation and degeneracy of the peasants prove to be insuperable obstacles. And it is because she is disillusioned in the programme, rather than in Misail, that Masha leaves him. For all her talk of her desire for freedom, one suspects that it was in fact the hardships of this particular way of life which were too much for her, and that the marriage would have worked had they settled down to a life of ease and satisfaction in their occupation (although then Chekhov would not have written about them). 'My Life' is a rather special case, in that the plot is a sort of amalgamation of the foundering-marriage and lost-love themes—for Masha leaves Misail before he has time to comprehend how fragile their love really is. Misail lives in an introspective world: Masha is his fairy princess rather as Misyus is the artist's. But the narrative is firmly rooted in what Chekhov saw as the sordid reality of rural life, where resentful peasants crowd into the manorial courtyard shouting abuse. There is no tiresome witch-hunt; because if there is a villain it is the peasant, not Masha, and the story is the better for it.

Here then love is destroyed by prosaic and intelligible factors. Both 'On Account of some Apples' and 'My Life' consist of something between a comment on the nature of human relationships and a sociological tract, but in both stories the dénouement is seen to be the direct consequence of the tract-type part of the story, which last would appear to have been the primary component of the plot. Hence it seems somewhat less than likely that either story was motivated by Chekhov's views on love, whether derived from personal experience or not.

One might compare with these 'The Artist's Story'. This too is based on a graft between a love-story and sociological polemics, but the self-complementing introduction and conclusion, which are pure lyricism, provide the framework of the plot and in so doing establish its dominant romantic key. The argument concerning the individual's duty to society, in the course of which Lida's hostility to the artist emerges, could have been an argument about anything: the point of it is, basically, to indicate the animosity which makes Lida veto her sister's marriage, so destroying the artist's romance. Before the argument begins it is clear that the artist has inspired in Lida some feeling of enmity, and the story retains its artistic wholeness even if we do not extend the author's meaning, as one critic has done, by the

Chekhov, Shchepkina-Kupernik (left), and Yavorskaya. This studio
portrait was entitled by the subjects 'The Temptation of St. Anthony'

Chekhov in the 1890s

explanation that Lida is jealous.[8] That Lida's dislike should be instinctive and her hostility motiveless is satisfyingly interpreted simply as an irony of fate.

'The Artist's Story', then, is fundamentally a narrative of the introspective type. Nor is this to be wondered at: for this is one of the rare instances where we know there to be a link between Chekhov's fiction and his biography. 'The Artist's Story' is the first clue in any search for a real romantic heroine whom Chekhov might have loved and lost.

In 1895 Chekhov wrote to his friend Elena Shavrova: 'I'm now writing a short story called "My Fiancée". I was engaged once —my fiancée was called "Misyus". It's this I'm writing about.'[9] So here we have the origin of 'The Artist's Story', as 'My Fiancée' was to become. But was this Misyus, this fiancée, also re-evoked and poeticized in many other stories and plays, starting with 'Lights' in 1888, and throughout Chekhov's life thereafter?

Possibly this was indeed the case; but we can only speculate, for the reference itself remains obscure. Shavrova in her reply to Chekhov's letter invited further information by expressing interest in Chekhov's remark,[10] but apparently never received it: at least, neither she nor any contemporary has left any specific suggestion as to who this fiancée might have been.

Confusion is added to obscurity by the fact that some years previously Chekhov had been referring to a 'fiancée', who was almost certainly one Efdokiya Isaakovna (Dunya) Efros, a Jewish fellow student of Masha Chekhova's.* But it is extremely unlikely that Misyus and Dunya Efros were one and the same. Chekhov's liaison with the latter seems to have been a turbulent affair. Our knowledge of it is derived from certain of his letters to his friend V. V. Bilibin. Chekhov's résumé of the affair is comprised in the comments that follow.

In January 1886 he writes: 'By the way, yesterday as I was taking a certain young lady home I proposed to her. Give me your blessing on my marriage.'[11] By February however he had

---

* The generally held supposition that Dunya Efros was the fiancée to whom Chekhov referred in early 1886 is based on the facts that the alleged fiancée was Jewish, as was Dunya, and that in 1886 Chekhov mentioned Dunya several times in his letters to his siblings and to his friend Mariya V. Kiseleva, in the bantering tone which he usually adopted when speaking of or to girls with whom he flirted.

this to say: '—my marriage probably—alas, alack, the censor won't pass this. My "girl" (*moya "ona"*) is a Jewess. If this rich Jewess has the courage to accept Orthodoxy with all it entails—fine. If not, we'll forget it. Anyway we've already quarrelled. Tomorrow we'll make it up and in a week we'll fall out again. Vexed that religion is a problem, she has broken pencils and photographs on my desk. This is typical of her. She's a terrible spitfire. I shall undoubtedly part from her within one or two years of marriage.'[12] A fortnight later Chekhov was still referring in the same correspondence to his 'marriage';[13] but by the end of the month all was over. 'I've parted from my fiancée *for good*,' he wrote. 'That is, she's parted from me. But I haven't bought a revolver yet. . . . Everything in this world is unstable, mutable, approximate, and relative.'[14] And soon after he concluded his account of the affair decisively: 'I've parted with my fiancée: *nec plus ultra*,' he affirmed, adding: 'I shan't write to you any more about her. Perhaps you are right in saying that it's too early for me to marry.'[15]

At first glance some aspects of this affair may suggest the romance of 'The Artist's Story': the secrecy of the man's intention of marrying, the obstacle to happiness (which could be, in Chekhov's case, his fiancée's religion), the fact that it was the girl who broke off the romance. But how is one to reconcile this 'spitfire' of the apparently violent temper with the meek Misyus of the story? Even physically there is little suggestion of a resemblance: although Misyus is sketchily described, she does not sound like Dunya, who was a young Jewess with a large nose. (Dunya Efros was a co-pupil of Masha Chekhova's at the 'Guerrier Courses' (of higher education for women), which suggests that when Chekhov knew her she was at least in her twenties, i.e. not as young as Misyus is in 'The Artist's Story'.) Chekhov was apt to refer to her as 'The Israelite' or 'Nose' in a way that scarcely brings to mind the artist's passion for Misyus.

It seems in fact fairly clear that Chekhov's liaison with the Jewess was the outcome of one of his many flirtations, an engagement entered into precipitately which he was perhaps even glad to escape from: his letters suggest that his attitude to the affair was relatively casual. This, at any rate, was the opinion of his older friend Mariya Kiseleva, who took a vicarious interest in Chekhov's flirtations. In a letter to Chekhov of 1887 she wrote: 'The other day I dreamt of you as Dunya's bridegroom. Your face was sad and you admitted that you didn't want to marry, but Mama Efros commanded it . . . they dragged you both to the synagogue, and I was so sorry I wept . . .'; but, Kiseleva added, had it been real, she would have laughed and said: 'He got what was coming to him! Serves him right!'[16] Chekhov in her opinion had carried the flirtation far enough to warrant Dunya's having some claim on him: but he had not intended to commit himself to her.

There are extant a very few letters from Dunya herself to Chekhov, unpublished, and marked (in Chekhov's hand) '1886'. They are dignified and reserved, and tell us nothing, with the exception of one revealing comment: 'I was thinking about a rich bride for you, Anton Pavlovich, even before I received your letter: here we have the daughter of a Moscow merchant, not bad-looking, rather short (your type) and rather stupid (another good point).'[17]

This, written in June 1886, shows that any engagement was by then at least a thing of the past. The sarcastic, impatient tone of Dunya's letter is illuminating. One can well imagine that she, whose reaction to obstacles was to smash things, would, if she ever read 'The Artist's Story', have considered the wilting Misyus 'rather stupid'.

If, then, Dunya Efros was not the fiancée who inspired 'The Artist's Story', and possibly also 'Lights', who was? Other clues to possible prototypes for Misyus are even less substantial. In the summer of 1882 Aleksandr Chekhov referred to a 'fiancée' of Chekhov's who lived in the Tula region with her mother.[18] Perhaps that was Misyus: but we know nothing else about her. Similarly, two items from Misha Chekhov's reminiscences catch our attention in this connection, but remain unelucidated. In one of his books on his famous brother Misha Chekhov states that 'Lights' was inspired by its author's experiences in the Don steppe country, while staying with his friends the Kravtsovs in the summer of 1887.[19] However, it seems unlikely that he meant by this that Anton had some romance there involving a prototype Kisochka, as he was certainly referring in chief to the steppe scenery which forms the background to the introductory part of 'Lights': Ananiev's story within a story, the one in which Kisochka figures, takes place in a seaside town. In another book about his brother, Misha writes: 'Anton Pavlovich told me about some affair when he was staying with his fat friend but unfortunately I cannot relate it in these memoirs.'[20] Chekhov's fat friend was V. I. Zembulatov, and Chekhov stayed with the Zembulatov family from time to time during the years 1876–9. They lived near Taganrog, a seaport, so that it is much more probable that this 'affair' could have inspired the story of Kisochka: particularly since Chekhov had gone to school in Taganrog, and therefore could have encountered a girl there whom he had known from classroom days. Perhaps he even played as unpraiseworthy a part in the affair as did Ananiev. A friend has noted that Chekhov told him 'about one of his student loves what others would have preferred not to tell.'[21] Was this confession transformed into 'Lights'? This would explain why Misha felt unable to go into details about the 'affair'. It would not necessarily have prevented Chekhov from referring to the girl sentimentally in his letter to Shavrova, fifteen years later: for this affair must have been fleeting, and if Chekhov later thought of 'Misyus', 'Kisochka', or whoever it was as his fiancée, then he was clearly romanticizing the past and doubtless exaggerating in retrospect the significance of what had been a casual affair. At fifteen years' distance and in the maudlin mood in which 'The Artist's Story' was evidently written, any mishandling of the affair on his part, whether deliberate or not, might well have undergone in Chekhov's imagination a metamorphosis into a blow of fate, the concept of which is so attractive to the romantic mind.

Mention must finally be made of a fragment of a letter from Chekhov to a person unknown, which is possibly relevant to an investigation of Misyus's origin. The fragment is dated 11 December 1888, and runs: 'in such and such a town lives Petr Ivanovich Bobchinsky. If this Bobchinsky dies or goes off his head, or marries a witch or is carried up living into Heaven . . . in a word, if by the will of the fates he finds himself over the hills and far away from you, then forget him. However, once a year, reading these lines and yawning, remember, suddenly, that he loved you with all his heart and deeply respected you—A. Chekhov.'[22] This expression of sentiment sounds remarkably sincere, the more so for the verbal inventions which precede it (Chekhov rarely wrote a love-letter to his wife in which sentiment was not juxtaposed with humour, as we see here). But who was the recipient, or intended recipient, of this letter? Given its tone, we can safely assume that it was a woman; but at this period of his life there is no other indication whatsoever that Chekhov might have been deeply in love.

It is to be hoped that fresh facts will come to light and elucidate the mystery of Misyus's identity. Until then one can but speculate whether this girl played a significant part in Chekhov's emotional life.

From about 1889, Chekhov's relationships with women were fewer in number and incomparably better documented—but there is little point in searching for the 'real' Misyus in this or the following years. The fictional romantic heroine had come into being before that: Kisochka, whose appearance and fate suggest that she derives from the same inspiration as Misyus (although she is made of sterner stuff) was created in 1888.

This shroud of mystery over nearly all the 1880s is perhaps not entirely to be deplored. For, if the real Misyus were found, might she not be as blurred a figure as her fictional counterpart? And the more closely she resembled the Misyus of the story, the less her personality would seem to invite discovery.

Of course it would be satisfactory to learn the facts of Chekhov's relationship to his 'fiancée'. Yet it certainly cannot be assumed from the term 'fiancée' that this relationship was a crucial one in Chekhov's life. Even if the girl could be identified as the original heroine of the lost-love stories, an explanation would still seem to be required for the fact that the theme of lost love, instead of finding extensive and highly emotional expression in Chekhov's work of the latter 1880s, does so in the latter 1890s.

Chekhov had taken his first serious look at the problem of love between persons who were not free to marry in 'Neighbours', written in 1892. 'Neighbours' opens with the words: 'Petr Mikhailich Ivashin was in very low spirits: his unmarried sister had gone to live with Vlasich, a married man.' The simple and blunt statement of the problem, in contrast to the rather weak phraseology 'was in rather low spirits' (*byl sil'no ne v dukhe*) immediately produces an impression of the faintly absurd. And as the story develops it becomes apparent that it is basically humorous, for it is chiefly concerned not with investigating the fate of the lovers, but with examining Ivashin's muddled shilly-shallying attitude to them. Although believing that he ought to be liberal-minded, Ivashin dislikes hearing his sister's lover refer to her as a 'woman'—the term is too plain for him—and he tells himself that whereas free love is all right, *this* is depravity. Though he rides over to reason with the couple full of indignation, he meets them shamefacedly. He feels they never can be happy; but if this judgement is intended to be taken as prophetic, it is lost to the reader as Ivashin pathetically and absurdly assures his sister that after all she is not doing anything wrong. There is no suggestion in the story of Chekhov's personal involvement, and the only mention in it is the scorn directed at Vlasich's absent wife, whose existence is the cause of his troubles.

Not much to rend the heart in this. But the problem is posed. And several years later Chekhov was to write two further stories on the theme of lovers who cannot marry: 'About Love' (1898) and 'The Lady with the Dog' (1899).

The plots of these two stories are rather similar, and as in 'Neighbours' the block to happiness lies in the fact of previous marriages—of the woman in 'About Love', of both lovers in 'The Lady with the Dog'. But in tone they differ sharply from the earlier story. There is no humour in them, only pathos and bitterness towards the fate that has brought about this situation. The emotional climax of 'About Love' is reached as the hero, Alekhin, parts with his beloved for ever: 'oh, how wretched she and I were! I confessed my love to her, and with a searing pain in my heart I realized that everything that stood in the way of our love was irrelevant, petty, and false.' A similar, if more restrained, emotion is expressed in 'The Lady with the Dog'. Gurov and Anna Sergeevna have fallen in love for the first time in their lives: 'they felt that fate itself had predestined them one for the other', but in reality fate has brought about the incomprehensible fact of their being married to different people, so that 'it was as if they were two migrant birds . . . which had been caught and made to inhabit separate cages.' The image is a good example of Chekhov's narrative style at its most restrained and moving.

It has been shown that the theme of love being destroyed by a cruel fate did not always have for Chekhov the appeal of the tragic: that it could also serve him as a good framework on which to build farce. Nor could one claim that the theme of illicit passion found its source in Chekhov's own imagination, let alone experience: Tolstoy's *Anna Karenina* had been published in the later 1870s, before any of Chekhov's work. None the less the coincidence of plot and emotion found in 'About Love' and 'The Lady with the Dog', together with the fact that the theme occupied Chekhov chiefly in the 1890s, has given rise to some speculation as to whether in fact Chekhov's own love-life during those years suffered as one critic puts it from the interference of a *force majeure*.[23] Since in this period Chekhov's private life is no longer a closed book (although many pages are indecipherable) the search for the romantic heroine becomes more complex. It becomes feasible to try to connect with her image certain women whose relations with Chekhov are at least partially illuminated and illuminating. Of Chekhov's female friends three in particular must now claim our attention.

4

There is a case both *pro* and *contra* the theory that Chekhov was, during a considerable period of his maturity, in love with a married woman, who loved him, and that their mutual happiness was prevented chiefly by the existence of her husband and children. The theory finds its source in the reminiscences, written not long before her death in 1943, of Lidiya Alekseevna Avilova.[24]

In these reminiscences Avilova tells the story of her relationship with Chekhov from 1889 until 1894, admits that she was in love with him, and gives some evidence to suggest that he was in love with her.

Avilova's belief that Chekhov returned her love is based upon a series of events—the version of these which follows being *that which she recounted in her memoirs*. On 24 January 1889 she—an attractive young married woman—met Chekhov at the house of her brother-in-law in St. Petersburg. Avilova was herself an aspiring writer of fiction and admired Chekhov's work greatly. Now she was captivated by his personality. The attraction, moreover, appeared to be mutual. When they looked deeply into one another's eyes, Avilova felt 'an explosion' in her soul, and she 'was in no doubt that the same had happened to Chekhov'.[25]

On 1 January 1892 they met again at a party. This time Chekhov singled Avilova out to keep him company and almost immediately suggested in a jocular manner that they had known, nay loved, each other in the past—that their previous meeting had been the scene of a recognition after long separation. After this Avilova sent Chekhov one of her manuscripts. He returned it with a pleasant letter of criticism, and in this way a correspondence between them was initiated.

On a further visit to Petersburg in 1895 Chekhov told Avilova that they ought to see one another every day. She asked him to come to her house on the following evening, when she would be alone. Chekhov did come (13 February 1895), but the *tête à tête* was spoilt by the arrival of unexpected visitors. However, when they were at last alone, Chekhov declared to Avilova that he had loved her on the occasions when they first met (*v pervykh vstrechakh*), saying that on the second of these she had appeared even more beautiful and lovable than previously. He told her that she was for him something sacred, and that the only way to love her was with a pure, sacred, lifelong love. However, Chekhov's mood as he spoke these words seemed to be one of anger, and having had his say, he made an abrupt exit.[26]

At a subsequent meeting in a theatre they decided to meet in Moscow. This they did, but Chekhov was at the time in Ostroumov's clinic, seriously ill (March 1897). He talked to Avilova none the less, deploring the unsuccess of their rendezvous, and wrote on a scrap of paper: 'I'm very [fon] grateful to you' (*Ya vas ochen'* [*lyu*] *blagodaryu*)—striking out the crucial uncompleted word (here in brackets), with a smile.[27]

Avilova last saw Chekhov in 1899, but when she heard of his marriage in 1901, she sent him a letter of congratulation signed with the pseudonym 'Luganovich': Luganovich being the surname of the young married heroine of 'About Love', which story Avilova believed to have some connection with her relationship to Chekhov. Chekhov, she said, replied, and signed himself 'Alekhin': thereby, the implication is, tacitly admitting to the connection Avilova suspected.

What basis, apart from the above events as recounted by Avilova, is there to the theory that Chekhov returned her love?

Their correspondence certainly existed. The most recent edition of Chekhov's 'complete' letters include thirty to Avilova. Many of these contain a personal note. In his first letter to her (21 February 1892) he adopts a frankly flirtatious tone: 'Really, in return for your refusing to see me, I ought to tear your story into little bits, but—may Allah forgive you!' Much later he writes, in apology for some harsh criticism of her writing: 'You want only three words, but I'd like to write twenty. . . . You and I are old friends; at least, I should like this to be the case.'[28]

His letters to her during the 'Yalta period' of his life show a similar desire to keep on good terms with Avilova, although this may have been quite difficult, since she seems to have been easily offended. On 27 April 1899, when Avilova had been helping him in matters concerning the publication of his work, he wrote most warmly to her: 'When shall we see one another? I must meet up with you in order to put into words how infinitely grateful I am to you and how much, indeed, I'd like to see you . . .'. And his last letter to her, written not long before his death and when he had been married for nearly three years, shows that even then Chekhov was interested enough in Avilova to give her a friendly word of advice.[29]

Chekhov's letters to third persons are a notoriously poor source of information about his affairs of the heart, and one searches his correspondence in vain for revealing references to Avilova. It is however perhaps worth noting a remark he made to his friend Leikin on 22 May 1889, a few months after first meeting Avilova: 'When I start living like a human being, i.e. when I have a place of my own and my own wife, not someone else's, when, to put it briefly, I'm not bothered by trivia and petty worries, I shall take up comic writing again . . .'. It is not impossible that the words 'someone else's wife' referred to Avilova: Chekhov might well have mentioned to Leikin that he thought Avilova attractive; for after the party of 1 January 1892 Avilova heard—so she says—a rumour that Chekhov, while drinking with friends, had talked of 'abducting' her. The rumour may have been true, but Avilova later, for reasons that she does not give, concluded that Leikin had invented the story.[30]

The theory, which might be deduced from the letter to Leikin quoted above, that Chekhov had a desire for a home and domestic bliss which ruled out the possibility of his taking up with a married woman, is of course of prime importance for the defence of Avilova's story. And we have seen that there are what could be reflections of a *grande passion* in Chekhov's work of the 1890s. There is of course a parallel between Avilova's relationship with Chekhov, as she saw it, and 'About Love'; moreover, Avilova resembled Luganovich in so far as the latter is described: both were young, pretty, and fairhaired. Anna Sergeevna, the heroine of 'The Lady with the Dog', was also a blonde, and like Avilova despised her husband. Perhaps it was in view of this latter fact that one critic linked Avilova both with Anna Sergeevna and with Masha in *Three Sisters*.[31]

Avilova's story, the fact of the correspondence, and the inferences to be drawn from Chekhov's work form the basis of the theory that Chekhov was in love with Avilova. It is not much to go on. Yet her story has won a number of adherents, including Chekhov's friend Bunin who did not suspect the existence of a romance in Chekhov's lifetime, but envisaged it all in retrospect when he read Avilova's story in the first published versions.[32]

The best defence of Avilova's case is made by David Magarshack in his biography of Chekhov.[33] This defence is based on the premise, derived from Chekhov's correspondence, that Chekhov intended to settle in St. Petersburg at the end of 1888 or the beginning of 1889, and that his meeting with Avilova drove him back to Moscow; and that it drove him ultimately to Sakhalin Island. The theory is that he was passionately in love, but prevented from doing anything about it by his disapproval of extramarital union and the difficulties of obtaining a divorce and of supporting Avilova and her children, these being the greater since he was not in good health. In so far as it goes, Magarshack's defence has something to be said for it, and of particular interest are some sentences he cites from a letter of Chekhov's to Natalya Lintvareva of February 1889. Chekhov apologizes for not leaving St. Petersburg in the company of Lintvareva's brother, and writes: 'Tell him I *could not* wait. I had to leave no matter what. I fled to escape violent sensation (*Ya bezhal ot silnykh oshchushchenii*) as a coward flees from the field of battle.'[34]

Magarshack believes that Chekhov was obsessed with the necessity of blotting out Avilova's image from his mind, even to the extent of undertaking the Sakhalin trip in order to do so. That no one suspected how Chekhov felt at this time Magarshack explains by the hypothesis that Chekhov suffered in silence (a hypothesis which would also account for the dearth of documentary evidence for Chekhov's being in love with Avilova).

The hints of this motive for the Sakhalin journey which he

discovers in Chekhov's correspondence are surely not convincing.[35] And at this point Magarshack expounds what he could not know to have been the truth, saying that Chekhov, who caught influenza during December 1889, 'during those awful nights of illness and terror . . . fought in vain against a feeling he could not overcome.'[36]

Magarshack's defence of Avilova is, as a hypothesis, not implausible, but it is marred by a number of dubious claims. He asserts for instance that Chekhov's behaviour on the occasion of his second meeting with Avilova was something she 'could not possibly have invented'. Why not?[37] Also, although Magarshack reports Chekhov's alleged declaration of love, which is the linchpin of Avilova's case, he does not describe the attendant circumstances, which must be taken into consideration.

None the less, Magarshack's defence of Avilova's story is much more convincing than are those of her other supporters. Alja Rachmanowa in her biography of Chekhov resorts to unproven statements about Chekhov's feelings without adducing any concrete evidence in support of her theories. A much more honest attempt to justify Avilova appeared in 1960 in an article by Cyrille Wilczkowski. His argument is based largely on an analysis of certain themes in Chekhov's fiction, but it is invalidated by certain fundamental flaws,[38] and there are one or two factual inaccuracies in the text—some admittedly due to the fact that his article is based on an earlier abridged account of Avilova's story.

Thus, attractive though the theory may be that Chekhov was in love with Lidiya Avilova, and suffered himself at the hands of the blind destiny which ruins many of his fictional romances, the fact remains that little concrete evidence has been found to support this theory. The only indication that Chekhov loved Avilova is contained in her account of ten meetings with him. Of these, six indisputably took place. But what exactly occurred between her and Chekhov on any one of these occasions could be known only to the two of them.

The evidence for Chekhov's not having been in love with Avilova is on the other hand considerable, although not conclusive. It has been accepted by the majority of commentators on the question.

The case against Avilova has been best put by Ernest J. Simmons. Although his attitude sometimes seems to be one of bias against Avilova,[39] the facts to which he points do much to cast doubt on the overall reliability of her account.

There are of course some obvious weaknesses in Avilova's case. Firstly, in all Chekhov's letters to his family and friends, there is no indication that he had any special feeling for Avilova. This alone need not strike us as odd, because it was not Chekhov's habit to reveal his personal feelings on such matters, not on paper at any rate. But none of Chekhov's contemporaries has confirmed Avilova's story, on the basis of observations made *at the time* of the romance's supposed duration. Without undue lack of charity, we may point out that Avilova was an old woman when she wrote her memoirs and, being an authoress, was presumably accustomed to using her imagination.

Chekhov did not reply to Avilova's first letter, written after their initial meeting (but which she makes no mention of in her memoirs), because, he said later, he had forgotten her married name and did not realize whom the letter was from.[40] There is no reason to disbelieve this explanation: if he had not written because he wanted to blot out Avilova's image, he would not have subsequently entered into a correspondence with her. If the violence of his feeling for her drove him to Sakhalin, it seems most improbable that he would run the risk of being once again attracted by her, even if he believed himself cured of this passion.

It is not impossible that at their second meeting on 1 January 1892 Chekhov propounded to Avilova the whimsical and banal theory that on the first occasion they had met again after a long separation. Chekhov could be both whimsical and banal in what he said to women. However, on this same trip he did not see Avilova again, and he was spending time with an actress, Zankovetskaya.

In the early months of 1892 Avilova wrote twice to Chekhov and received two replies, which facts, as Simmons points out, she omits from her reminiscences. From what Chekhov says in the second of these replies,[41] it is clear that she was angered by some of his well-meant criticism of her work. Four days afterwards he wrote to Suvorin, perhaps with Avilova's resentment in mind: 'Women are most of all unsympathetic because they're unfair, because a feeling for fair play doesn't seem to be one of their natural attributes.'[42] Next month he wrote: 'I've grown old not only physically, but in spirit too.'[43] These are hardly the remarks of a man absorbed by a sacred passion. Perhaps Chekhov had just received, on 6 or 7 March, Avilova's letter objecting to his insulting her while drunk. His reply to her (19 March 1892) is polite, but dignified: 'Think what you will of me.' He seemed particularly upset that she should imagine he could ever talk 'filth' about any woman. The letter ends with Chekhov casually stating that he is resolved not to come again to St. Petersburg that year—a remark which, whether meant to be facetious or discouraging, could not be intended to raise Avilova's hopes. And if Chekhov wished *not* to encourage Avilova (because he regarded his love for her as 'pure') why should he deliberately have sought her company on subsequent occasions? In this year Chekhov's letters to his friend Lika Mizinova demonstrate that he could write in an intimate vein; but his next letter to Avilova is pleasant, filled with desultory news, and absolutely devoid of any intimate note.

Simmons appears to question whether a third meeting, mentioned by Avilova, and supposedly in the winter of 1892–3, ever took place; and his arguments, though not conclusive, further shake confidence in Avilova's memory.[44] He likewise questions Avilova's statement that she met Chekhov at Leikin's in February 1895, when she invited him to visit her the following evening. However, one feature of Avilova's story at this point adds to its credibility. Chekhov, escorting her home, behaved rather rudely, taking the nearside seat in the sleigh first, so that Avilova was forced to walk round to the far side.[45] This is an odd detail for Avilova to have invented, since it makes it appear that Chekhov's attitude to her was one of disrespect. At any rate, Chekhov's letter to Avilova of 14 February 1895 verifies that they did meet at her house on 13 February, as Avilova says. But this letter is also an indication that no dramatic scene such as she describes ensued between them. In it Chekhov makes not the slightest allusion to the passion he was said to have admitted. This might be interpreted as the drawing of a veil of discretion over what had occurred. But why should Chekhov then lie to Avilova, saying as he does that he left because he felt she was tired and because he felt depressed? (In Avilova's account he leaves in a highly excited state.) That Chekhov's letter of 14 February gives the lie to Avilova's account is implied, moreover, by the very fact that it is omitted from that account.

Was the declaration of love then a complete invention? Very possibly not. There are some interesting aspects of Chekhov's 'confession'. He states that he 'loved' Avilova (*Ya vas lyubil*), something she has to grapple with later in her account, as the present tense of the verb would have fitted better into her story. Chekhov also stresses the chaste aspect of his passion, and thereby avoided any such complication as the seduction scene Avilova might have been expecting. (Otherwise why should she feel, as she says she did, that to offer Chekhov champagne would be 'an insult' to her husband?) Chekhov expressed his passion in what strikes one as an unusually lofty manner. His words: 'it was possible to love you only with a pure, saintly, lifelong love. You were for me something holy' are distinctly reminiscent of the nonsense talked by Trofimov ('we are above love') which is satirized in *The Cherry Orchard*. Chekhov seemed angry—presumably because he was overwrought—but he let go of Avilova's hand when they parted with the curiously flippant words: 'Oh! What a cold hand!'—and left at a run, in order to have time to have supper with Suvorin. It seems more likely that what Avilova took to be a sincere declaration of passion was simply Chekhov putting on a display of the facetious gallantry with which he was accustomed—as his letters constantly demonstrate—to treat pretty young women. Chekhov may well have referred to a former attraction to Avilova, and then, curious perhaps to see her reaction —or simply carried away by the dramatic scope of the situation (Chekhov loved acting, and farcical humour came naturally to him)—he lapsed into a mock-heroic declamatory style. Even if he did express his love in terms as strong as those Avilova quotes, he probably had no idea that she would take him so seriously. This explanation seems the only plausible one, since it accounts both for Chekhov's offhand reference to the evening in his letter of the following day, and for the element of bathos in his confession, which by virtue of its incongruity lends Avilova's story credibility.

Avilova, as it was, was not discouraged, especially as she thought that only shyness had prevented Chekhov from declaring his love in the present tense. Now in no doubt about her feelings for him, and prompted by his confession, she sent Chekhov a watch-chain pendant inscribed with a page and line reference to his story 'Neighbours': 'If ever you need my life, come and take it.' Chekhov however neither took up the offer, nor acknowledged the gift, nor even kept the pendant for himself: he gave it to his friend the actress Kommissarzhevskaya to use in the production of *The Seagull*.[46]

Avilova appears to have continued her pursuit of Chekhov. She does not mention in her memoirs, however, that in March of the same year, 1895, she inquired for Chekhov in Moscow, having told him she was to be in that city, and was informed at the office of *Russkaya mysl'* ('Russian Thought') that he was in Taganrog. But Leikin was truthfully informed by the same office that he was at Melikhovo.[47] It is not impossible that Chekhov arranged for Avilova to be misinformed.

Although again Simmons seems to question the fact, Gitovich has found some evidence that Chekhov attended a certain masked ball in St. Petersburg on 27 January 1896, where he met Avilova.[48] She was wearing a mask, and his friendliness to her caused her to wonder whether he might not be mistaking her for Lidiya Yavorskaya, with whom his name was still linked. But she was thrilled when he promised to give her an answer to 'many things' from the stage, on the opening night of *The Seagull*.[49] Avilova's doubts as to Chekhov's recognition of her were dispelled when she saw the play. In *The Seagull*, Nina Zarechnaya gives Trigorin a pendant with the reference 'page 121, lines 11–12'. Trigorin looks up the reference and finds the words: 'if ever you need my life, come and take it'. The words, then, were those Avilova had referred to on her pendant: but the actual numbers of the page and lines stated in the play were different from those of the page and lines in her text of 'Neighbours'. What book did they refer to? At home, after a considerable search, Avilova finally found in a book of her own authorship (of which she had given Chekhov a copy) a sentence corresponding to the reference given in the play which made some sort of sense. It was: 'Young girls should not go to masked balls.' This reply bewildered her (though, characteristically, she made the best of it), and indeed it would seem to be an obvious snub.[50]

A further flaw in Avilova's story is her assertion that they then met in a theatre, since Chekhov does not appear to have been in St. Petersburg in the interval between the opening night of *The Seagull* and the next meeting after the one in the theatre that Avilova describes—that which took place in Ostroumov's clinic.[51]

At this point Leikin once more contradicts her story: he says she told him Chekhov did not speak to her,[52] and in fact it is recorded that he did not even speak to his sister on the day of Avilova's first visit.[53]

Their correspondence continued. But when Avilova caught at a reference to 'About Love' in one of Chekhov's letters, concluded that here was a hint at Chekhov's feelings for her, and taxed him with this, ostensibly objecting to his having made use of their relationship in that way, Chekhov's answer was even more vague than the purpose of Avilova's somewhat cryptic letter. 'As to the rest', he wrote, clearly referring to something she had said, '—indifference, boredom, gifted people living and loving only in the world of their ideas and fantasies—I have only one thing to say: another person's soul is darkness.'[54]

As Simmons notes, the first time Chekhov took the initiative in writing to Avilova was when he wanted her to do something for him: namely, to help him with some work that had to be done for his publisher.[55] His letters during this year (1891) do not give the impression that Chekhov was conscious of higher things between them. Avilova herself admits in her account that they contained no 'call'.

It is none the less very likely that Chekhov was glad of an opportunity to see Avilova and thank her for her help, when she was passing through the city with her children on 1 May 1899. But even on this self-sought occasion Chekhov appears to have behaved strangely, for they had what seems to have been a rather snappish conversation. Chekhov said he would not visit Avilova in St. Petersburg and left abruptly. Perhaps he was afraid that she would be so emotional as to embarrass him in public. Certainly—for she admits it—she was thinking at the time of the last meeting between the would-be lovers Alekhin and Luganovich.[56]

Whether Chekhov actually did reply, under the pseudonym of 'Alekhin' to 'Luganovich's' letter of congratulation (on his marriage) is not proven, since Avilova did not give Chekhov's sister the letter to publish. As Chekhov had not replied to a previous letter of hers, in which, she says in her reminiscences,[57] she could no longer conceal her love and yearning, it seems unlikely that he would have joined her subsequently in this rather coy charade.

Avilova asked Masha not to publish one letter Chekhov did send her, as far as one can judge, after he must have received her love-letter. Chekhov's letter is in answer to some question Avilova put him concerning her brother's treatment for tuberculosis. It begins: 'You write that it is "excessively difficult" for you to make a request of me, and I feel excessively sad that this should be so.'[58] This faint note of mockery might be Chekhov's way of replying to some over-ardent letter such as Avilova mentions. In any case, his letter contains no personal message and is in fact rather curt.

As for Chekhov's last extant letter to Avilova, this might well contain his answer to 'Luganovich's' letter: 'I wish you all the best,' he wrote. 'Most important of all, keep your spirits up, and don't look for such complexities in life; it's probably much simpler in actual fact. After all, is this—life, which we know nothing about—worth all the tortuous reflection with which we Russians rack our brains—that is the question.'[59]

When Chekhov wrote 'don't look for such complexities in life' (*ne smotrite na zhizn' tak zamyslovato*) he surely had in mind precisely the *zamysel*—the underlying meaning—which Avilova thought was the link between their relationship and the would-be lovers in Chekhov's story. In other words, Chekhov was telling Avilova not to look for non-existent meanings in things—a tendency she appears to have displayed throughout their relationship.

Avilova's reaction to Chekhov's reply was to indulge in further tortuous reflection. 'I read this letter hundreds of times. What had incurred this new mood of Chekhov's? "Life is simpler, it isn't worth tortuous reflections . . .". And it seemed to me that he was smiling at himself with bitter scorn as he looked at himself in the past. He has not lived, nor thought, nor felt as he should have . . .' (*Ne tak zhil, ne tak dumal i chuvstvoval. . .*).[60] The next words, which conclude the whole story, are: '*Propala zhizn'!*' ('A lifetime wasted!') and are slightly ambiguous. Whose life was wasted, hers or Chekhov's? The implication is: Chekhov's. Perhaps here Avilova was trying to imply that Chekhov regretted not having become more deeply involved with her.

One must however point out at this stage that Chekhov's sister Masha reported that Avilova herself showed some diffidence when speaking to Masha about her relationship with Chekhov.[61]

This is understandable when one remembers that Masha—who in the same context stated that there was nothing between her brother and Avilova—must have been an intimidating and relatively knowledgeable opponent of the idea that Chekhov loved Avilova.

It is unfortunate that Avilova stresses to an unnecessary extent the unpleasantness of her jealous (and unfaithful) husband, the charm of her children and her passionate love for them, her application to her writing, and so on, for all these circumstances are too obviously intended to enlist the reader's sympathy. Moreover, they dramatize Avilova's situation, and consequently tend to make one look for dramatization in her presentation of the facts.

The possibility cannot be ruled out that Chekhov did love Avilova, that this was for him a tragic blow of fate such as he describes in his work of the 1890s. The reasons Avilova finds to justify the passive role Chekhov played in their friendship—the 'sacred' quality of his love, his bad health, and responsibility towards his family; and especially Magarshack's theory—that Chekhov deliberately tried to forget her, until the Sakhalin trip cured his obsession—are all in themselves fairly plausible hypotheses. It is however factual evidence that must chiefly concern us. The many instances where Avilova omitted relevant facts, withheld letters, or where her chronology is as Simmons points out 'garbled',[62] do her case no good. In view of this, and until there appears some more positive proof of the theory that Chekhov loved Avilova, it would seem wisest to conclude that this theory is simply a myth, and to deny it great significance in our examination of Chekhov's unhappy picture of love.

5

A much more substantial role in Chekhov's life was played by Lidiya Stakhievna Mizinova. And yet this woman, who knew Chekhov much better than did Avilova, and who is more generally recognized to have been an object of Chekhov's affection, has probably even less claim than Avilova to recognition as a prototype of the romantic heroine.

Mizinova, a friend of Chekhov's sister Masha, was known to the Chekhovs as 'Lika'. She appears to have made Anton's acquaintance in the autumn of 1889, when she was nineteen years old and he twenty-nine. By the time of his departure for Sakhalin they were good friends. Lika came to see him off, and Chekhov gave her his photograph, with the inscription: 'To the best of creatures, from whom I am fleeing to Sakhalin, and who scratched my nose. I beg her suitors and admirers to wear thimbles on their noses. A. Chekhov. P.S. This inscription, likewise the exchange of photographs, doesn't bind me to anything.'[63] These lines are typical of the correspondence between Chekhov and Lika during 1891 and the first half of 1892.[64] Their letters reveal that the relationship between them at this period, when Lika was a constant guest of the Chekhov family, was based on an affectionate familiarity, the chief characteristic of which was a cheerful brand of rudeness and vilification. 'I . . . will be glad of your death,' Chekhov wrote in his first extant letter to Lika. 'I'd like to pour boiling water over you. I want your new fur coat (8 r. 30 kop.) to be stolen, also your felt boots and galoshes, and your salary to be cut, and Trofim (*Trophim*) when he marries you to contract jaundice, chronic hiccups, and a tic in the right cheek.'[65] 'Trophim'—as Chekhov spelt it sometimes in the Roman alphabet—was one of several invented characters, supposed lovers of Lika, of whom Chekhov pretended to be jealous, and to whom he referred with pseudo-vehemence. 'When you and Trofim go to the Alhambra,' he writes on one occasion, 'I hope you accidentally gouge out his eyes with your fork.'[66]

He also touched fleetingly from time to time on the question of marriage. 'How about my marrying Mamuna?'[67] is the guileless postscript to his first letter to Lika. And five days later he writes to Masha: 'Rumours have reached me that Lidiya Stakhievna is marrying *par dépit*. Is that so? Tell her that I shall take her away from her husband *par dépit*. I am an insolent fellow.'[68]

It was in fact Lika herself who had stated in a letter to Chekhov that she was marrying *par dépit*.[69] This was a joke: Lika was playing her part in the mock romance they had elaborated. She did so, however, with considerably less enthusiasm than her correspondent. She never, for instance, used absurd pseudonyms such as those with which Chekhov was wont to sign his letters (e.g. 'Your famous friend: Guniyadi-Yanos'; 'Master of the

Watchdogs Golovin-Rtishchev'; and even, on one occasion, 'Lika's lover').[70] Chekhov very probably used these pseudonyms expressly to emphasize the imaginary nature of the romance. It is noteworthy that he did not use them in two friendly but sober letters he wrote to Lika in the summer of 1892, when his purpose was to transmit messages from Masha.

Lika, on the other hand, found herself faced with the same problem that later confronted Yavorskaya: without wishing to seem too serious, she wanted to define the terms of their relationship. She referred jokingly to 'Trofim' etc., but also to real admirers. Twice she declared her intention of marrying: the first time *par dépit*, the second time to the seventy-two-year-old owner of a wine-factory who had proposed to her. 'As to whether the men here are courting me—naturally!' she wrote to Chekhov while on holiday in 1892.[71] Often her comments on her admirers were unflattering or rueful: one of them had stolen her purse, on another occasion she found them particularly 'nasty'; her object in mentioning them, whether conscious or not, was to remind Chekhov that she was a beautiful girl who was much sought after. She never meant to suggest that Chekhov had a rival in her affections. In one letter to him she commented that her writing was shaky, because, perhaps, Levitan (Chekhov's friend, the artist) had escorted her home. She could not however be totally disingenuous. 'You know,' she admitted towards the end of the letter, 'if Levitan looked the least bit like you, I'd have asked him to supper!!'[72] When Chekhov, similarly facetious, once began a letter to her with the words: 'Having fallen for the Circassian Levitan, you . . .'[73], Lika's reaction was swift. In her next letter she both objected to Chekhov's remark and pointed out that, thanks to the vigilance of his mistress (Kuvshinnikova), Levitan did not dare to approach her too closely, and in any case was never left alone with her for one moment.[74] In a later letter she asked more heatedly: 'Why is it you so insistently like to remind me of Levitan and of my so-called "dreams"? I'm not thinking about *anyone*, I don't want or need anyone.'[75] In fact, it was plain to both parties whom Lika wanted.

There was a pathetic awkwardness in Lika's manner as she strove to conceal her true feelings while uttering the bantering words which no doubt stuck in her throat. Once she responded to Chekhov's flippancy ('I love you passionately, like a tiger, and offer you my hand')[76] with a mock love-letter,* addressing Chekhov as *ty*—for the first and only time—and using such expressions as 'my dear Anton' and 'Thine for ever'. But the love-letter is a self-conscious and apologetically inept essay in the genre: 'I'm writing the letter in this tone, I mean, I can bring myself to do it only because you ordered me to send the stamp in a love-letter. And such letters I do usually write in a familiar tone!!' (*na ty!!*).[77]

Lika was not really capable of entering into the elaborate fiction established by Chekhov's 'love-letters' to her. She was much more in her element when responding to his outbursts of rudeness, for this came naturally to her: she was a vivacious and quick-tempered girl. In her letters of 1891–2 expressions abound such as 'devil take you' (*chort Vas zadavi*); 'what pleasure it would give me to slap you'; and 'although you're the famous Chekhov, you write rubbish, or else you know nothing about medicine'[78]—this last in reply to some sincere advice about her health. As in this case, Lika's rudeness (unlike Chekhov's) was often the expression of genuine, if slight, irritation. Almost always Lika gave free vent to her feelings—in this lies the chief charm of her letters, and because of this characteristic they tell us much more about the relationship than do Chekhov's.

That Lika was in love with Chekhov is indicated in her very first extant letter to him. Ostensibly written to give him some information about primary schools which he had requested, it contains the engagingly candid remark: 'of course this is only a pretext!'[79] She must have hoped that by her constant visits to the Chekhov family, her good-natured execution of Anton's many commissions in Moscow, her readiness to supply him with news, gossip, or practical advice as the occasion demanded, she would eventually become an indispensable adjunct to his life. Meanwhile by frank admissions of how she felt and attacks on him when he fell short of her standards of friendship, she sought to awaken some emotional response.

It seemed, indeed, that there were grounds for hope. Members of the family testified that Anton liked Lika very much. Masha Chekhova believed for some time that her brother's feelings for

* With this, as with all Lika's letters, care has been taken to render accurately into English her conversational, somewhat haphazard epistolary style, not excluding her occasional lapses in grammar and punctuation.

Lika were stronger than hers for him.[80] Nor would this be surprising: Lika was an acknowledged beauty, described by Tanya Shchepkina-Kupernik as a 'real swan-queen out of a Russian fairy-tale, with ash-blonde curly hair' and 'clear grey eyes' beneath 'sable brows'.[81] Misha Chekhov, confirming this impression, commented: 'everyone used to stare at her'.[82]

Misha also states in the same context that 'Anton was attracted to [Lika] as a woman' (although elsewhere he claims to be unable to say that any of the brothers 'were consumed with ardour' for her).[83] It was in fact obvious from Chekhov's continual references to Lika's looks that he was well aware of her physical attractions. There is no reason to suppose that he had not had some form of mild flirtation with her. A biographer states that, before Chekhov met his wife, '[es war] sein Prinzip gewesen, es bei Frauen, die in ihn verliebt waren, niemals bis zum Küssen kommen zu lassen.'[84] No evidence is offered, however, in support of this rather implausible hypothesis.

In any case, whether or not Chekhov let matters reach the kissing stage, there are indications that Lika's physical attraction to him was not entirely discouraged. In June of 1892 a mysterious incident occurred between them. In a letter written on the next day after a visit to Melikhovo, Lika apologized for having behaved 'like a little girl' and continued: 'It's ludicrous actually, forgetting oneself so far as to misunderstand a joke and take it seriously. Still you surely won't blame me too much, because you've probably been well aware for ages that that's the way things are . . . I shan't calm down till I get at least a line or two from you and see that your attitude to me hasn't changed and that you don't condemn me too much for my lack of restraint.'[85] Did this mean that Lika, misunderstanding something that Chekhov had done or said, took the opportunity of letting him know that she was willing to sleep with him? The unusually embarrassed and reticent tone of the letter suggests that it was something to do with sex. Moreover, she and Chekhov had been talking of a trip to the Crimea and Caucasus together in August, which appears to have been Lika's idea, and which had inevitably a suggestion of impropriety about it, so that Lika told her family that she was going with 'a lady'.[86] Whatever the incident at Melikhovo was, Lika was not deterred from continuing her plans for this trip. To abandon them would have been to make a mountain out of what was clearly in Chekhov's eyes a molehill —and to ruin a chance of having Chekhov all to herself.

For—and this is significant—Chekhov did not take the incident seriously. In his reply to Lika's agitated letter about her 'lack of restraint' he made light of the matter, implying that he had no reason to blame her. 'Dear Likusya,' he wrote, 'instead of moping and scolding yourself and myself for bad (?) behaviour like a governess, you'd do better to tell me how you are, what you're doing, and how your affairs are in general.'[87]

Whether with relief or not, Chekhov could not honour the arrangement to go south *à deux* with Lika: a widespread epidemic of cholera prevented him from leaving his medical duties. The fact that he asked Suvorin to make a trip to the Crimea with him, in the autumn when the cholera had died down, does not necessarily mean that he was unwilling in principle to go travelling with Lika, whom, it is evident, he was capable of dealing with under any circumstances.

Poor Lika found Chekhov impervious to her physical charms. In July, reduced once more to fruitless jocularity, she informed him of her decision to marry the wine-factory owner, adding with perhaps a touch of wryness: 'I must have become infected with your good sense and caution . . .'.[88] Lika's was a passionate nature, and an excess of caution was something in Chekhov with which she could not cope. Whatever Chekhov could offer her, it was not what she wanted.

Her disappointment was the more complete because Lika had been more favoured than most of Chekhov's female admirers. For at least the first four or five years of their acquaintance Chekhov showed that he bore Lika a strong affection and that he took a genuine interest in her personality and activities. His letters to her do not consist entirely of heavy witticisms. In particular in the first half of the year 1892 one is impressed by a difference in his letters to her. There is a greater warmth in them. In March he lists a string of complaints, ending with, 'and worst of all, Melita isn't here, and there's no hope that I shall see her today or tomorrow.'[89] Despite the ubiquitous banter ('When is the spring coming? Lika, when is the spring coming?' Chekhov asks, adding: 'Take the last question literally, and don't look for any hidden meaning in it')[90] one senses that Chekhov is writing with greater ease, because the result is more natural and his letters altogether more 'normal'. In reply to a letter from Lika in which she told him that writing to her did not bind him to anything, he wrote with a gentler humour than usual: 'Canteloupe, I know what—now you've grown up you've fallen out of love with me'; and, apropos of nothing in particular: 'Inside you, Lika, there's a big crocodile, and indeed I do well to listen to common sense, and not to my heart, which you've taken a bite out of.'[91]

'You do nag, Lika,' he wrote on 16 July, but finished the letter by asking her to come to Melikhovo for the winter, and begging her to write. During of the summer of 1892 and on into late autumn Chekhov renewed his invitations to Melikhovo and his demands for letters. In November he wrote several times. On 19 December he wrote, rather pathetically, to 'Likusya': 'I'm frozen and not very well,' and, later in the month, he wrote from Petersburg, having heard she might be coming there and obviously delighted to think so. In January, still in Petersburg, he wrote: 'I'm hellishly bored. Write, angel.'[92]

But, alas for Lika, Chekhov's sudden adoption of a kinder, more intimate tone did not mean that he had suddenly discovered a soulmate in her. He had wanted, previously, to keep her at bay, and his humorous style of writing had assisted him to do so. Now, however, he had less need to resort to the infuriating banter: by about 1892 Chekhov knew that Lika was in the process of realizing that her pursuit of him was hopeless.

Lika's letters, never published in full, but none the less the key to the whole relationship, prove conclusively that, from a relatively early date, there was emotional involvement on her side only. And it is clear that from about the middle of 1892 she began to suspect this. Within a month of the unexplained incident at Melikhovo which so embarrassed her she seemed to be beginning to give up the idea of capturing Chekhov. On 28 June 1892 Chekhov had written her a semi-mocking, semi-affectionate letter in which he referred jokingly to the noose she had thrown round his neck. She replied with an ostensibly cheerful, resigned letter. Referring in it to Chekhov's good sense and caution (as quoted above), she attempted to appear jolly and indifferent herself. 'In memory of our *former friendship*,' she wrote, 'write more often ... how I should like (if I could) to draw the noose tighter. However, this is not for me! For the first time in my life I've no luck in this field.'[93]

A similar jocularity, which ill disguised Lika's underlying nervous diffidence, characterized her letters as the months passed: 'don't forget the girl who thinks of you constantly. (That's a pretty phrase, isn't it? But I'm afraid it'll alarm you, so I hasten to add I was joking.)'[94] By November Lika had put her cards on the table, but was pathetically eager to assure Chekhov that she was not taking seriously his protestations of love: 'As regards my having turned your head to the extent that you're prepared to swear to me that two times two is five, what am I to say, poor thing, if you've turned *my* head to the extent that I'm actually prepared to believe it, and actually to believe you want to see me.'[95] On 30 December 1892 she signs herself: 'The girl you have abandoned'.

Not however until the middle of the following year did Lika finally give up hope. 'I . . . know you,' she wrote in July of 1893, 'and I know only too well what your attitude to me is to claim you should remember about me.'[96] A week later she wrote an apparently cheerful and gossipy letter, inserting, as it were casually, the questions: 'What are you doing? Who has taken my place?'[97]

Then, suddenly, her letters become painfully frank. 'I shall be infinitely happy,' she wrote in August of 1893, 'when finally I become totally indifferent to you . . .'[98] And by November her tone was one of desperation. 'I'm familiar with your attitude—either you feel condescending pity for me or else you ignore me completely. My most ardent desire is to be cured of the horrible state I find myself in, but it's so difficult by oneself—I implore you, help me—don't invite me to come to you—don't see me! It doesn't matter all that much to you, but it will perhaps help me to forget you.'[99] Lika cannot have had the courage of her convictions. Next month Chekhov was in Moscow and they arranged to meet. Chekhov might not have suggested it, but he seemed in any case to ignore Lika's request for help. Having failed to keep the rendezvous, on account, he said, of his bad health, he wrote Lika a note of apology which finished: 'I'm leaving for Melikhovo now. I'll expect you on Friday. Be sure to come. You know how much I need you. Don't let me down, Likusya, for Heaven's sake come!'[100]

And Lika did come. But she came in the company of another man, Ignaty Potapenko, also a writer, who soon became a fairly close friend of Chekhov. For it was at this point, when she was finally convinced that her friendship with Chekhov had reached an *impasse*, that Lika turned to Potapenko, who although married, was willing to undertake an amorous adventure. In 1894 Lika and Potapenko both went to Paris (although not together); but they saw little of one another there, owing to the presence of Potapenko's dominating wife. After some months Potapenko left Paris with his wife, leaving Lika, who was pregnant. Lika stayed abroad and her daughter was born when she was living alone in Switzerland. The child died at the age of about two. Therefore, viewed from a distance at least, the whole sequence of events formed a wretched episode in Lika's life; but at the time she must have obtained release from the frustration of her one-sided passion for Chekhov.

Lika's name had none the less been closely linked with Chekhov's, and it is understandable that their relationship was liable to misinterpretation. An unpublished letter to Chekhov from A. A. Lesova, a friend of the family and at one time fiancée of Ivan Chekhov, shows that she believed Lika to have jilted Chekhov. 'What are you doing, abandoned by cruel Lika?' she asked.[101] And a little later she wrote: 'Forget Lika and love me. Didn't Lika ruin your plush waistcoat when she extracted your heart?'[102] These words indicate, however, that Lesova suspected Chekhov of not being deeply hurt and she was shrewd if she did not take his plight seriously, even while believing him to be the injured party. M. T. Drozdova, a friend of Masha's, on the other hand, clearly took Chekhov unnecessarily seriously when he told her that he 'used to be very jealous' of Lika; this being some time after Lika's love-affair with Potapenko and her return from abroad.[103] For Chekhov, far from bearing Potapenko any grudge, remained on the friendliest of terms with him. In the summer of 1894 he went for a short holiday with him, when the latter came home. He also saw Potapenko in the following December and spoke with warmth of him to Suvorin in March 1895.

In subsequent years Chekhov and Lika resumed their former friendly relationship. Chekhov's letters to Lika never, indeed, expressed anything but goodwill. She, however, was from time to time unable to suppress an echo of her earlier resentment. When Chekhov, writing from Biarritz in 1897, referred coyly to his French Margot, Lika retaliated with more than a tinge of mockery: 'I hope she really stirs you up a bit (*Pust' ona Vas rasshevelit khoroshen'ko*) and awakens those qualities in you which have been long in hibernation. Suppose you came back to Russia not a sourpuss but a living person—a man!' And she continued, taking up a cryptic reference in his letter of 18 September to 'cheese-making'—a word which apparently embraced some *double-entendre* for them both: '. . . you don't know a thing about cheese, and even when you're hungry you only like to gaze at it from a distance, not eat it (remember this theory of yours?). If you stick to this with your Margot too, I'm very sorry for her, tell her that a companion in misfortune sends her regards! I once foolishly played the part of the cheese you didn't fancy eating.'[104]

We know, of course, from the evidence of his liaison with Yavorskaya that Chekhov did not apply his theory of looking and not touching to all women. But the history of his friendship with Lika demonstrates plainly that he was not prepared to have an affair with any girl who crossed his path and showed willing. On the contrary. The constant availability of Lika put him off.

Poor Lika, aware of this but unable to forget Chekhov, wrote to him in 1898 in a tone of exasperated humility: 'I'd write every day if I didn't think you'd tell me to go to hell!'[105]

Thus the evidence is that from an early stage in their friendship —if not always—no strong emotion of any sort entered into Chekhov's feelings for Lika. She herself knew this, and in 1898 she summed up the whole relationship for her own satisfaction: 'You were always afraid of [my love] even before you had cause, and ran away.'[106] This was the epilogue to Lika's ambitions to be more than a companion to Chekhov.

In the light of this knowledge we may return to consider briefly the connection between Lika and Nina Zarechnaya, heroine of *The Seagull*: a tiresome connection, let it be said immediately, which nevertheless cannot be overlooked, particularly because of the great significance which certain critics and biographers have given to it.[107] There is, for instance, a chapter-heading in Zaitsev's biography of Chekhov: 'Lika—"The Seagull" '; and Grossman entitles his long article on Lika's life and her relations with Chekhov 'The Romance of Nina Zarechnaya', although in his second paragraph he admits that the genesis of *The Seagull* is more complicated than is suggested by the simple scheme of prototypes: Nina/Lika; Treplev/Chekhov; Trigorin/Potapenko.

It is strange however that anyone should claim, as does Nemirovich-Danchenko, that Nina Zarechnaya was not connected with 'a friend of Masha's' (i.e. Lika).[108] Of course the Lika–Potapenko affair formed the framework of *The Seagull*'s plot. Lika herself knew it, and she was not alone in knowing it. 'Everyone here is saying that . . . *The Seagull* . . . is taken from my life,' she wrote to Chekhov in 1896.[109] Yet there is much more intrinsic interest in the relationship between Lika, Potapenko, and Chekhov than in the Nina–Trigorin–Treplev triangle, which is simply an unsubtle device in an insignificant plot. *The Seagull* is not a dramatized real-life story. Like all Chekhov's plays, it is more concerned with ideas and with demonstrating a dramatic technique than with the plots that Chekhov implemented.

The part Trigorin plays and the fact of his being an author, in addition to the connection claimed between Arkadina and Potapenko's wife, make it possible to equate Trigorin with Potapenko. But as for Treplev, the only aspect, so far as concerns the love-intrigue, in which he could be said to be a projection of Chekhov himself, is that of the rejected lover, and this was one part which we know Chekhov did not play *vis à vis* Lika. Of course Lika looms larger in Chekhov's biography than Nina does in the genesis of *The Seagull*. But she was not the girl Chekhov loved and lost, not the girl who inspired his stories of unhappy love.

Lika's character and history have appealed to the sympathies of many students of Chekhov's life. But even Grossman, one of her most ardent admirers, who states—with a rather exaggerated enthusiasm—that Lika's biography is of interest to us 'as an historical document of striking significance, as evidence of the spiritual crisis of an entire generation, as a memorial to one of Chekhov's loftiest inspirations'[110]—even Grossman is concerned with pointing out not that Chekhov loved Lika, but that he ought to have done so. In yielding Lika to Potapenko, Grossman says that Chekhov 'lost the most important thing—life'[111]; and, of the phrase in one of Chekhov's letters to Lika: 'I've obviously let my health slip through my fingers, as I did you'[112]—Grossman writes: 'In all the many volumes of Chekhov's correspondence there would seem to be no lines more hopeless than these. And they sound the more poignant in that here we have not merely a tragedy of fate, but a tragedy of guilt.'[113]

To judge Chekhov in this way seems strange. It is to blame him for not doing something which he had neither the obligation nor the inclination to do. For Chekhov quite simply did not want Lika's love.

What was it about Lika that prevented him from responding to her touching devotion? Masha Chekhova, who probably knew more about both sides of the relationship than did any other third party, evolved her own theory about her brother's attitude to Lika. According to Masha, Chekhov kept down his real feeling for Lika—who was 'weak-willed and disorganized'—because he felt calm and equilibrium were of paramount importance to his creative life, and that he would not find these in marriage to Lika.[114]

Lika's temperament may well have made her difficult to live with. Her letters show that she alternated between fits of black depression—'*Akh, kak skuchno!*' ('Oh, I'm so fed up') is one of her most frequently reiterated phrases—and boisterous high spirits. One would be inclined to think that it was the depressive side of her nature that Chekhov found unattractive, rather than her high spirits. However, there was a Bohemian side to Lika's character that very possibly did not appeal to him. Lika liked singing and dancing—all very well: but she also smoked and drank rather more than was fitting,[115] and, as in larger issues of conventional morality, so in more trivial matters her behaviour was not always 'ladylike'. Olga Knipper, meeting Lika at a party in 1901, was shocked when the other, intoxicated, buttonholed her with the proposal that they should drink '*Bruderschaft*'.[116] It is the potential vulgarity of Lika's behaviour, as indicated by these facts, rather than the possibility of his not leading a calm life, which suggests itself as a likely cause of Lika's lack of appeal for Chekhov.

Furthermore, there is considerable significance in the fact that the concept of purity in women—or *Reinheit* as they called it—became the subject of a joke between Chekhov and Lika. He wrote to her in 1893: 'The schoolmaster Kryukovsky hasn't returned your photograph yet. He says he's given it to Kochetkov, the industrialist, who apparently has hung it in his drawing-room and written under it: "A Swan". What swine! Decidedly they have no respect for *Reinheit*.'[117] To which Lika responded: 'You can leave my picture at Kochetkov's—it's more the place for it there than with you or Kryukovsky the schoolmaster, because he quite rightly doesn't see *Reinheit* where it doesn't exist.'[118]

There is a certain irony in Lika's reply because, in view of her subsequent affair with Potapenko, she was indeed not, potentially at least, the embodiment of *Reinheit*; and although Chekhov may have continued to see *Reinheit* in some women where it did not exist, in Lika's case his apprehension of the truth was inevitable. And Lika perhaps even before she went off to Paris already supposed that Chekhov might have a fundamentally different attitude to *Reinheit* which could preclude his serious involvement with her. Some years after the end of her affair with Potapenko, she wrote to Chekhov in a tone of wry amusement: 'I feel as though the past few years hadn't happened, and I'd found again the erstwhile *Reinheit* which you prize so much in women, or, more accurately, in young girls! [?]'[119]

Lika, aware that Chekhov did not love her, may have made a grave tactical error if ever she let him think that she would settle for a purely sexual relationship with him—albeit *faute de mieux*. For in the concept of *Reinheit* that Chekhov valued so much there was doubtless implicit a recognition of the essentially spiritual quality of what he considered to be the desirable relationship between man and woman. This, at any rate, is what is implicit in the 'purity' of his romantic heroines, who are inseparably associated with the concept of spiritual love.

There is another point. Lika may have made a further error in seeing too much of Chekhov, in opening her heart to him, and in short, letting him come to know her too well to be able to 'poeticize' her in any way. For Chekhov had not set his sights on a homely presence, on the 'girl next door'. On what was possibly the very day that he received Lika's letter saying that he feared her love, Chekhov wrote to his brother Misha: 'Marriage is an attractive proposition only if it's for love. To marry a girl just because she's nice is the same as buying some useless article in the market just because it's pretty. In family life the most important thing is love, sexual attraction, being of one flesh, the rest is undependable and a bore, however you look at it. So it's not a question of a nice girl, but of one you love: the rest, as you see, counts for little.'[120] All Lika's attractions, therefore, went for nought: they were not precisely what Chekhov was looking for.

6

What, indeed, was Chekhov looking for in a woman? He stated once, in a letter to Suvorin: 'In women I love beauty above all things'.[121] However, although these words certainly reveal Chekhov in a more sympathetic light than do his pompous assertions concerning what he did *not* like in women, it would be a mistake to take this statement too literally. Lika and Lidiya Avilova in particular would have found a certain irony in it. Both possessed physical attractions well above the average, and Chekhov found neither sexually irresistible. True, neither had the brittle, fragile quality of the romantic heroine: Lika was decidedly plump, Avilova tall and rosy-cheeked—both physically robust, in appearance at least.[122] Was this to their disadvantage from Chekhov's point of view?

It seems highly unlikely. Moreover, Yavorskaya, to whom Chekhov was sexually attracted, does not appear to have been notably evocative of the romantic heroine either. According to her friend Tanya, Yavorskaya was 'attractive but not beautiful', with a harsh voice, 'a complete inability to keep still', 'strange eyes with a sort of emptiness in them' and 'a kind of reptilian grace':[123] more reminiscent of the anti-heroine than the romantic heroine, in other words, although elsewhere Tanya is less critical of Yavorskaya's looks; photographs show the latter to have been attractive in a rather modern style, with big eyes and a wide mouth: a face of character rather than beauty.

In any case, given the vague nature of Chekhov's allegation concerning beauty in women, it seems best to approach it in a spirit of conjecture. It does appear safe to say that the sort of beauty which captivated Chekhov had a quality of transience or remoteness. We recall that Chekhov's boyhood encounter with the girl at the well was fleeting; and in a letter to his sister Chekhov once described a 'wondrous vision' of a languid beautiful girl in a white blouse whom he glimpsed at a railway station on the steppe.[124] Although the reference is casual enough, the incident is believed to have inspired the story 'Beautiful Women'. Lika, a beauty in the hand, as it were, and Avilova also, seem to have had less grip on Chekhov's imagination than beauties more remote from him.

This hypothesis receives some support from what we can surmise of the nature of Chekhov's feelings for the actress Vera Kommissarzhevskaya, who created the part of the *ingénue* Nina in *The Seagull* in a way that won Chekhov's enthusiastic approval, and perhaps his heart also. Vera, who, photographed playing Nina, appears as a waifish figure in a light-coloured dress with long dark hair and huge eyes, certainly corresponds to the physical type of the romantic heroine, and perhaps it was this, together with her successful interpretation of the character, that aroused in Chekhov a special tenderness for her. Such a feeling is clearly discernible in his letters to her, which are devoid of banter, but always respectful, solicitous about her health and warmly appreciative of her artistic talent; and at times humble—for Chekhov—in his gratitude for her attentions. Thus, when she wrote recommending him a certain doctor,[125] Chekhov—although accustomed to the solicitude of feminine admirers—replied: 'Your letter touched me deeply and I thank you with all my heart. You know what I feel for you (*Vy znaete, kak ya otnoshus' k Vam*) and so you will understand how much I thank you and how glad I was to have a letter from you.'[126] Several years later he made the following comment to her on his marriage: 'You saw my wife, whereas I shan't see her till the spring. Either she's ill, or I'm away, and so nothing is as it should be.'[127] Such a confidence about the unsatisfactory state of his private life is very rare in Chekhov's correspondence with friends at this period.

Kommissarzhevskaya, however, was bound to have been more interested in another part of this letter, where Chekhov wrote: 'Shall I not write a play *for you*. Not for this or the other theatre, but for you. This has long been an ambition of mine.' Kommissarzhevskaya had had no scruples in asking Chekhov to give the play he was then writing—*The Cherry Orchard*—to a theatre which she was opening.[128] She was in fact quite single-minded in the pursuit of her acting career, and in her letters to Chekhov, although these are full of genuine goodwill, there are indications that she had no qualms about exploiting the friendship of an important playwright. (And not just in connection with the stage: she at one point reminds Chekhov of a promise to find her land for a house.)[129] There is no evidence at all that she felt more than affectionate friendship for Chekhov. The ardour with which she pursued her career doubtless left her little time for other attachments.

One critic has suggested that her relationship with Chekhov constituted a *romance manquée*,[130] and from Chekhov's point of view this may have been the case: quite possibly, however, he preferred to admire Kommissarzhevskaya from afar (they met infrequently, owing to his health and her career): perhaps this preserved the poetic quality of his feeling for her. That he should have 'poeticized' Kommissarzhevskaya would help to account for his regard for her—who was possibly the only woman for whom Chekhov's feelings were stronger than hers for him.

Curiously enough her independent character and her relative maturity—she was thirty-two when she met the thirty-six-year-old Chekhov in 1896—make Kommissarzhevskaya more like the Nina Zarechnaya who appears in the last act of *The Seagull* than the character as she appears in Act I. This is interesting because, firstly, most of the other women whose relationship with Chekhov has been discussed were in their early twenties or younger when Chekhov's name was linked with theirs, and in this particular respect one would think that they suggested to Chekhov the type of the romantic heroine more strongly than Kommissarzhev-skaya; secondly, because the quality of toughness, which Kom-missarzhevskaya must have possessed to some extent to have carved a career as she did, is distinctly lacking in, say, Misyus or Kisochka.

Yavorskaya also must have possessed the same quality, for the same reason, and the other women in Chekhov's life are not notable for their helplessness: Avilova, like Kisochka, felt ill-used by a boorish husband, but she took—so it appears—more deliberate steps than Kisochka to involve herself in a liaison; and Lika, who found herself in a wretched predicament when Pota-penko abandoned her pregnant and far from home, proved herself capable of living through this and subsequent trials without her spirit being crushed. But do we ever find Chekhov commending Lika's courage? No. His last letter to her tells her patronizingly: 'Your letters, and indeed your life, show that you are a most interesting woman':[131] all the praise he could muster, it would seem.

What Chekhov probably did appreciate in Lika, and in his other female friends, was vitality and a sense of fun. Misha Chekhov, among others, spoke of Lika's 'gay personality', and Masha Chekhova said that Anton was always cheerful and

K

pleasant when Lika's presence enlivened the household.[132] Chekhov was also fond of Natalya Lintvareva (the girl whose political opinions he scorned) and said of her: 'she roars with laughter so that you can hear her a mile away.'[133] He also liked one Sasha Selivanova, who was a 'noisy, rip-roaring maid' who played and sang 'incessantly'.[134] In 1888 Chekhov wrote to Suvorin: 'I'm tired of the golden mean, I'm loafing around and regretting that there are no original, wild-spirited women about.'[135] One might have thought that Chekhov would have been repelled by boisterous women, so different from the timid heroines he described. There is no evidence that there was anything particularly childlike in the high spirits of Chekhov's female friends, nor indeed anything especially childlike about them,[136] with the possible exception of Tanya Shchepkina-Kupernik, who at nineteen was naïve enough to believe Chekhov when he told her that his coffee-coloured doves were a cross between a dove and a cat of that colour[137]—an ingenuousness worthy of Misyus—but there is absolutely no suggestion in Chekhov's correspondence or in the memoirs of contemporaries, including Tanya's, that Chekhov was interested in her as a woman. It was much more typical of what we can surmise to be his taste that he should have been attracted by Yavorskaya, whom, it may be remembered, was described as 'sometimes . . . intelligent' and 'well dressed'. It has been shown that Chekhov appreciated intelligence in women, but it may at first seem odd that he should have thought the way in which they dressed important: his romantic heroines mostly seem too unsophisticated to be smart. None the less, in one of his last letters, written in Berlin a month before his death, Chekhov commented disparagingly on the appalling taste in dress of German women.[138] And at this point we remember the connection implied between the tasteless dress of Natasha in *Three Sisters* and her mediocre set of values. It becomes apparent that Chekhov would have prized in elegant women the absence of vulgarity which suggests the spiritual refinement of the romantic heroine.

The fact remains, however, that there is a distinct disparity between the type of woman with whom Chekhov consorted in his daily life and the type whom he glorified in his fiction. None of the women with whom we know him to have been on relatively close terms corresponded in many significant particulars to the romantic heroine—none of these women, that is to say, *as they really were.*

But this is only to be expected. The vital connection is the connection in Chekhov's own mind. The romantic heroine, who as an individual is mysterious and seems remote from the real world, is so because she is simply a projection of an idea in the mind of her creator. The romantic heroine is the symbol of love. Beautiful and pathetic she may be, but she acquires a human depth and complexity only when love acquired for Chekhov a human face.

5 Love

If we seek to clarify Chekhov's attitude to love, we are immediately confronted, as in so many other aspects of his life, with ambiguity. What is by no means certain is that Chekhov, during those years when Lika, Avilova—and perhaps other women—hoped to win his heart, was actively seeking to fall in love with anyone. True, he wrote to Suvorin in October of 1892: '. . . I wouldn't at all object to falling in love. It's a dull life when you're not madly in love';[1] and to Elena Shavrova in 1896: 'You write that you want fame much more than love; and I the contrary: I want love much more than fame.'[2] But these words cannot be taken entirely at face-value: they are unmistakably tinged with the bantering tone into which Chekhov so readily fell in his correspondence.

He could go further and be downright cynical. In 1896 Suvorin noted in his diary the following sentiments, under a general heading, 'Some of Chekhov's ideas': 'Friendship is better than love. My friends are fond of me, I am fond of them, and through me they are fond of one another. Love makes enemies of those who love the same woman. When in love, men wish to possess a woman entirely, to let no one else have her, and they consider anyone who conceives the urge to attract her as their enemy. Friendship knows no such jealousy. For that reason friendship is better than love, even in marriage.'[3]

Now, despite the unequivocal tone, these words do not mean that Chekhov was uninterested in love, and they need not invalidate attempts to find a love-object in Chekhov's past. Only two years later, Chekhov, as we have seen, urged his younger brother Misha in equally direct language to remember the supreme importance of love in marriage.[4] A sudden *volte-face*? Perhaps. But the same sober, apparently so rational tone in which

Chekhov puts friendship before love in 1896 had been heard before: in 1888 he wrote to his elder brother Aleksandr: 'You . . . know perfectly well that family-life, music, caresses, fond words, aren't to be had by marrying the first woman you come across, even if she is a decent girl, but by *love*.'⁵

A fluctuating attitude, indeed. Yet not for a moment need we doubt Suvorin's accuracy when he set down the contrary opinion as Chekhov's. For upon examination of the theme of love in Chekhov's fiction, it will be seen that the existence of love-friendship side by side with love-passion was for Chekhov a fundamental and fascinating fact of life.

'Friendship is better than love.' The remark is intriguing on several counts. Perhaps most of all because it sounds like the comment of a man who has never been passionately in love. Most men (and women) would after all find natural the typical lover's less than altruistic attitude, of which Chekhov here speaks so disparagingly. That he should do so suggests that he was clinging to an abstract ideal of love, based on no experience that can have approximated to the typical lover's sexual passion. The insight is hypothetical, but it is reinforced by the recollection that sexual jealousy plays only a very minor role in Chekhov's fiction.

Aside from his jocular remarks quoted above, which one must hesitate to take literally, there are scarcely any references in the whole of Chekhov's correspondence which suggest that he personally wanted to fall in love. However, as in his dealings with female admirers, so in other matters Chekhov was adept at concealing what he really thought, whether he did so by being facetious or by keeping silent. Thus there is some justification for the speculation of critics who say that Chekhov was dreaming of '*un grand amour romantique*'⁶ or talk of his 'hunger for love'.⁷ Certainly, Chekhov's general pronouncements on love—those which were not intended to be taken as a comment on his personal affairs—show that he took love very seriously. Even more significant than the homilies addressed to his brothers are a couple of lines written in 1889 to Suvorin—towards whom Chekhov felt no such strong pontificatory urge: 'Love is no joke. If people shoot themselves because of it, it means they take it seriously, and that's important.'⁸ The earnest tone of this comment suggests that Chekhov had stronger views on the subject of love than his correspondent might have suspected. In any case, at least one critic, H. P. Collins, is shown to have been badly misled when he writes: '[Chekhov's] marriage with the Alsatian actress Olga Knipper . . . remains rather puzzling. Though in his later stories he wrote with increasing poignancy of frustrated love, the love for women seems to have had little serious part in his life.'⁹ The implication would seem to be that Chekhov somehow stumbled into marriage as he might have stumbled into a hole in the ground; and it is surely much more likely that Chekhov wrote poignantly about frustrated love because love did, in some sense at least, have a serious part in his life. Whether or not Chekhov dreamt for years of a great romantic love, he did experience love towards the end of his short life: and it was a love which we know he took seriously, because at this point Chekhov dropped his reticence. The evidence of his feelings is to be found throughout his correspondence, from the day he encountered the woman who was to become his wife.

2

Olga Leonardovna Knipper was in her late twenties when Chekhov made her acquaintance at a rehearsal of *The Seagull* on 9 September 1898. A month later, after seeing her play Irina in A. K. Tolstoy's *Tsar Fedor Ioannovich* he wrote from Yalta to Suvorin: ' . . . best of all was Irina. If I'd stayed in Moscow I would have fallen in love with that Irina.'¹⁰

In May of the following year Olga visited Chekhov at Meli-khovo: after this, in June, their correspondence began. Chekhov's letters were full of the inevitable banter, but they also contained more than a suggestion of serious involvement. His second communication with her began: 'Hail, last page of my life . . .'.¹¹ Few phrases could provide a more substantial indication of Chekhov's desire for a permanent relationship.

In the summer of 1899 he and Olga stayed in Yalta, he at an hotel and she with friends. They travelled back to Moscow together in August, going over the Ai Petri range and through the Kokkoz valley together in a carriage. It was almost certainly on this journey, within less than a year after their first meeting, that they agreed to marry: for in a letter some months later Olga wrote, saying that she had heard that Chekhov was going to marry someone else: 'Congratulations, dear writer, so you couldn't hold out?'—and adding that she will come to upset his domestic tranquillity: 'After all, we came to an agreement—remember the Kokkoz valley?'[12]

By late August of that year Chekhov was back in Yalta, settled in the south more or less permanently, while Olga was kept in the north by her work. The romance continued by correspondence. From the start, Chekhov's letters show an enormous enthusiasm for his love, which expressed itself in uninhibited affection: 'Hello, dear, precious wonderful actress! . . . Hello, my joy!'[13]

Olga came to Yalta on tour with the Moscow Arts Theatre in April 1900, and in July on a private visit to Chekhov. It was on this second visit that they apparently became lovers; for a switch from '*vy*' to '*ty*' in their correspondence began at this point.

The sexual side of Chekhov's relationship with Olga Knipper has already been discussed. The romantic side, as revealed in Chekhov's correspondence, was no less satisfactory for him. He was joking when he wrote to Olga in January of 1901: 'I wish you . . . still more love, to last even longer, about fifteen years. What do you think, is love like that possible? For me it's possible, but not for you . . .';[14] but his tone expresses his confidence in his new situation. Now that he had found a relationship in which he was free to do so Chekhov referred to his love repeatedly, even quite openly, in a telegram: '. . . well, in love . . .'.[15]

They married on 25 May 1901, and throughout the rest of their life together Chekhov continued to assure Olga of his devotion. 'Believe that I love you, love you profoundly,' he told her. 'Whatever might happen, even if you suddenly turned into an old hag, I'd still love you—for your soul, for your disposition.'[16] 'No one in the world loves you as I do,' he told her on another occasion.[17] And on another: 'My dear, good, splendid gifted little actress, God bless you, I love you very much.'[18]

Although there is nothing particularly remarkable about the way in which Chekhov expressed his love, it is necessary to underline the written evidence of his affection for Olga Knipper, because a certain faction seems to regard Olga in her position as Chekhov's wife at best with surprise, at worst with animosity. For example: Collins, in the remainder of his article, implies that the marriage was entered into without love on Chekhov's part and with an 'uncomprehending' attraction[19] on Olga's; Chekhov's friend Bunin claimed that until he read Avilova's reminiscences—and believed her story—he had thought there to be no great love in Chekhov's life:[20] which is as much as to say that Chekhov did not love Olga Knipper. The same is implied by Altshuller, Chekhov's doctor in Yalta, who wrote: '. . . when I read about [Chekhov's] especially "deep and tender" love for anybody, I think that one must take this in a very relative sense.'[21] Other contemporaries and critics of Chekhov have voiced or implied their disapproval of Olga.*

Unfortunately this dislike is more graphically expressed than the reasons for it: but these seem fairly obvious. Olga herself took violently against certain people and could be a malicious enemy, as her letters to Chekhov show. Many must have been jealous of her, whether on account of her own success or her influence on Chekhov. Anyone who reads it in context will recognize the undertone of jealousy in Bunin's remark (relating to Easter 1901): 'Chekhov, even when Olga Leonardovna was there, insisted on my spending every day at his house.'[22] Altshuller disapproved of Olga because he thought that her irruption into Chekhov's life ruined his patient's health.[23] Similar feelings were no doubt entertained by others, less directly involved in Chekhov's well-being, who regarded Chekhov as society's, or Russia's, property rather than as master of his personal affairs. It is extremely interesting to note in this connection the far greater amount of interest and sympathy shown by most of Chekhov's contemporaries and biographers towards Lika Mizinova, which is out of all proportion to the interest Chekhov showed in her. This of course is partly due to the fact that Knipper was alive until 1959, whereas Lika was dead and her life-

* See, e.g., Shchepkina-Kupernik, p. 326, where she describes how not long before Chekhov's death Olga went off to the theatre with Nemirovich-Danchenko, telling her husband 'not to be bored and to be a good boy'. Chekhov then turned to Shchepkina-Kupernik and said: 'Yes . . . it's time I was dead'. The anecdote is not intended to reflect well on Olga. See also: Nemirovich-Danchenko, *Chekhov*, p. 426, where he refers to Olga's jealousy of Chekhov's sister. This point was often made against Olga. See also: Rachmanowa, *passim*: Rachmanowa appears to be conducting a personal vendetta against Olga Knipper, in a tone which would invite a libel action from the latter, had she still been alive.

history open to speculation and elaboration by 1937. It is also an excellent demonstration of the audience-appeal of unhappy love.

If the tone of Chekhov's letters to Lika suggests that he was fond of her, the tone of his letters to Olga puts it beyond doubt that he loved her very dearly. If further proof of this love be demanded, it can be found in the affection that Chekhov's sister Masha showed towards Olga Knipper. Masha Chekhova, as we shall see, was passionately devoted to the cause of her brother's well-being: and that she and Olga became lifelong friends in spite of the jealousy they felt for one another is conclusive proof that Chekhov's love for his wife was obvious to those who observed them together.

Olga Knipper can no more easily be equated with Chekhov's fictional romantic heroines than can his other women friends. Like most of these, and as one would indeed expect of the actresses among them, Olga was sociable and vivacious rather than timid and retiring. Like Lika, she became depressed and elated easily. She was ten years younger than Chekhov, but she was no adolescent when he met her. Her letters to Chekhov sometimes reveal a trait of immaturity—but not the kind of pure uncorrupted childlike vision that Chekhov depicted in his fiction. Olga's immaturity is revealed rather in a tendency to worry over trivial matters—and in a childish sense of fun, which she herself was the first to admit to: 'Do you remember taking me back as far as the stairs, and the stairs creaking so treacherously? I adored that. Heavens, I'm writing like a schoolgirl',[24] she wrote to Chekhov with reference to the early stages of their love-affair.

It is not in fact particularly rewarding to speculate why Chekhov loved Olga. The important thing is that he believed that he had found love, and he once told her that the longer he lived with her, the broader and deeper his love would become.[25] In being identified with Chekhov's concept of true love, Olga Knipper corresponds symbolically to the romantic heroine, even if not in other respects.

It was for Olga Knipper that Chekhov wrote the part of Masha in *Three Sisters*,[26] one of Chekhov's finest creations and the last of his romantic heroines. 'Oh, what a part you've got in *Three Sisters*! What a part!' he told her as he was writing the play.[27]

The charm of Masha as a character lies in her possessing both the 'poetic' attributes of the romantic heroine and a strong personality which can easily be 'put across' to the audience. Her part may be compared with the part of Nina Zarechnaya in *The Seagull*, which is very difficult to play well.* Nina's role is too dependent upon the symbolic significance which others are supposed to see in her. Her speaking-part does not bear the imprint of individuality, and so she fades into the symbolic pattern of her fate: beauty injured, hope triumphant.

By contrast, Masha's individuality is emphasized and the pattern of her fate, which also resolves itself into love–disappointment–hope, is toned down. Her personality is dramatized: she wears black; swears and whistles; is blunt to the point of rudeness; hot-tempered (she even snaps at her pathetic old nurse); her behaviour is moody, unpredictable and odd: she intends to leave before Irina's party, and then abruptly changes her mind; she is asleep during the fire scene while her sisters are in a state of great agitation; she is preoccupied and bursts into snatches of song. In a word, she is mysterious—different from her sisters. (And what is more, Chekhov intended her to be aware of this: in the confession scene, he told Knipper, Masha feels that she is more intelligent than her sisters.)[28]

The drama of her love for and forced renunciation of Vershinin is, on the other hand, underplayed. Masha is shown not to feel bitter about her marriage to the absurd Kulygin: she speaks about it in a calm, matter-of-fact way: 'I'm used to him . . .'. Vershinin's love for her is expressed in his highly emotional speech of Act 2: 'I love you, love you, love you . . .' (there is nothing very subtle about the way he is depicted), but we do not finally know Masha's mind until Act 3, when the fact of their complete knowledge of one another is revealed in the interchange, meaningless to outsiders, 'Tram-tam-tam . . . Tam-tam', etc. When Masha tells her sisters of her love, the scene is again underplayed: or should be, as Chekhov was at pains to point out to Knipper: 'it's not a confession at all, just a frank talk . . . the main thing . . . is to put across that it's been an exhausting night.'[29] And at the climax of the play Masha's present grief—as is Irina's—is domin-

---

* Lykiardopoulos, reviewing *The Seagull* (p. 239), commented: 'The Moscow Art Theatre has today come to the conclusion that, even in Russia, a good Nina Zarechnaya is almost impossible to find.' How flat the play can fall if the audience cannot appreciate its symbolic atmosphere was demonstrated by its first-night failure on 17 October 1896.

ated by the question of the future: 'They're leaving us . . . we're left alone, to begin our lives from the beginning again. Life must go on . . .'—thus runs Masha's last speech.

This deliberate synthesis of the dramatic and the non-dramatic in the presentation of Masha does not sound subtle, but it is peculiarly effective on the stage. Masha's predicament, as befits a romantic heroine, is not devoid of pathos: 'When you take happiness in little snatches, bit by bit, and then lose it, you gradually become thick-skinned and bad-tempered', but never does she appear to be sentimentalized. The part played by Irina helps here. It is Irina who possesses, at first glance, the character-istics of the typical Chekhovian romantic heroine. In Act I Irina is dressed in white, filled with a childlike *joie de vivre*. Chebutykin 'poeticizes' her into a little girl; Tuzenbakh and Soleny poeticize her as the woman they love; although none of those people really know Irina: she has her symbol—the locked piano. But her sisters—and the audience also—see the unromantic side of her—see her as an ordinary girl, growing older and disillusioned as the years pass.

Irina however could be said to take over, to a certain extent, in place of Masha, the pure childlike aspects of the heroine which seem to have obsessed Chekhov. Masha is devoid of these characteristics, which are not always easy to put across sym-pathetically to audience or reader.

Masha is mature, and not 'pure', at least not in terms of conventional morality. She shocks her sister Olga by glorying in her love for another man. Yet Masha is the most 'heroic' of the play's three heroines, because it is she who chiefly represents true spiritual values, as Chekhov saw them. It is she who comes out with the strongest tirade against vulgarity, in Act 2; it is she who most sharply criticizes Natasha, the incarnation of vulgarity, before Natasha makes her appearance; she who expresses dislike of 'that Mikhail Potapych, or Ivanych'—Protopopov, who later becomes Natasha's lover. Conversely, she is attracted by idealism: after Vershinin's visionary monologue on the values of culture in an uncivilized world, she decides to stay to lunch after all. She falls in love with him: and, what is most important, her heightened sensitivity makes her the most aware of what love should be. She knows that Kulygin's expressions of devotion to her are as automatic, sterile, and intrinsically as meaningless as is the

chanted paradigm of *amare* which she repeats in her irritation
with him. She believes that love has tremendous importance: it
places one in a different frame of experience, where all considerations are subject to the demands of love. 'When you read a novel,
you think it's all old hat, and there's no mystery about it,' she
tells her sisters, 'but when you fall in love yourself it becomes
obvious to you that nobody knows anything, and everyone must
take decisions for himself . . .'.

Is it to Olga Knipper that we are indebted for this at one and
the same time credible, interesting, and poetic heroine? Chekhov
may well have endowed Masha with certain of Olga Knipper's
traits, but there are no striking points of resemblance between
Masha and what we know of Olga Knipper. Nor is it to be expected that there should be, for Chekhov created the role of
Masha for Olga with the intention of providing her with a good
part to play, rather than of portraying her character. Masha's
personality, whomever it is derived from, is not the motivation of
the play; *Three Sisters* contains themes, characters, and situations
which Chekhov had used before; it was written as an experiment
in dramatic technique, as were his other major plays. The
credibility of both Masha and Irina as romantic heroines is due to
Chekhov's increasing mastery of his dramatic technique.

3

All Chekhov's romantic heroines of the stage have an inherent
advantage over their counterparts in his fiction: they have, when
they are on the stage, a physical presence and cannot be shadowy
or totally insipid. Moreover, the success of Chekhov's dramatic
technique is mainly dependent upon sureness of characterization;
to a lesser extent, on the creation of an atmosphere; to a still
lesser extent on the plot, which tends in the case of Chekhov's
major plays to be minimal and very simple.

The technique which Chekhov used in most of his love-
stories is more conventionally dramatic. In these the plot is also
simple, but it is much more important. We are presented with a
schematic pattern: love is thwarted by extraneous circumstances,
as in 'The Artist's Story' and 'About Love'; or the chance of
finding love is thoughtlessly thrown away, as in 'Miss N.'s

Story' (*Rasskaz gospozhi N.N.*, 1887) and 'Lights'; or love ends in disillusionment, as in 'The Story of an Unidentified Person' and 'The Teacher of Literature' (*Uchitel' slovesnosti*, 1894): this occurs when one of the partners is shown to be, or to become, a *poshlyak*. The essential feature of these works is what happens to love, and the actual nature of the love relationship is not investigated. We have, for example, in 'The Story of an Unidentified Person' the heroine, Zinaida Fedorovna, who is 'good', the villain, Orlov, who is 'bad': the action is set in motion by Zinaida Fedorovna's leaving her husband, and a gloomy *dénouement* inevitably follows. Like the narrator, we never really understand why Zinaida Fedorovna loves Orlov. Here the characters as individuals are interesting, but not in their relationship with one another, which remains mysterious. More frequently, only one partner is interesting at the other's expense—usually the heroine's.

The absence of an analysis of the *nature* of relationships between human beings—an omission perhaps imposed by the restrictions of the short-story form—is compensated for by atmosphere, which in the Chekhovian love-story is all-important: this type of story depends almost entirely for its effect on 'poetry'—on the ability of the reader to enter into a world of nostalgia and anguish and to find something in it which touches him personally. Chekhov's treatment of love relies heavily for its effect on sentences such as: 'What enormous happiness it is to love and to be loved, and how dreadful it is to feel that one is about to topple from this lofty tower!' ('My Life') or: ' . . . at times when I feel melancholy and weary of solitude I have vague memories and gradually for some reason the idea takes hold of me that someone is remembering me too, and waiting for me, and that we shall meet. . . . Misyus, where are you?' ('The Artist's Story'). The effectiveness of Chekhov's love-stories depends upon our appreciating the mystique with which he surrounds love. That the romantic heroine is in danger of seeming insipid—unless Chekhov specifically makes a feature of her non-poetic aspects—is due to the fact that the heroic role is really played by love. Love, rather than any character, stands for the ultimate in desirability.

In the world of Chekhov's fiction love is regarded not merely as an embellishment of existence, but as indispensable to existence. 'Without love there would be no life; he who fears it and evades it is not a free man': the words are those of Dr. Blagovo in 'My Life', who has seduced Kleopatra, the narrator's sister. Blagovo is very sympathetically portrayed and the implication clearly is that the importance of love justifies his action. In 'About Love' it is again emphasized that love should take precedence over everything else: the climax of the story is reached when Alekhin, saying farewell to his beloved Anna whom he has never claimed, realizes that 'when you love someone, all considerations regarding your love must take as their starting-point something higher and more important than happiness or unhappiness, sin or virtue in their everyday sense, or else you must take nothing into consideration at all.'

These words would seem to sanction a dangerous egocentricity, were it not for the fact that idealized love is presented in Chekhov's work as a power for great good, even as a regenerative force. In the original published version of 'About Love' Chekhov wrote: 'When you love someone you discover such riches in yourself, such a bottomless well of tenderness and kindness, that you can scarcely believe you are capable of such love.' Later, he cut this sentence out, probably because such asides interfered with the pace of what is essentially a fast-moving narrative: but the idea is developed more fully in the in many ways similar theme of 'The Lady with the Dog'. Gurov's love-affair with Anna Sergeevna inspires in him a feeling of disgust for the tenor of his day-to-day life: 'the frenzied card-playing, the gluttony, the drunkenness, the continual discussion of the same topics . . .'. In 'The Artist's Story' there is an implicit contrast between the beauty of the artist's love for Misyus and the unromantic cohabitation of his host Belokurov with his pompous housekeeper who looks like a fatted goose. The weakness and cynicism of Chebutykin, the doctor in *Three Sisters*, is redeemed to a great extent by the one uplifting and ennobling feature of his character —his genuine and touching love for Irina. Andrei's love for Natasha, on the other hand, while it may strike us as touching, is not uplifting or ennobling, because, as we have seen, only by his excessive stretch of imagination is she a romantic heroine. For love in the world of Chekhov's fiction is only a great force for good when the loved one is worthy: the ideal of love demands an ideal love-object. So Chekhov would seem to be saying when he jotted in one of his notebooks: 'Love is a blessing. It is not for nothing, indeed, that at all times amongst practically all civilized nations love in the broad sense and the love of a husband for his wife are both alike called love. If love is frequently cruel and destructive, the cause of this lies not in love itself but in the inequality of human beings.'[30] People, therefore, must live up to the concept of love.

Of no one more aptly than of Chekhov could it be said that 'the dramatist cannot afford to question the absoluteness of the emotions out of which his drama is concocted'.[31] The critic who wrote these words was discussing Tolstoy the novelist, and he is making a point about the difference in this respect between Tolstoy's work and that of a dramatist. Tolstoy's treatment of love in his two greatest novels is markedly different from Chekhov's treatment of love within the 'dramatic' framework of his short stories, and it would seem apposite to indicate briefly the nature of the difference.

At the end of *War and Peace*, when Natasha Rostova, the romantic heroine *par excellence*, has changed into a fussy demanding matron, we may feel that her love and Pierre's has devolved into some more mundane emotion. But do we find Pierre kicking against the traces of domesticity, crying, like Chekhov's teacher of literature (in the story of that name): 'I must escape from here, escape this very day, or I'll go mad!'? Far from it. Similarly, in *Anna Karenina*, it is clear that the love of Kitty and Levin is not, and never has been, ideal and pure: in Kitty it originally contained an element of her fear of spinsterhood, and after marriage it is threatened by the evolution and alteration of emotions in both partners. This causes them, the protagonists, pain, but it is the author's vision which is dominant, and the author's vision remains in this connection serene: life and love are like that, Tolstoy knows it and he assumes that we realize it, whether we like it or not. There is no suggestion of anguish or irony. Tolstoy could adopt this attitude to changes in the nature of love because his novels, as far as the love-stories in them are concerned, have as their hero the family. Still with the same apparent detachment, Tolstoy leads the love-story of Anna Karenina herself to its conclusion of turmoil and tragedy. Anna neither can nor wishes to see her relationship with Vronsky devolve into peaceful domesticity. She has only the ideal of 'love' to cling to.

Significantly Chekhov, in his two essays in the novel genre,

'The Duel' and 'Three Years', was to examine relationships in evolution: the conclusions he came to in these isolated works will be discussed in a later chapter. But in by far the greater proportion of his fiction the view of love propounded is that of his favourite Anna Karenina herself: love has the immutable quality of the ideal.

In Chekhov's later work, this ideal of love was to become increasingly associated with the concept of something above and beyond the transient, or more precisely, with a quasi-philosophical speculative interest, and a quasi-mystical faith, in the future of mankind. In *Three Sisters*, Masha's relationship with Vershinin arouses our sympathy because it is a predicament of immediate 'human interest'; but we note that Masha is initially attracted to Vershinin by his idealistic vision of the future. There is no 'human interest' in the romance between Anya and Petya Tro-fimov in *The Cherry Orchard*, because it is devised merely as a prop to their interest in and ambition for the future; and the chance of making a dramatically poignant minor tragedy of the *romance manquée* of Lopakhin and Varya is made little of. This is because the plot-scheme of *The Cherry Orchard* is as follows: youth's innocent love and hope for the future is contrasted with their elders' corruption and nostalgia for the dying past. In 'Betrothed', Chekhov's last short story, and in which more than in any other there is a recognition of the social forces that were changing women's lives, there is a fusion of the social and the romantic theme—or rather, the lack-of-the-romantic theme, because Nadya does not love her fiancé: she does not love him because he is smugly content to regard his social inactivity as a 'sign of the times'. Even in 'The Lady with the Dog', in which the actual nature of the human relationship described is of paramount interest, the awakening of love forms a bridge to idealistic philosophizing: 'As he sat beside the young woman, who was looking so lovely in the dawn light, calmed and en-chanted by the fairytale setting of the sea, the mountains, the clouds, the vast sky, Gurov thought how, if one came to think of it, essentially everything on earth was beautiful, everything save our own thoughts and deeds, when we forget the higher aims of existence and our human worth.'

This feeling of involvement with the future of mankind which Chekhov seems to be seeking to transmit in his late works is of course especially interesting when viewed in the light of subsequent events in Russia, and much has been written by both Soviet and Western writers on the development of the theme in Chekhov's work and its significance. On the basis alone of the optimistic outlook expressed by so many of Chekhov's characters one can challenge the view that Chekhov was a gloomy cynic which was held by many early critics of Chekhov, notably by Shestov.[32]

But, however great Chekhov's interest in man's future may have been—and it is possible that the theme was introduced into his stories and plays only to uphold the theory expressed in one of his plays that 'a work of art must express some great idea',[33] rather than that his stories and plays were to any extent inspired by the theme itself—love, in Chekhov's work, is not regarded as an emotion secondary or subordinate to sociological zeal or preoccupation with the future. Chekhov makes it clear, for instance, in *Three Sisters* that Irina Prozorova is not looking forward to happiness when she marries Tuzenbakh although she is to lead a 'new life' as a teacher. Why? Because she does not love Tuzenbakh, and she has made the sacrifice of the imaginary figure she calls her 'real' husband. There is no question in her view—or ours—of the new life being in any way a substitute for love. Nor, in *The Cherry Orchard*, is there any doubt as to who is meant to be the moral victor in the splendid clash of philosophy between puritanical Trofimov, who pompously declares himself to be 'above love' and the down-to-earth Ranevskaya: 'I am above love!' she reiterates in mockery. 'You're not above love, you're just . . . half-baked.' The absurdity of Trofimov's position is promptly underlined by his falling downstairs. As for Ranevskaya, it is felt that if anyone's sins are to be forgiven on account of having loved much, hers will be.

Given his preoccupation with the subject of love, it is not surprising that Chekhov entitled one of his works simply 'About Love'. In the opening paragraphs of this story Alekhin philosophizes on love: 'we, when we love someone cannot stop asking ourselves questions: whether we are behaving honourably or dishonourably, sensibly or stupidly, what our love will lead to, and so forth. Whether this is a good thing or not I don't know, but one thing I do know—that all this is an interference, a pest, and it detracts from one's satisfaction.'

L

Alekhin illustrates his point by describing how his love for a married woman and hers for him is thwarted by their scruples with regard to her husband and family. Love, the story suggests, ought to be untrammelled by such considerations—should rise above petty human conventions. There is however no suggestion of rebellion against these conventions, but simply a thinly concealed yearning for the ideal world in which such an ideal love could flourish. 'The Lady with the Dog' conveys a similar feeling.

Love, as Alekhin sees it, is in fact almost divorced from human circumstances and reality. He refers to the case of a pretty servant-girl whose love for the brutish-looking cook seems inexplicable. Love, the implication is, is not an emotion to be implemented by man's reason, capable of being fitted by man into a scheme of things that would further his interests. This conception of love is commonplace enough; but Alekhin goes further. 'We do not know,' he says, 'how much questions of personal happiness matter in love.' It is no secret that love can lead to unhappiness, but Alekhin is saying that 'love' is of greater importance than the happiness it can bring: that it is, in fact, an end in itself. Nor is he talking of love for the divine—he is talking of love in the context of human relationships. What is the point of this love, it may be wondered, if questions of personal happiness do not come into account?

Chekhov himself would not perhaps have gone so far as to say this. When characters, even those whom he portrays sympathetically, start to 'talk philosophy', we may expect to hear extreme opinions which are not necessarily Chekhov's. Nevertheless, since in Chekhov's fiction the romantic heroine is overshadowed by the concept of an idealized love, the possibility springs to mind that Chekhov personally might have found this idealized love more alluring than the physical relationship or the 'human interest' that any specific liaison could offer him.

In the face of this possibility one of Chekhov's last stories leaps into significance. In December of 1897 Chekhov wrote 'A Visit to Friends' (*U znakomykh*). This story tells how one Podgorin is invited to spend a few days on the estate of Tatyana Loseva, an old acquaintance. He had as a student been in love with the younger sister, Nadezhda, although he had never actually proposed to her. Podgorin is still a bachelor: he has dealings with loose women on Malaya Bronnaya St. and other such parts of

Moscow, but without any sense of involvement and even with some distaste. Nadezhda, or Nadya, who meets Podgorin at the station, at once suggests the romantic heroine: next to her brother-in-law, Tatyana's husband, she 'seemed ethereal': she is a pale-faced blonde of twenty-four, wearing a white dress with an open neck. But—and here is the surprise—Podgorin is displeased: 'her long bare white neck struck him as something new and not altogether agreeable': Nadya's behaviour strikes him as affected and unnatural. This is therefore no Misyus, the reader concludes: and indeed the climax of the story is in direct contrast to that of 'The Artist's Story'. It becomes apparent to Podgorin that he is expected to propose to Nadya. Walking in the garden one night, he realizes that Nadya is nearby, that she senses his presence and that 'white, pale, slim, very beautiful in the light of the moon, she was waiting to hear tender words'; but Podgorin 'felt irritated, and all he thought was that here on a country estate on a moon-lit night, so close to a beautiful young girl dreaming of love, he was so unmoved that he might have been on Malaya Bronnaya St.—because, evidently, this sort of poetry had served its time for him, as had the other crude prose. Meetings on moonlit nights, white, slim-waisted figures and mysterious shadows . . . had served their time . . .'.

Here then, in plain terms, we have a categorical rejection of the romantic heroines of Chekhov's earlier fiction—a rejection of both their physical trappings and of the aura of poetry which surrounds them.

The unexpectedness of such a statement demands some explanation. Podgorin, it might be alleged, is not necessarily Chekhov himself. But if Chekhov's apotheosis of a certain type of heroine and his poeticization of her has hitherto been, as it appears to have been, a strikingly idiosyncratic sentimentalization —idiosyncratic to the extent that it becomes monotonous to the reader who cannot share in the 'poetry'—it seems unlikely that Chekhov would shatter this private vision just for the sake of appearing unbiased. Podgorin is surely expressing something that Chekhov himself felt.

The critical point is that Podgorin is not averse to thinking about love; but only as something remote from the idea of a love-affair with Nadya, or indeed from any love-affair: 'he would have preferred . . . some other woman, who standing . . . where

6 The Cynical Hero

The theme of the rejection of the romantic heroine had in fact made its appearance several times in Chekhov's work before 'A Visit to Friends', although never previously was the message so explicitly stated as in that story. In order to achieve a better understanding of Chekhov's treatment of this theme, it must be borne in mind that, for all his propagation of an idealized view of love and high-minded approach to the baser aspects of hetero-sexual relationships, the integrity of Chekhov's outlook on the entire field of art is marred by a curiously idiosyncratic approach to certain matters.

We take as an example a minor episode in Chekhov's corres-pondence. In 1887, in a letter to Leikin, Chekhov objected to a sketch of a prostitute that had appeared in Leikin's journal *Oskolki* ('Fragments'). 'The *décolletée* woman in the centre of Erber's drawing,' wrote Chekhov, 'is so coarse and vulgarly repellent that the editors and the artist should be clapped in gaol.'* These are strong words, and Leikin must have protested, justify-ing himself in the name of realism: for in his next letter Chekhov felt obliged to air his views on the subject further: 'In a journal like *Oskolki*,' he countered, 'realism should confine itself to the signatures, and the drawings must be as refined as possible, make no mistake. The ugly, moreover, is in no respect more real than the beautiful. Thirdly, not only in a *café chantant* but even in the lowest den of depravity they're not all as grotesquely corpulent

* Letter to N. A. Leikin, 21 August 1887. Chekhov's description of the prostitute runs in Russian: '*Dekoltirovannaya baba . . . do togo neiz yashchna i kukhonno-gnusna . . .*'. The adjective *iz yashchny* which figures in this and in the following quotation was a word which Chekhov attributed particularly often to his romantic heroines; hence it seems appropriate to take it as implying refinement when translating it in this context.

as in Erb[er]'s drawing. Fourthly, if you like, a refined-looking prostitute will sooner arouse the sympathy and compassion of the reader than a filthy one—in short, I can't think of a single reason why it should be edifying and appropriate to depict reality in precisely its worst aspect: *Oskolki* is light reading, after all.'[1]

The last words summarize Chekhov's rational justification of his point of view; he had Leikin's interests at heart and was probably right in his assessment of the reading public. But it is a curiously unscrupulous justification from one who felt strongly that prostitution was an evil and is reported as having said: 'One mustn't deceive in art.'[2] Chekhov's aversion to the drawing, expressed in such remarkably emotive language, and his image, which he considered was to be preferred, of a 'refined-looking prostitute', suggest immediately the workings of that part of his mind which could shut out unpleasant facts of life. We recall his exhortation to his brother Aleksandr: 'protect at least the poetry of life if the prose is already done for'.[3] Here, in his letter to Leikin, Chekhov seems to be as good as admitting that, whereas in the written word the truth is necessary, in pictures (which appeal to the imagination rather than to the intellect) all things must be bright and beautiful. The impression made by his comments to Leikin, as by his injunctions to Aleksandr, is one of astonishing cynicism: particularly since Chekhov said that it was the duty of a writer to be an impartial witness[4] and that 'a man of letters is not a confectioner, a cosmeticist, a comic entertainer . . . he is duty bound to fight his squeamishness, to soil his imagination with the dirt of life'.[5]

This last statement occurs in Chekhov's defence of his story 'Slime', the anecdote about a Jewish *femme fatale* which his correspondent (M. V. Kiseleva) had criticized on the grounds of its being sordid. The other assertion—that a writer is an impartial witness—occurs in his defence of 'Lights', in which story, Suvorin had complained, no solution was offered to the 'pessimistic' outlook of the youthful narrator Ananiev.

Chekhov's defence of the artist's right to impartial observation in connection with these particular two stories is interesting, for the following reasons. In the first instance, when he was talking of 'Slime', he was defending his right to show up woman's sexual power in a very harsh light: he did this in 'Slime', and even more single-mindedly in, for example, 'Ariadna' and *The Seagull*. We have seen how anti-heroines such as these pervert the concept of 'love' into something squalid, or meaningless, just as we have seen how the intervention of fate can make love appear impotent. Chekhov is depicting reality, as he saw it, but he makes plain his partiality—for love, the 'victim', as it were.

But in 'Lights' it is the man who ruins love. Ananiev's outlook on life prevents him from acknowledging that what has happened between Kisochka and himself is of any importance, and thus he is capable of abandoning her. Therefore when in defending 'Lights' Chekhov defends his abstention from judgement, he is in effect refusing to judge a situation where cynicism gains the upper hand over love. The 'objective' Chekhov regards the immoral man impassively, whereas in 'Slime' the immoral woman is 'the dirt of life', to be exposed at the expense of good taste.

It would therefore seem pertinent to examine further Chekhov's treatment of male characters who, like Ananiev, reject the love that the romantic heroine offers them.

2

Among those themes that are concerned with relationships between the sexes rather than with sociological relationships, this theme of rejection is the only theme recurrent in Chekhov's mature work in which the focus of interest is the state of mind and/ or behaviour of the *man* involved.

Early expositions of this theme are to be found in 'The Shooting Party' (1884) and in two rather similar sketches of peasant life, 'The Huntsman' (*Eger'*, 1885) and 'Agafya' (1886). In each of these stories the hero responds with cold indifference to the woman who loves him.

In 1887, however, the theme seems to have exercised a stronger grip on Chekhov's imagination, for in this year it finds in both the story 'Verochka' and the play *Ivanov* a much more graphic exposition. In each case a pure young girl offers the hero her love, and in each case he reacts with unexpected violence: Ognev by a panic-stricken retreat, Ivanov—even more dramatically—by shooting himself on his wedding morning.

'Lights' was written in 1888: in 1889, the theme reappears in a somewhat different guise. Nikolai Stepanovich, the hero of

'A Dreary History' is not offered the love, in any romantic sense, of the heroine Katya—but she offers, and asks for, a profound friendship, like the love between parent and child; and this he proves unable to give her.

Later, in the 1890s, a situation similar to that of 'Lights' is depicted in 'Terror' (*Strakh*, 1892). Here the narrator seduces his friend's wife—a young, slim, pale-faced blonde beauty, who does not care for her husband—a true romantic heroine, it would seem. But here is the difficulty: whereas for her their affair is 'a great and serious love, with tears and pledges', he wants none of this—no tears, pledges, or talk of the future. He regrets the incident and cannot understand how he could have become involved.

In the following year, 1893, Chekhov reintroduced the theme in 'The Story of an Unidentified Person'. Zinaida Fedorovna, the heroine, leaves her husband for her lover, Orlov, but Orlov remains unappreciative of her action. He spends less and less time at home, until the narrator, Orlov's servant, finally persuades Zinaida Fedorovna to come abroad with him, where she dies, as is thought, by her own hand, after giving birth to Orlov's child. Compared with the narrator, Orlov is strikingly unmoved by Zinaida Fedorovna's sad fate, and makes amends only to the extent of putting the child in a kindergarten.

This is the last full exposition of the theme before 'A Visit to Friends', although it appears again in a less emphasized form in *The Seagull*, in the abandonment of Lika by Trigorin. As has been described in an earlier chapter, Wilczkowski made of the re-emergence of this rejection-theme in *The Seagull* a crucial point in his case for Chekhov's having loved Avilova. The flaws in his marshalling of the facts to this purpose have been pointed out, but it is none the less interesting to read his account of the significance in Chekhov's work and life of what he describes as the theme of '*égoïsme masculin*' or '*indifférence coupable*'.[6]

To describe the theme in these terms seems at first appropriate: 'egoism' and 'culpable' suggest a reaction on the reader's part of moral indignation which Chekhov doubtless intended us to feel. But whether he himself felt this with regard to his protagonists is less certain. His treatment of the theme is notably devoid of the harsh moralizing tone with which he dealt with erring females.

It seems moreover preferable to call the theme that of masculine 'cynicism' for the following reason: this, rather than the egoism of the man concerned was what primarily interested Chekhov. There are a number of 'selfish' male characters to be found in Chekhov's fiction in addition to those mentioned above. But no one could say that, for example, those suave ladykillers, Panaurov and 'little' Volodya or the morose seducer in 'Misfortune', Ilin, constitute the centre of interest in the narratives in which they figure. Plain complacent selfishness is not a characteristic capable of providing the psychological drama which is an essential feature of many of Chekhov's short stories. To be cynical, however, one must be aware of what idealism is, and this may imply a conflict in the mind which can be dramatic. Thus cynicism is the more rewarding state of mind for the writer to explore.

However, it would seem that Chekhov was interested in cynicism not merely as a fruitful source of plot material. His recourse to the theme of masculine cynicism was, it would appear, connected with an area of his own mind in which there was a strong conflict between idealistic and cynical attitudes to love. The clue to the existence of this conflict is to be found, firstly, in the way Chekhov depicts those characters who reject the romantic heroine, and secondly in the apparent motivation of this rejection.

The most obvious feature of Chekhov's method of depicting them is the fact that none of them is shown to be an out-and-out villain. The contrast with his treatment of women whose attitude could be described as similarly cynical is remarkable.

The degree of the author's involvement in his characters' feelings varies considerably in Chekhov's treatment of the theme. Where the protagonists are peasants he is at his most detached and remote: the heroes of 'The Huntsman' and 'Agafya' are seen to be spoilt and casual in their behaviour towards women, but even in 'Agafya', where the story is told by a narrator, no moral judgement is passed. But when Chekhov is dealing with his own social stratum his involvement in the psychological phenomenon of male cynicism would seem to be considerably greater.

The impression of involvement is of course heightened by the fact that in many of the stories concerning masculine cynicism Chekhov writes in the first person. This approach, which he did not use in his depiction of heroine and anti-heroine, helps the reader to feel sympathy for Ananiev.

In many of the stories Chekhov invites us to feel sympathy for his heroes by an even more obvious expedient: simply by having his heroes feel remorse. In 'Lights', Ananiev feels so guilty that he actually returns to ask Kisochka's forgiveness, and his awareness of the wrong he has done her is what impels him to tell the story, many years later. 'Terror' ends with the hero asking himself 'in despair' why he has seduced his friend's wife, and with his subsequent, final departure from their house. Nikolai Stepanovich is deeply distressed by his inability to help Katya when she comes to him in the hope of comfort, at the end of 'A Dreary History'. Ognev's inability to respond to Verochka's need for love provokes a similar reaction: 'He was conscience-stricken . . .'.

However, among Chekhov's male characters there are other cynical lovers who do not evince such touching, if futile, remorse, or, if they do, remorse is not enough to whitewash what they have done. Orlov in 'The Story of an Unidentified Person', Ivanov in the play of the same name, and Trigorin in *The Seagull* all seem to embody egoistical feeling *vis-à-vis* women, because what they do is obviously wrong: Orlov ungallantly deserts an adoring mistress who has thrown herself on his mercy; Ivanov is cold and even cruel to his dying wife, and subsequently lets his fiancée down by committing suicide on the wedding-day; Trigorin seduces and later abandons Nina Zarechnaya.

It would be unrealistic to say that Chekhov intended none the less that most of these characters should inspire great sympathy. The respective plots concerned depend upon their fulfilling the role of villain. Even the most sympathetic, Ivanov, is interesting precisely because Chekhov depicts him as a basically good man afflicted with depression and an acute perception of reality, which make him blunt to the extent of brutality.

And yet it is difficult not to feel at least some sympathy for them: for Ivanov particularly, because the interest of the play is so concentrated in his personality, and also, surely, for Orlov and Trigorin. In the case of these last two this is partly because the 'rival' male character cuts such a wretched figure. One is hard put to it to find sympathetic traits in the prim narrator of 'The Story of an Unidentified Person', and Konstantin Treplev is effectively shown to be a tiresome neurotic.

But—and this is the crucial point—there is also the implication that the egotistical male may himself be a victim. Trigorin, a weak man, is completely at the mercy of Arkadina: her force of character dominates him and her sense of ownership virtually imprisons him.

The woman in the case need not be as obviously tyrannous as Arkadina. The narrator of 'The Story of an Unidentified Person', commenting on Zinaida Fedorovna's relationship with Orlov, talks of the 'treasure' and the 'rarity' that is 'the love of a refined, intelligent, and decent young woman' which is going to waste— but even he occasionally lets a false note of cynicism drop into his pompous sentiments: recounting Zinaida Fedorovna's description of how she parted from her loathed husband, the narrator says: 'when he [the husband] wailed, "Oh God, when will there be an end to all this?" and went into his study, she pursued him like a cat a mouse, and, preventing him from locking the door behind him, shouted that she hated him with all her being . . . her husband answered her with reproaches, threats, and finally with tears, and it would be truer to say that he, not she, had been attacked.' This sounds almost as if the narrator disliked Zinaida Fedorovna; the reader at any rate glimpses her momentarily in a different guise from that of the forlorn dis- illusioned romantic heroine: she, in place of Orlov, assumes the role of predator.

Orlov is not weak and not afraid of Zinaida Fedorovna. But he cannot bear her living with him. Why? Because she has turned his bachelor existence upside-down. We are encouraged by the narrator to think that this had been a rather barren existence; but Orlov's own description of his mistress's effect on his life is an appeal for sympathy which is barely resistible: 'she wants my flat to smell of cooking and washing up . . . she has to count my shirts and worry about my health, she has to interfere every moment in my private life and observe my every step, and at the same time sincerely assure me that I can preserve my habits and freedom.'

The confrontation between Ivanov and the young girl Sasha has certain features similar to that between Orlov and Zinaida Fedorovna. Sasha, like Zinaida Fedorovna, is in love and is determined to insinuate herself into her beloved's life. Ivanov, like Orlov, is unable to resist her physical encroachment—but resists her in spirit to the last.

Like Zinaida Fedorovna, Sasha is in some respects a touching figure. She has indeed been called 'a wonderful and charming girl',[7] but this aspect of her is perhaps the least obvious. At first sight, it is true, she appears attractive: young, naïve and earnest, proclaiming to the world-weary Ivanov the power of love: 'Only love can regenerate you'; and Ivanov is drawn to her 'youth' and 'freshness'. However, as the play progresses and Sasha pursues her suit, her naïve speeches become merely tiresome: Ivanov talks of her 'trite phrases' and punctures her pronouncements with savage bathos: 'I have this sensation again of having eaten too many toadstools.'

Sasha's tiresomeness seems to have irritated even her creator. Chekhov, discussing her part in the play with Suvorin, speaks of Sasha as though he thought her not charming, but exasperating. He describes her in letters to Suvorin as 'not a girl but a maiden',[8] 'a wretch' (*merzavka*),[9] 'a female (*samka*) whom males conquer not with their gaudy plumage or grace or bravery but with their complaints, their moaning, their failures'.[10]

In the same correspondence with Suvorin, however, Chekhov analyses Sasha's character without the malice that is implicit in the above expressions. Sasha's fault as Chekhov sees it is that she is in love with the idea of regenerating Ivanov, not with Ivanov himself. Ivanov realizes this, and taxes her with it, but Sasha is determined to go through with the wedding. Her reply shows just how right Ivanov's estimate of her motive is: 'How can I give you up? How shall I give you up? You've no mother, nor sister, nor friends—you're ruined, your estate's squandered, everyone's gossiping about you.' Under these circumstances it is difficult to sympathize with anyone other than Ivanov on the day of the wedding.

If we feel an impulse to side with Ivanov, Trigorin, and Orlov, this is because the threat to their independence represented in Sasha, Arkadina, and Zinaida Fedorovna is seen to be a very real threat: something greatly to be feared and to be avoided only by flight, or by death. It is worth recalling at this point Chekhov's dislike of Turgenev's 'ardent, voracious, insatiable tigresses': Odintsova and Irina would for Chekhov certainly fall into the category of dominating women who attempt to command and thus to threaten men.

The predatory female, intent on ensnaring a man, provided a rich vein of satirical humour in Chekhov's early works. In the pseudo-mystery story 'The Swedish Match' (*Shvedskaya spichka*, 1883) a man—who is thought to have been murdered—has actually been kidnapped by one such woman. Chekhov also made much use of the comic possibilities of the proposal scene. Usually the humour in such scenes lies in the girl's disillusionment: the supposed suitor turns out to be asking for her cooperation as his model, or for a glass of vodka.[11] Such stories are however a mocking comment on society rather than an attack on woman-kind; they find a parallel in the theme of the mercenary suitor: if the would-be bride is a romantic empty-head, the would-be groom is a calculating cynic. Chekhov's eager spinster is a figure of fun, and in no way resembles the predatory female who is motivated by sexual desire, whom, as we have seen, Chekhov depicted harshly, as something to be despised.

In portraying a third variation on the type of woman who is to be regarded with alarm, Chekhov conceals what were possibly his own feelings more successfully than in, say, 'Volodya' or 'Ariadna'. It is perhaps because of this that this third type of woman—though met with rarely—appears much more abhorrent and to be feared than an Ariadna or a Nyuta: and, at her most developed, she inhabits an enclave of Chekhov's fictional world as far removed from that of his starry-eyed spinsters as the other side of the moon.

This type of woman is domineering—domineering, usually, to the point of tyranny. As with other female types in Chekhov's work, the earlier examples are comic in inspiration: 'the last of the female Mohicans',[12] for instance, a large woman aptly named Olimpiada, who is going to the authorities to complain about her hen-pecked husband's failure to behave like a member of the upper classes. Then there is the wife who forbids her husband to wear the trousers in his own home—so literally that he goes about in his underwear 'for economy's sake'.[13]

But the seriously depicted, memorable characters of this type belong to Chekhov's later work. They are three in number: Lidiya Volchaninova in 'The Artist's Story', Aksinya in 'In the Ravine', and Natasha in *Three Sisters*.

It may seem hard on Lidiya, or Lida, to group her with the latter two, for she is in some ways actually sympathetic—more so, perhaps, than she was intended to be, by virtue of the contrast she makes with vapid Misyus and the artist. Moreover, the artist himself to some extent admires her as a 'vital, sincere young woman with convictions' whom 'it was interesting to listen to'; and in their arguments Chekhov puts intelligent opinions into Lida's mouth, so that it is difficult to tell whose side in these arguments he actually supported.

However, any liking we might feel for Lida is subtly undermined by the emphasis laid on her sternness; by the reiteration of the epithets 'severe' and 'serious' in descriptions of her; by reference more than once to her 'small mouth', 'beautifully shaped' but 'stubborn'; and—particularly successfully—by the sharp and sarcastic tone of her arguments: Lida's pronouncements are peppered with sentences like: 'even you smart landscape-artists, it seems to me, ought to have some sort of opinion on the subject'; and: 'You don't like that, but then one can't please everybody.' This sort of thing makes her speech much more vivid than her sister's; and it enhances the strong impression Lida's personality makes on us.

The strength of this impression derives principally, however, from Lida's function in the plot as the destroyer of love. She uses her influence on Misyus to prevent the latter from marrying the artist. Her final appearance in the story, when she tells the artist brusquely that Misyus has gone away—without seeing fit to mention her part in the affair—shows Lida at her most anti-pathetic. Significantly, during this scene she is giving dictation to a child—just as she dictated her wishes to Misyus.

Lida's fault is that which she has in common with Aksinya and Natasha: she has power and abuses it to harm others. The parallel between Aksinya and Natasha is closer, although Natasha suggests an everyday type of villain,[14] while the figure of Aksinya suggests, rather, a symbol of evil. Both of these anti-heroines represent the ascendancy of the petty bourgeoisie, in the one case over the peasants, in the other, over the gentry. Aksinya, married to the feeble-minded younger son of the Tsybukins—incipient *kulaki*[15]—murders her father-in-law's infant heir by throwing boiling water over the child, in front of its mother. She not only gets away with this crime, but comes to rule her husband's family, to part-own a brick-works and to attain a position of power in the village. Natasha marries Andrei Prozorov and becomes mistress of the three sisters' house, where she turns the old order upside-down. If the monster Aksinya represents the power of darkness, petty-minded Natasha represents the power of vulgarity (unlike, it is worth noting, Lopakhin in *The Cherry Orchard*, who fulfils a not dissimilar role as far as the play's sociological content is concerned).

Although both Lida and Aksinya are described as 'beautiful', and Natasha is seen to use her sexual attractions to her own advantage, it is not by their sexual power that these women make a dominant impression: it is by the power that they wield by encroaching on other people's lives and property, be the latter material—Irina Prozorova's bedroom, which Natasha demands for her child—or human—Lipa's little boy, or the artist's Misyus.

We are put in mind of the outline of a story in one of Chekhov's notebooks, which runs as follows: 'A country house. Winter. N., an invalid, is sitting at home. In the evening there suddenly arrives from the station a stranger, Miss Z., a young girl who introduces herself and says she has come to look after the invalid. He is embarrassed, alarmed, refuses—then Z. says she'll spend the night all the same. One day and then another passes and she's still there. Her personality is intolerable, she poisons his existence.'[16]

The theme of a woman taking over a household thus appears several times in Chekhov's work. A very early variant on it, in 'Belated Blossom' (*Tsvety zapozdalye*, 1882) is remarkable for the savagery with which Chekhov describes the mistress of a degenerate nobleman, Prince Priklonsky: 'She was the wife of a billiard-scorer at the club and nothing better, but that did not stop her from making herself completely at home at the Priklonskys. The slut liked to rest her feet on the table.' Kaleriya Ivanovna, 'the slut' (*svin'ya*), soon moves in with Priklonsky and his genteel, hard-done-by mother and sister.

These invaders of the fireside, taken as a group, are liable to strike the reader as being a more formidable crew than Ariadna, Nyuta, and their like (although this latter type may be, and usually is, a domestic tyrant). This is perhaps because the hands of the invaded party are bound—for reasons anyone can appreciate —by social conventions and forces still in operation today. It is easy to see that the three sisters cannot get rid of their brother's wife, whereas it is difficult to appreciate the notions of chivalry which bind Shamokhin to Ariadna. But there is surely also a less logical basis for the alarm that they inspire in us. For a woman to ensnare a man with her charm is a commonplace: but to take over a home and establish herself in the man's position suggests a woman who is larger than life: it is unnatural and sinister.

Reverting to Chekhov's treatment of the theme of masculine egoism, we find that many of Chekhov's villains are afraid for their independence—or regret its loss. Orlov and Ivanov feel trapped in the institutions of cohabitation and marriage. The huntsman was, it turns out, wed to the woman he neglects against his will, when he was drunk.

The characters who feel trapped in a relationship have usually married young. The 'teacher of literature' is warned not to do this (he is in fact twenty-seven, but looks younger). He disregards the advice, and soon comes to regard his marriage as a prison. Significantly, Dr. Blagovo, the sympathetic seducer of the narrator's sister in 'My Life', was married young and no longer lives with his wife. Gurov, hero of 'The Lady with the Dog', made the same mistake. But most wretched of all would seem to be the position of Vlasich in 'Neighbours'. He married his wife out of pity, when she had been seduced and abandoned by his battalion commander: but virtue was ill-rewarded: marriage did not prevent her from going to the bad, from leading an immoral life and ruining Vlasich. Now Vlasich is living with his neighbour's sister, unable to marry her because his wife will not grant him a divorce. Vlasich graphically sums up the situation to his neighbours: 'Terrible woman! There's a fly, old boy, that lays its larvae on a spider's back so that the spider can't throw it off. The larva attaches itself to the spider and sucks its blood. It's just like that that the woman has leeched on to me and is sucking my heart's blood.'

Is it such a situation that all Chekhov's cynical, 'egoistical' men envisage when they reject the romantic heroine? The fact that these men are not condemned in anything like the measure in which Chekhov condemned the anti-heroine and that many of them do in fact invite us to take their part suggests that Chekhov himself felt emotional, if not rational, sympathy for them. And the stark depiction of the type of woman or situation with whom in his work such men are seen to contend suggests possible emotional grounds for Chekhov's sympathy.

If, as would appear to be the case, Chekhov himself could be illogical and cynical, in order to preserve untarnished his vision of the poetic, it is not entirely surprising that his cynical heroes should seem to act illogically when threatened by the advent of the romantic heroine in the flesh. Did Chekhov himself fear that the intrusion of women into his private life would spoil the vision?

3

In 1887, not long after the end of his liaison with Dunya Efros, Chekhov did in fact say, in a letter to Mariya Kiseleva, that the 'symbol of love and domestic bliss' was 'a noose'.[17]

But the remark was facetious, and no more than characteristic of any young bachelor who, like Chekhov, did not wish to risk serious involvement with girls who were the object of casual flirtations. Mariya Kiseleva, who had gleefully observed Chekhov in the act of avoiding such involvement, gives a graphic description of his technique for doing so: 'sometimes I picture you face to face with some young maiden! Those eyes—like those in the photographs, your maliciously penetrating words, and the poor girl is simply squirming. She feels that any moment she'll fall on your neck, but you are—shy, and you realize this, and—*ein* [*sic*], *zwei, drei*—a metamorphosis! Your eyes begin to ache with nes—neur—Heaven knows the name of the disease! An anxious look comes on to your face, and off you go to your writing. Subsequently—the same story all over again, and the victim, brought to the ultimate stage of love and despair, falls ill with some interesting ailment . . .'.[18]

This method of self-defence was clearly adopted for show and afforded Chekhov himself, at least, some amusement. But it was not simply a question of playing a game. Chekhov, it seems, could not help putting up a shield between himself and others. A man who is, as Chekhov was, attractive and successful is likely to shy away from women who pursue him but who do not measure up to his ideal.* How much more likely is this to happen when a

---

* Chekhov, whose admirers haunted the promenade at Yalta when he lived there, was also pursued from a less discreet distance. There exist in the Chekhov archive several pathetic letters to Chekhov from one A. A. Pokhlebina, a pianist, who was desperately in love with him. On one occasion

man can resent the intrusion into his privacy made by friendship
—let alone by love. That Chekhov could seem to fear the romantic
heroine and sympathize with those of his heroes who reject her
is explained by his being such a man.

It is no secret that Chekhov's was a reserved nature. Chekhov
himself admitted as much in a revealing letter to Nemirovich-
Danchenko: 'My dear friend, I shall answer the main question
you brought up in your letter—why we tend to have serious
conversations so seldom . . . . Are we to discuss our private lives?
Yes, that can sometimes be interesting, and we might perhaps
talk about that, but on this topic we're embarrassed, secretive and
insincere, restrained by the instinct of self-preservation, and we
are afraid. We're afraid that as we talk we are being overheard by
some uncivilized Eskimo, who doesn't like us and whom we
don't like either; I personally am afraid that my friend Sergeenko
. . . will be discussing the question . . . in every house and railway
compartment . . . of whether I had an affair with N. while Z. was
in love with me . . .'.[19]

Chekhov's reticence was evident from his early youth. According to one Dr. Shamkovich, Chekhov's contemporary at the
Taganrog Gymnasium, the schoolboys there were chiefly
interested in the significance of sensual pleasures, or alternatively,
of politics. But Chekhov did not attach himself to either faction:
his only observed leisure interest was the theatre.[20]

Clearly the fantasy-world of the theatre can serve as a refuge
to a person who finds real life in any way oppressive. In fact,
Chekhov was very shy: we have the attestation of his contemporaries to confirm this. Olga Knipper referred to his 'retiring
personality';[21] V. I. Kachalov, the actor, says that he only once
saw Chekhov angry, and that was when some students wanted to
organize an ovation for him.[22] Kornei Chukovsky talks of Chekhov's 'unparalleled reticence';[23] and M. M. Kovalevsky describes
him as 'taciturn'.[24] A priest, S. N. Shchukin, felt this when he and
Chekhov first met. He found Chekhov's gaze cold and his manner

she wrote: 'The mere thought that you don't care about my suffering drives
me out of my mind . . . at least pretend, act as if I wasn't antipathetic to you,
deceiving myself is my last escape-route, there's no harm, you see, in deceiving me, otherwise I can't live . . .' (letter to A. P. Chekhov, 9 March 1893:
Otd. ruk. 331.56.38). Chekhov's infrequent references to Pokhlebina in his
correspondence express at best indifference and—more often—amusement
and exasperation. Her plight, evidently, did not touch him.

of talking 'brief, curt and abrupt'. '*This* man,' he thought, 'could not have written *those* stories.'[25]

The coldness which Shchukin took for a want of humanity came not from Chekhov's dislike of him—for Chekhov on further acquaintance proved extremely kind—but from the reserve which made him appear withdrawn even to his family and friends of long standing. Aleksandr Chekhov, who always wrote to his brother in a very intimate vein, asked Anton in a letter of 1888 how his affairs were progressing, adding with a touch of annoyance: 'You're so obstinately shut up in yourself that I don't know a damn thing about you.'[26] Gorky told Chekhov that he was 'colder than the devil himself.'[27]

The result of this reserve was to leave Chekhov rather isolated in the midst of his friends and acquaintances. 'I do not think,' wrote Potapenko in his reminiscences of Chekhov, 'that he had a single friend.'[28] Nemirovich-Danchenko makes a similar comment.[29]

There is abundant evidence that to those whom he liked Chekhov could be an agreeable and sympathetic companion. But, as Potapenko continued in his assessment of Chekhov, although others probably told Chekhov about themselves, 'he never laid bare his [soul] to anybody.'[30] A minor but not insignificant fact about Chekhov is that, even when ill, he disliked to appear before his friends *en déshabille*: he was always properly dressed.[31]

It is interesting that Suvorin, who was for many years probably Chekhov's closest friend, despite the twenty-six-years' difference in their ages, described Chekhov as 'very conceited'.[32] (This was in 1896 or 1897, when he and Chekhov were still on excellent terms.) Lika thought Chekhov was spoilt, but nowhere else do we find any reference to Chekhov's conceit: he has the general reputation of having been a rather modest man. Perhaps Suvorin detected something arrogant in Chekhov's aloofness. If what he said were true, it is an indication of how few people knew the real Chekhov.

So strong was the impression that Chekhov gave of self-sufficiency that his biographer Zaitsev states: 'it is doubtful whether Chekhov was fond of any one person in particular. In his life certain friends are replaced, without fuss, by others, substitutes, if not friends.'[33] The second, somewhat equivocal, remark could probably be made about most people's lives; and many friendships come to grief in political differences as did the friendship of Chekhov and Suvorin, which is probably what Zaitsev has in mind.

However, Zaitsev's exaggeration contains an element of truth. For, although we know Chekhov to have been capable of feeling love, his ability to express love seems to have been impaired by his tendency to remain wrapped up in himself. It was a tendency encouraged, no doubt, by admiring friends who were too much in awe of Chekhov to attempt to reach him in his ivory tower. It was with a touch of mockery, however, that one of these admirers expressed the following view of Chekhov: 'I'm very interested in your fiancée "Misyus",' wrote E. M. Shavrova. 'The name alone is delightful! Besides, I'm glad to hear that it's possible my *cher maître* loved someone once and therefore that he could know and understand this mundane feeling. Don't look so surprised, I really somehow feel that you analyse everything and everybody too closely to fall in love, i.e. to be dazzled, even temporarily.'[34]

Shavrova, in seeing Chekhov as a detached observer incapable of deep emotional involvement, had a valid point. And yet this is only half the truth. Chekhov was not a feelingless man. As has been indicated, there is plenty of emotion in his *work*, and particularly in those works in which women play a prominent part. A. I. Kuprin, one of those who take the line that there is great reserve in Chekhov's work, makes a comparison which comes much closer to the truth than Shavrova's remark. Kuprin, commenting on Chekhov's restraint as a writer, states that he is like a man who cannot bring himself to make a declaration of love.[35] Now, while obviously one cannot claim that it was Chekhov in his private life who was incapable of making a declaration of love, none the less the withdrawn aspect of his nature was that which played the most significant part in Chekhov's relationships with women.

Rumour and reminiscence have indicated that in society Chekhov was a success with women, a lively and amiable companion: particularly, one imagines, when the women were young and pretty and flattered his self-esteem. His correspondence with women friends and acquaintances—doubtless a more accurate, although tantalizingly inadequate, testimony to his feelings—supports this. Chekhov's letters to women are generally cheerful, almost cocky in tone, reading like a transcript of social small-talk. They contain gossip, remarks about the weather, remarks about Chekhov's activities, inquiries about the addressee's health, and so forth. They are rarely serious in tone, except, for example, when Chekhov is discussing literature with those women whose opinions he appeared to respect—such as Mariya Kiseleva or Elena Shavrova.

However, also typical of his letters to Shavrova and Kiseleva are remarks such as the following: to Kiseleva: 'You're not Shakespeare, nor Chekhov, although you are dreaming (oh, I'm aware of your machinations!) of giving your daughter my name some day, so as to publish your work in her name and sign them instead of Kiseleva—Chekhova. But you won't succeed!'[36] To Shavrova: 'You ought to go on a trip to Australia! With me!!'[37] and 'If you'll say "yes" to luncheon with me . . . wire me "yes". The telegraph operator may think I've offered you heart and hand, but what care we for the world's opinion?!!'[38]

This banter is the most striking feature of Chekhov's correspondence with women. With 'a million kisses!!'[39] he concludes a letter to Tanya Shchepkina-Kupernik, and writes to her five years later: 'As before, I seethe with passions, but am fighting them quite successfully.'[40] To the artist A. A. Khotyaintseva he sent flowers with the comment: 'I imagine that Nemirovich has already turned your head so much that you are in no state to appreciate my gallant gesture.'[41]

Even when he addressed older women who were acquaintances rather than friends a coy tone often crept into Chekhov's letters. Thus to A. M. Evreinova, the editress of *Severny vestnik* ('The Northern Herald'), a woman in her forties, Chekhov wrote: 'The time is ripe for a romance (in the literary sense, of course, not in a bachelor's).' ('*Nastupilo samoe podkhodyashchee vremya dlya romana (literaturnogo, konechno, a ne zhenikhovskogo)'.*)[42]

One could adduce similar examples of this superficial banter *ad lib*. Few will find it one of the most attractive features of Chekhov's epistolary style. But it constitutes none the less an important pointer to Chekhov's real personality. It suggests, first of all, the amiable, sociable side of Chekhov's nature, the side that made him eager to please people and to amuse them: no doubt this banter, so exasperating when reviewed *en masse*, did amuse, most of the time, most of the individuals to whom it was addressed. But it also indicated Chekhov's withdrawnness: by making flirtatious remarks and references to his bachelor state so obviously facetious, Chekhov effectively erected a barrier between himself and anyone who might be seriously interested in his compliments.

Lika Mizinova showed that she was aware of these two aspects of Chekhov's personality when, in a letter to Chekhov of 1894 she groped, for her own satisfaction, for a clarification of Chekhov's personality. 'You live for others,' she wrote, 'and it seems as though you don't even want a private life.'[43]

By this Lika acknowledged the fact that Chekhov presented to the outside world what one contemporary described as 'the image of an intelligent, good, infinitely righteous man'.[44] Any adequate biography of Chekhov supplies details of Chekhov's services to his fellow-men: of the humanitarian enterprise of his Sakhalin trip and subsequent activities towards the improvement of conditions there; of his efforts for the cause of famine relief and the control of a cholera epidemic in the early 1890s; and of a great many more philanthropic deeds. His correspondence and works bear witness to his liberal views and compassionate social conscience, and show him to be concerned with the lack of freedom and culture in Russia, and in particular, with the plight of the peasants. Also in the more circumscribed context of his personal relationships, by and large, Chekhov appears as a kindly, lovable man, generous with money and advice, and with help, the latter especially through string-pulling, and where it was a case of assisting other writers.

Lika, however, knew another side of Chekhov's character. The evidence of Chekhov's correspondence would suggest that only two other women knew Chekhov as well as Lika did over a prolonged period of time: his wife and his sister. Each of these three women offered Chekhov wholehearted love and companionship. But his relationship with each of them is indicative of the extent of his introversion—an introversion through which he was capable of injuring others, as did his cynical heroes.

4

When Lika made remarks to Chekhov such as: 'You couldn't care less what people think of your actions',[45] or: 'you think only of yourself'[46]—and she made such remarks frequently in her letters to him—was she simply making the ritual grumbles of the injured party she considered herself to be, or was she justified in these accusations of selfishness? One must be wary of taking all Lika's evaluations of Chekhov's character at their face-value. However, some commentators on the relationship seem to consider that Chekhov dealt Lika a wilfully cruel blow in not coming to Montreux in Switzerland to see her when she was pregnant.[47] Certainly Lika's letters to him at this time make pathetic reading. She reiterates how unhappy she is, complains that he and her other friends have forgotten her, and begs him to come. No doubt she really was very miserable. Potapenko had abandoned her, and Varya Eberle, her companion in Paris, had gone back to Russia. 'I feel I'd give half my life,' she commented later, in December of 1894, '. . . to feel that this whole year hadn't happened and that everybody and everything remained as they were!'[48]

The tone of her letters is frequently hysterical. In one of them almost every sentence ends with an exclamation mark. Lika's distress was increased by the fact that Chekhov, who was at this time travelling from place to place in Europe, never seemed to receive her letters, which she sent frantically to Paris, to Abbazia, even to Melikhovo, talking in every one of his coming to see her.

Her letters caught up with Chekhov in Nice on 2 October 1894. On that day he replied briefly, but not unkindly, explaining that he would have come to Switzerland if her letter had reached him in Abbazia, but that he now was with Suvorin who wanted to go to Paris and whom it would be awkward to 'drag along' to Switzerland. (Lika had insisted that Chekhov bring no one to see her.)

It is difficult to see why it should be implied that Chekhov's refusal to visit Lika at this point was in some way morally reprehensible. His reason as stated for not doing so was perfectly valid. The matter was not after all of life-or-death importance. And what could he have done for Lika if he had gone? She wanted either love, to make her able to face the future, or a magical obliteration of the past. Chekhov could fulfil neither demand.

Moreover, Chekhov was very probably somewhat irritated by Lika's reproaches. In her letters which reached him at Nice Lika had written: 'I think you have always been indifferent to people and to their faults and weaknesses . . .',[49] and: 'your attitude to people is one of condescension and indifference, so that you won't pass judgement as others would!'[50] That these statements offended Chekhov is clear from a brief comment in his answering letter: 'You need not have talked of my being indifferent to people.' He was probably the more offended because these remarks of Lika's were nearer to the truth than the accusations of selfishness and disregard for the opinion of others that she was accustomed to hurl at him.

Chekhov's only recorded comment on Lika's predicament, in a letter to Masha also of 2 October was: 'Potapenko is a (. . .) and a swine.'[51] Which apparently put the matter, as he saw it, in perspective.

It seems unlikely that Chekhov consciously pursued a policy of putting himself first. But, while it cannot be said that he ought to have come to Lika in Switzerland, Chekhov's attitude to Lika throughout this unhappy period in her life showed a certain lack of thoughtfulness.

At the beginning of March 1894, both Potapenko and Lika set off for Paris, one within a few days of the other. Lika intended to study singing there. But she may also have known, or suspected, that she was pregnant. In any case, before reaching Berlin she wrote Chekhov an odd letter, mainly cheerful but referring to herself as 'rejected' by him and containing a cryptic sentence: 'I can't wait to reach my destination, and I also want to have a look at Berlin, for I shall soon die and see nothing more.'[52] To which Chekhov replied briskly: 'I know very well that you won't die and that no one has rejected you.'[53]

This apparent lack of sympathy can be explained by the fact that Chekhov did not know that Lika was pregnant. As for her reference to dying, she was homesick at the time and might have been merely depressed: she was apt to make dire pronouncements of this sort. In a letter of the previous autumn, when she was trying to break away from his influence, she had told Chekhov: 'I have only two or three months left in which to see you, after that perhaps never again.'[54]

Chekhov's proposal in his letter of 27 March 1894 that she should come to Melikhovo in June suggests that he suspected nothing, as does his fraternizing with Potapenko that summer: at that time he did not know that Potapenko had been so ungallant as to abandon Lika pregnant.

Nevertheless it is odd that he should not have guessed at Lika's pregnancy. He knew Lika well enough to know that she was no paragon of virtue. He knew of her affair with Potapenko: she had virtually apprised him of it herself in a letter of December 1893: 'I have finally fallen in love with Potapenko!'[55] It was obvious that Lika ran the risk of pregnancy.

If Chekhov did not guess the truth, one can only conclude that he thought about Lika even less than she imagined, especially since Lika would almost certainly have confessed all at the slightest encouragement. If he did guess, then his letter of 27 March was unnecessarily flippant, suggesting that he had decided to turn his back on her misfortunes. That this is what he in fact had done is indicated by his apparently remaining in ignorance until 2 October, when he read Lika's letters, full of such transparent allusions that he was forced to realize what had happened.

Lika felt and resented Chekhov's indifference. 'How mean of you,' she wrote in July, ' . . . not to have stopped me from coming to Paris! Don't think . . . I say this because of my singing . . . it's going all right, but in general . . .'.[56] And in September: 'Not a vestige remains of the old Lika, and as I see it, and I can't help saying it, it's all your fault!'[57]

Obviously, this was rather an extreme view: but there is something in what Lika said. Chekhov had let himself be loved by her when he could have refused to see her: and then, if he had not, as Lika put it, actually 'dumped her on somebody else',[58] he had turned a blind eye to her predicament at a time when she plainly wanted and needed moral support. If, at the time when she became pregnant, he had felt even the measured sympathy he felt for her in Nice in October, Chekhov might have spared Lika much unhappiness. Instead, while Lika 'howled'[59]—to use her own expression—in Paris, depressed at seeing so little of Potapenko, Chekhov wrote to a French friend, Jules Legras: 'Be so good, when you are in Paris, as to look up Mlle. Mizinova and find out from her the address of Ignaty Nikolaevich Potapenko, who is also living in Paris, and ask him to come to Melikhovo. He is very bored in Paris.'[60] Lika, if she had known of this letter, might well have considered that her need of Potapenko was greater than Chekhov's.

Nevertheless, even if Chekhov's treatment of Lika does strike us as uncharitable, in view of his attitude to women who pursued

men too ardently, his behaviour was more than understandable
—it was only to be expected.

Chekhov had his brainchild Orlov witness with horror the
attempts of Zinaida Fedorovna to unite her life with his; and the
fate of Shamokhin who succumbed to Ariadna's wiles speaks for
itself. In 1894 Lika was apparently trying to do exactly the same
thing—to claim rights that Chekhov did not consider were hers.
Ariadna, when she wanted to lure Shamokhin to Abbazia, signed
herself: 'Your abandoned . . . ' and again, 'Your forgotten
Ariadna'. After Lubkov deserted her she reproached Shamokhin
'with having failed to extend to her a helping hand, having
instead looked down on her from the height of his virtue and
abandoned her in her hour of peril'. These words echo so accurately the tenor of Lika's letters to Chekhov after Potapenko's
desertion of her that the connection in Chekhov's mind seems
indisputable—particularly since he wrote Ariadna within a year
of receiving those letters.

Lika, to be sure, asked only for Chekhov's friendship. But had
Chekhov come to see her during her pregnancy, he would certainly
have found himself more involved in her situation than he would
have cared for. In Paris, although her pregnant condition could
not yet have been unmistakable, Lika passed herself off as a
married woman; and she told Chekhov that her landlady believed
that a photograph of him represented her husband. In a later
letter she remarked that his pictures were distributed all round
her room.[61]

It can readily be imagined that Chekhov's photograph would
fulfil the same function when transferred to Montreux; that
Chekhov would realize this, and that the idea of keeping up the
deception when he arrived there would strike him as an intolerable abuse of his friendship. It is perhaps not even too far-fetched
to suppose that Chekhov had this distasteful scenario in mind
when he had Shamokhin comment: 'I don't like the idea of
pregnancy and childbirth.'

Be that as it may, one thing is clear: the more desperately Lika
tried to involve Chekhov in her difficulties, the more resolutely
he withdrew from her clutches. That he should so obviously
draw upon her letters for his portrayal of the arch-villain Ariadna
shows clearly that Chekhov's affection for Lika was, in such a
situation, considerably less than his fear for his own independence.

5

In comparison with the turbulent history of Lika's emotional involvement with Chekhov, the story of Masha Chekhova's relationship with her brother might on the surface appear to be peaceful, almost idyllic. And yet we are confronted, in Masha's case, with passions equally, if not more, intense, and with a situation that may strike us as comprising greater pathos. Lika's ups and downs were at least crowned by her marriage to a man she loved;* Masha's story has no happy ending.

The firm friendship between Masha Chekhova and her brother of which she writes in her reminiscences was apparent to all who knew the family. Masha's 'very deep devotion to Anton Pavlovich in particular struck one as soon as one met her', commented their friend Nemirovich-Danchenko, 'and Anton Pavlovich treated his sister with exceptional devotion.'[62] It was a friendship bred of long familiarity. Chekhov spent the greater part of his life under one roof with his sister, and when he was abroad it was to her that he—frequently—wrote, rather than to his father or mother. Naturally, they had much more in common with one another than with their less educated parents. Third and fifth children in the family respectively, Anton and Masha differed from their elder brothers Aleksandr and Nikolai in being alike more reliable, hard-working, and refined in outlook than the latter. It was Anton who largely paid for Masha's education— earning thereby her deep gratitude: their shared aspirations towards self-betterment doubtless played a large part in drawing them together.

Masha became the medium who interpreted Chekhov to his parents and attempted to smooth out any differences between them. If Chekhov complained that the soup was salty, then Masha would immediately exclaim: 'What excellent soup!'[63]

Ostensibly the relationship was charming. But one person was

---

* Lika married in 1902 the producer A. A. Sanin. Chekhov predicted in a letter to O. L. Knipper, 12 March 1902, that Lika would not love Sanin or be happy. But see Grossman, pp. 279–80, for details of a letter in which Lika tells her mother of her love for Sanin and her happiness.

not charmed by it. This was Chekhov's eldest brother Aleksandr, who after a short stay at Melikhovo in 1893 wrote to Chekhov: 'One thing I'm convinced of. Your relationship with our sister is all wrong (*otnosheniya . . . fal'shivy*). One kind word from you, with a bit of warmth in it, and she's all yours. She's afraid of you, and gazes at you with such humble and respectful eyes.'[64] Aleksandr might have exaggerated the situation; he might even have been jealous. But Masha in her own words confirms the essential accuracy of his observation. It is clear that her devotion to Anton was absolute. Describing how their friendship developed together with the growth of her admiration for him, Masha wrote: 'He attracted me more and more' (*on vse bolee i bolee uvlekal menya*).[65] And, as Aleksandr had noted, she was completely under Anton's thumb. She related on one occasion how once he had insisted she go to the Tolstoys' to repay a call. Masha did not wish to go at all, because it would mean missing a party at home; still Chekhov insisted, and he had his way.[66]

Masha seemed to submit with a good grace: she had in fact decided to sacrifice herself on the altar of Chekhov's fame and personal well-being. As the years passed, 'eventually I felt', wrote Masha, 'that I had a fresh purpose—to make my brother Anton's life easier in every way. I tried to do all I could to spare him unnecessary trouble.'[67]

And so Masha led a busy life, acting as domestic, nurse, and assistant to her brother as the occasion demanded, as well as running the household. She did not however lack opportunities to make a new life of her own: for she received, apparently, at least three proposals of marriage. The first, from an officer named Egorov, came when Masha was not thinking of marriage. She showed Egorov's letter of proposal to her brother. Chekhov said that he would attend to it. Egorov sent no more letters and no more was heard of the matter.[68]

However, to subsequent requests for her hand Masha was not so indifferent. She had a touchingly ineffectual romantic association with Chekhov's friend, the artist Levitan. K. G. Paustovsky has described how in telling him of her love for Levitan Masha had 'flushed with embarrassment, like a little girl'.[69] Levitan proposed; Masha asked her brother for advice; and Chekhov said: 'Naturally you can marry him if you want to, only bear in mind that he needs women the age of Balzac's women, not like you.'* Masha, although she did not know what Chekhov meant, did not accept the proposal. Whatever Levitan's true tastes in women may have been, Masha recorded that he protested on his death-bed that he would have married her sooner than any other.[70]

When Masha received a third proposal, from A. I. Smagin, another friend of the family, she seriously considered accepting it; but 'somehow made up her mind to have a word with Anton Pavlovich before doing anything else'.[71] She went to Anton and told him she was going to marry—which announcement was met with silence. In the course of the next few days Anton's attitude to her was one of reserve. Masha wept: she interpreted Anton's silence as clearly betokening his dislike of the idea. So then she made a momentous decision: 'My love for my brother, my attachment to him, resolved the whole affair.'[72] She refused Smagin and received a sharp reproachful letter from him. But Masha's main feeling seems to have been one of satisfaction that no one realized why she had refused.

Masha thus staked all her happiness on her brother's need for her and on the friendship between them. It is therefore not surprising that she reacted to Chekhov's marriage as she did— with hysteria and a surge of jealous possessiveness, followed by acute depression.

On the eve of Chekhov's marriage, in response to a letter in which he had hinted at the imminence of this event, Masha wrote: 'Personally, I'm shocked by the idea of marriage formalities! . . . You will always be able to marry . . . I wish you nothing but happiness. . . . If you don't answer this letter quickly, I'll be ill.'[73] Chekhov had said that he was obliged to go to Aksenovo, in Ufa province, for a *kumys* (fermented mare's milk) cure, and that he would find it dull to go alone: perhaps he might marry. Masha offered to join him forthwith. Although she disapproved of Olga's being her brother's mistress, it would seem that she infinitely preferred that to the finality of a marriage.

Her protestations came too late: the wedding had already taken

---

* Chekhova, *Iz dalekogo proshlogo*, p. 43. By 'women the age of Balzac's women' Chekhov was possibly referring to the heroine of Balzac's *La Femme de trente ans*, who was not only unfaithful to her husband, but sympathetically depicted by Balzac. Or perhaps Chekhov simply had in mind Balzac's preference for the woman of thirty to the *ingénue*.

place. On hearing of this Masha wrote to her brother: 'I feel very low. I want to see only you and nobody else . . . I can't eat a thing.'[74] To Olga however she adopted an epistolary style less like that of an abandoned lover, writing with a mixture of anger and conciliation which graphically expressed the duality of her feeling for Olga: 'Well, my dear Olechka, you alone have succeeded in marrying my brother! How firm the man stood, how he resisted—but his fate caught up with him, and there was an end to it! There was no getting round you. . . . Having a wedding ceremony struck me as such a dreadful thing—such a strain for Anton, who is a sick man after all—that I've asked myself several times what you had to have all that for? How I've suffered, if you but knew, my dear! What if our relationship alters for the worse. Now everything depends on you . . . I hope you will continue to be what you have always been to me . . .'.[75] For, ironically, Masha had herself encouraged Chekhov in his friendship with Olga Knipper, whom she had liked very much.[76] But the actual marriage upset her greatly, for several reasons, not all of which were selfish. As she implies in her letter to Olga, she had quite genuine fears for Chekhov's health, since he would probably share to some extent in the travelling and gaiety of theatre life. (Altshuller, Chekhov's Yalta doctor, was also alarmed by this prospect.)

Masha was also distressed by the way in which the news of the marriage was sprung upon her, as a *fait accompli* that came as a great shock to herself and her mother. That the couple's intention to marry had been kept a secret from her hurt her deeply.

It seems fairly obvious that at the root of Masha's objections to the marriage lay not those reasons that she voiced, nor even jealousy of Chekhov's love for Olga; but the fear that she would lose the important position she held in her brother's life as mistress of his household and ever-present companion. If he had married anyone other than Olga, she told Chekhov, she should have hated his wife.[77] After the marriage it in fact often appeared that there was little love lost between the two women: each was jealous of the other and more than ready to take offence.

Just how great a strain the marriage put on their relationship is fully revealed perhaps only in an unpublished letter—one of many which Olga Knipper wrote to Chekhov after his death, as a form of intimate personal journal—in which she describes

Masha's behaviour towards her when she and Chekhov returned from the *kumys* cure: 'We loved each other very much, you know,' Olga wrote apropos of herself and Masha. 'But she always felt that I had taken everything away from her, both the house and yourself, and she carried on like some kind of martyr. To begin with I was always having it out with her, having lengthy and heated discussions, trying persuasion and pleading, and the tears we shed, if you had but known! But still we didn't get on, and finally I gave up trying. If only she had known how much you and I talked, in Aksenovo, remember, about not letting her feel deprived in any way. I always considered Yalta her domain and hated to hear her say that now she had no home, no niche, no garden. If only she knew of the rainbow hopes I brought with me when I came with you to Yalta from Ufa. Things went wrong from the very first day . . .'. If things had turned out as she had hoped, Olga continued, she might in time have given up the theatre (which was probably what Masha, whether consciously or not, wished to prevent). But Olga realized at once that there could be no question of a harmonious existence at Yalta. 'Oh, how I suffered,' she concluded, 'during those six weeks in Yalta! And all those difficulties just because of a church ceremony!'[78]

Fortunately for both women—but especially for Masha—their friendship survived this critical period. In her reminiscences Masha is at pains to emphasize her affection for and approval of Olga, even when publishing letters that clearly show the tension and animosity she, for her part, felt at this time.

Chekhov made an attempt to deal tactfully with Masha's violent reaction to his marriage. He wrote her conciliatory letters and eagerly invited her to join him on the *kumys* cure. (Masha, now that it was a case of being *à trois*, not surprisingly declined.) He also explained patiently that their relationship would remain unchanged; he even gave reasons for his marriage, pointing out, *inter alia*, that Olga's family were 'nice people'—i.e. respectable—and that if it ever proved necessary to part from her, he would do so without misgivings, as if he had never married: Olga being independent and financially self-supporting.[79] Presumably the first explanation was intended to refute any suggestion that they should live in sin indefinitely. The second explanation is slightly ambiguous. One can take it, however, that Chekhov was not worrying about a future divorce at this stage, but had in mind his uncertain state of health. In any case, although they are no doubt valid as far as they go, there is no need to attach great significance to these explanations: Chekhov, who was particularly reticent on the subject of his marriage, almost certainly provided Masha with these explanations only to make her adopt a more sensible view of things. There is perhaps something rather distasteful in Chekhov's pandering thus to his sister's excessive complaining, but one must remember that it was in Chekhov's own interests to reconcile Masha with his wife. Bunin, with a touch of malice, records his impression that the strife between his womenfolk would kill Chekhov.[80] An exaggeration, no doubt: but Chekhov perhaps entertained similar notions.

Of course, his explanations were also prompted by pity. Chekhov was well aware of Masha's feelings towards him. He wrote with amusement of her reaction to his winning the Pushkin prize in 1888: 'My sister, as stern and painstaking a guardian of our reputation as a lady-in-waiting, being vainglorious and excitable, goes visiting her friends and spreading the glad news.'[81] Before he went to Sakhalin he remarked on how his absence would affect Masha: 'She'll have a bad time of it when I'm not there.'[82] After the lamentable first night of *The Seagull* Chekhov commented sourly: '[Masha] came rushing home from Petersburg, probably thinking I'd hang myself'.[83]

These remarks indicate that Chekhov's attitude to Masha contained an element of condescension. It is in fact apparent that, while his affection for his sister is indisputable, he could return her devotion only to a limited extent. His letters to her are warm and full of news, but that he kept no secrets from her, as Masha claims, is simply not true. For instance, in the summer of 1894 Chekhov warned Lika not to tell anyone in Russia where he was: 'I departed covertly, like a thief, and Masha thinks I'm in Feodosiya. If they know I'm abroad, they'll be upset. . . .'[84] He had already been abroad that year, and was much missed at home during these trips. Also Masha disliked and was probably jealous of Suvorin, Chekhov's travelling companion on this occasion.

It strikes one as absurd that Chekhov should be reduced to such subterfuges. Masha's clinging affection must often have been irksome to him. He, at any rate, had no objection to her leading an independent life. He had adequate reasons not to encourage Masha to marry Egorov (whom she did not love) or Levitan (who

Masha Chekhova

Lidiya Avilova

Vera Kommissarzhevskaya

Lika Mizinova

probably was unsuitable: for one thing, he was unbalanced). What of his attitude to Smagin's proposal? There are several possible explanations of what seems to have been a selfish abuse of his power over Masha. His silence may have betokened disapproval, and unwillingness to hurt Masha's feelings; he might not have realized that his active approval was so vital to her. Or he may have been merely exasperated beyond words by her inability to make her own decisions. It is even possible that Masha fabricated the story of her confrontation with him, perhaps finding herself, at the time, unable to commit herself to a decision and preferring to appear self-sacrificing, after the event. Be that as it may, Chekhov's contemporary appraisal of the Smagin affair is markedly out of tune with Masha's account. 'My sister has not married, but it seems the romance is continuing by correspondence,' he wrote to Suvorin. 'I don't understand what's going on. People are supposing that she has refused this time too. She must be the only spinster who genuinely doesn't want to marry.'[85] These lines patently indicate that Chekhov had at times less understanding—or sympathy—for Masha than she could have wished for.

Rachmanowa mentions, as if it were significant, that Chekhov wrote his last letter, from Badenweiler, to Masha who was 'the person closest to him'.[86] This last letter, like most of Chekhov's letters to Masha at this time, is in fact a cross between a progress report and a business communication, in which Chekhov asks for travel information and talks of his health and the weather.[87]

This letter indicates nothing about his relationship with Masha except how useful she was to him. But an earlier letter, written in the previous year, which Rachmanowa does not mention at all, tells us a great deal. Masha had written Chekhov a letter in which she sounded miserable.[88] It is hardly surprising that as she grew older she should feel that life had less and less to offer, especially as she saw less and less of Anton and as his health prospects were poor. This last factor Masha later claimed to have been the cause of her distress (in a footnote added to her letter when she published it). But Chekhov clearly did not understand her in that way: if he had, he would have brushed her fears aside with one of his usual vaguely optimistic remarks about his health, and left it at that. Instead, he wrote:

N

I don't understand why as you say in your letter you're feeling depressed and have gloomy thoughts. Your health is good, there's not a soul in the world who could have anything at all against you, you have an occupation and a future, like all normal people—so what's upsetting you? You should bathe and go to bed later, stop having wine, or else have it only once a week and not eat meat at supper-time. Pity the milk's so bad in Yalta and you can't be put on a milk diet.[89]

These precepts must have struck Masha as cold comfort, and they reveal in Chekhov a marked insensitivity to her emotional needs. As with Lika, Chekhov, it seems, was ready to let himself be loved; but when Masha needed his help and comfort, he shied away, although perhaps involuntarily, from acknowledging her need for him.

After Chekhov's death, Masha remained in the Yalta house, and eventually became custodian of the museum and archives there. She lived to a great age. In 1948 she wrote to Olga Knipper: 'On 13 August I was 85, and I think I haven't lived my life in vain, although I devoted it partly to my dear brother.'[90] There is a touching note of uncertainty in that 'although'. It would be sad indeed if, after a lifetime's service of her brother and his memory, Masha had come to realize that the rewards had not outweighed the sacrifices.

6

'Tchehov loved in no high romantic manner, but with the frank, facetious innocence of the child and the understanding of the genius.'[91] Thus the critic H. l'A. Fausset sums up Chekhov's relationship with Olga Knipper in his review of Garnett's translation of Chekhov's letters to his wife. Significantly Fausset, writing before the publication of *both* sides of the correspondence,[92] saw only one side of the coin. To read one set of letters without the other must inevitably lead to misapprehensions. And indeed, it would be hard to find a less appropriate description of that relationship. For—if 'romantic' can be said to imply a greater interest in the concept of love, as the experience of an emotion, than in the discovery of another person, then Chekhov's love for Olga Knipper was romantic. And that he loved either with the 'innocence of the child' or with the 'understanding of the genius'—two concepts which in this context would seem to be mutually exclusive—is open to doubt. There is certainly a facetious—some might call it superficial—element in Chekhov's letters to his wife, but there is also an element of disingenuousness. And, far from showing his wife the 'understanding of the genius', he not infrequently showed her what seems to have been insufficient understanding. He loved her, and tried to be kind to her, but his kind words were not always enough for Olga, as is illustrated by the following incident:

In August of 1902, they began a quarrel by correspondence. In the course of this quarrel Chekhov wrote to his wife: 'You are the person closest and dearest to me, I have loved you and I do love you immeasurably, but you describe yourself as "any old agreeable woman", a stranger to me and solitary . . . well, never mind, have it your own way.'93

As Chekhov's weary, or impatient, conclusion suggests, this declaration of his love resolved the problem and closed the matter, from his point of view. And yet, five months later, Olga was still brooding on this particular quarrel. 'You know, Anton,' she wrote, 'I suddenly remembered how terribly cruel it was of you to leave me at Lyubimovka in August. Why did that hurt me so much? Even just now it hurt me when I remembered it. Tell me, why? How I suffered at that time!'94 Thus, it would seem that what Chekhov could dismiss from his mind by an attestation of his love for his wife was for her a crisis in their relationship. He hurt her deeply and lastingly; and the more so, in all probability, because Olga must have felt that he had done this, and weathered the most stormy period in their relationship, ostensibly without putting himself in the wrong.

The exact details of the quarrel are irrelevant,95 since what concerns us here is Chekhov's reaction to it; but, briefly, the situation was the following: Olga had been very ill in 1902, first with a miscarriage at the end of March, and subsequently with peritonitis in June. Chekhov had nursed her, first in Yalta and then in Moscow. On 14 August he left her convalescing at Lyubimovka, the estate of Stanislavsky's mother, and returned to Yalta. Olga resented his going, apparently thinking that she was unwelcome in Yalta, and had not been invited to come. She wrote Masha a letter of complaint (which has not survived).

Masha—and Chekhov—found the letter extremely offensive in tone. Chekhov taxed Olga with rudeness: she retaliated by airing her pent-up grievances, and the quarrel developed.

The rights and wrongs of the incident need not delay us. It seems clear enough that Masha was not at fault,* and that Olga, on the surface of it, appeared to be making a childish fuss.

It should be remembered, however, that Olga, no less than her husband, had been exhausted and demoralized by her two illnesses. And Chekhov, although he nursed her assiduously and was full of solicitude for her health, might well have given her the impression that he was impatient to be off to Yalta; for, in the earliest days of her recovery in Moscow, Chekhov, who wanted a holiday, was clearly straining at the leash, as remarks to his friends show: ' . . . my summer can be considered if not ruined, then very much messed up'.[96] '[Olga] has already been sitting up in an armchair . . . and the main thing is, I am allowed to go and I leave tomorrow . . . with Morozov for Perm'.'[97] 'The pains have stopped, there's just the weakness now. Be that as it may, today I'm off with S. Morozov . . .'.[98] *En route*, he wrote blithely to Olga, 'I'm not worried about you, since I know, I'm certain, my dog is well, that she must be.'[99] And to Gorky: 'Olga was seriously ill, but now as you see I am set free, and can rest at ease.'[100] Reading these letters, it would be possible to conclude that Chekhov's own holiday mattered a great deal more to him than bearing Olga company.

However, at the real root of Olga's dissatisfaction in the quarrel that ensued lay two more fundamental grievances: her jealousy of Masha's clinging to Chekhov; and the nature of Chekhov's attitude to herself, as evinced in the quarrel.

Chekhov took Masha's part, believing her to be in the right, and scolded Olga like a child: 'What did you give Masha a row for? . . . Your letter was very very unjust.'[101] And again, on receiving Olga's protestations: 'It was a terribly rude letter, and

* Masha's letters to Chekhov of 1 and 6 June 1902 (as published in *Pis'ma k bratu*, pp. 204–5) make it clear that she expected them both in Yalta, although she did suggest (6 June) that he came alone for a week or two, failing Olga; however, she for some reason withheld letters that she wrote to him at Lyubimovka. Chekhov's letters to Masha of 6 and 10 June 1902 state categorically that Olga cannot come to Yalta, her doctor having forbidden her the journey. See also Chekhov's letter to K. S. Stanislavsky, 18 July 1902.

what's more, unjust.'[102] 'Masha is not to blame in any respect whatsoever, sooner or later you'll believe this.[103]

None the less, these reproaches were interspersed with sincere attempts at reconciliation: 'Of course I understood how you felt when you wrote, and I still understand. . . . Your letters are chilly, but all the same I pursue you with loving words and think of you incessantly. . . . Don't part from me [Olga had angrily suggested this course of action] so soon, before you've lived a proper life with me, before you've borne me a little boy or girl. When you've done that, then you can do as you like.'[104]

This last sentence would seem in the circumstances to risk inflaming Olga's anger again; but Chekhov, as the rest of his letter shows, was clearly trying to make the quarrel up. Indeed, from the start of it he had pursued a conciliatory policy—not apologizing for his censorious words, but dwelling much on other matters and writing in a kindly, affectionate tone.

Olga responded with a mixture of hysterical acrimony ('They [Masha and Chekhov's mother] probably avoid uttering my name')[105] and genuine efforts to be reasonable about Chekhov's being in Yalta. But the main issue in her letters is not that particular bone of contention: it is the way Chekhov reacted to her complaints.

Olga did not want kindness: she wanted to be better understood. She complained of being unable to tell Chekhov her thoughts: 'I keep imagining you'll laugh at me and won't understand me.'[106] A few days later she wrote: 'It has seemed to me that you need me only like any old agreeable woman, while I as a person lead my life as a stranger to you, alone.'[107] Olga was perhaps exaggerating, but the essence of her grievance was genuine enough. On the following day, she wrote again, begging her husband to understand her letter of the previous day. She implored him not to draw his 'usual conclusion': 'You're angry with me, darling'; she feared that with this remark he would dismiss her grievances from his mind. She felt, she said, that no change, no parting, no feeling had any effect on his calm character.[108]

Olga's pleas for understanding came too late. By the time he received the second letter, Chekhov had already answered the first: 'Darling, I feel neither you nor I are to blame in all this muddle, but someone else whom you've been talking to. . . . There's nothing, absolutely nothing I can do about it.' And he ended with the flat assertion of his love quoted above, which concluded the matter for him: while solving nothing for Olga.

'Cheer up,' he added, 'don't mope, or at least give an appearance of being cheerful.'[109] For poor Olga these words must have served as a confirmation of what she had suspected his attitude to be. His letter, kind as it was, showed no real sympathy for her: Chekhov, though offended at her accusations, simply did not take them, or her mood, seriously enough to examine their relationship or the cause of the quarrel.

But, before receiving this letter of his, Olga had evidently decided to cut her losses and be reconciled. To Chekhov's strange remark that she might do as she liked once she had a child, she merely answered reassuringly: 'I'll present you with a fine son next year.'[110] Her dissatisfaction with Chekhov's attitude during the quarrel, however, lingered on, and several days later she suddenly said at the end of a letter: 'Anton, must you keep silence always, whatever you feel?'[111] The quarrel had alarmed and injured her because it had shown how, suddenly, Chekhov could seem quite impervious to her demands, and unwilling to discuss their disagreements in depth.

It was however not the first time that she had felt conscious of a gap between herself and Chekhov. His letters to her dealt mainly with news of his health and activities, and with talk and gossip about the theatre—naturally enough. On a more intimate level, he jokes about his 'rivals'—Olga's male acquaintances—and referred to imaginary characters such as 'Nadenka', his supposed *petit bourgeois* wife. Much of this is strongly reminiscent of his correspondence with Lika, although the endearments which abound in Chekhov's letters to Olga are genuine, not teasing. As he did Lika, Chekhov called his wife by nicknames (so that once she asked him if he disliked the name Olga);[112] but, rather than 'Canteloupe' and the like, he mostly used for Olga the names of animals and birds; 'crocodile of my heart'; 'my tailless dog'; 'my dear little whale'; and a host of others, 'dog' and 'little horse' apparently being the favourites. There was a sexual element in this,* for Chekhov was not, *pace* Fausset, innocent, even in this

* So, evidently, thought the editor of the correspondence, for, e.g. there is omitted from Olga's letter to Chekhov of 7 November 1903 (as published in *Oktyabr'*, 1938, no. 7, p. 193) the phrase: 'I caress you with my hooves and wave my little tail' (see original, *Otd. ruk.* 331.77.4). Curiously enough

respect; and for all the naïvely childlike impression produced by his epistolary style, with its schoolboy epithets and heavy banter ('I certainly did not call you a little snake . . . you're a snake, not a little snake, a monstrous snake. Don't tell me that's not a compliment?'),[113] this style is in fact quite studied, the result of years of exercise in the art.

Olga Knipper, no less than Lika, entered into the spirit of the thing; but like Lika also, she wanted more than this. Lika wanted signs of emotional involvement on Chekhov's part. Olga had that, certainly, but she wanted Chekhov to treat her as an intellectual companion. The lightweight content of his letters from time to time irritated her, and perhaps she sensed in them an element of condescension. Chekhov—who shortly after their marriage had written to a friend: 'My wife is a very decent and intelligent being, and a good soul'[114]—would frequently adopt this perhaps unconscious air of patronage in his letters to Olga herself. 'Your long letters are very fine . . . I had no idea you were so intelligent,'[115] he wrote, and: 'I haven't received a single long letter from you, not one letter full of your opinions. And I love you so much when you give your opinion about something.'[116]

This was all very well, and indeed, it might be argued, only what Olga should expect, given Chekhov's superiority both in years and in the art of writing. But the trouble was that Olga was not content with uttering opinions in a void. She wanted a response, and not, surely, primarily because, as Simmons has it, she wanted to 'provoke an outpouring of profound thoughts and weighty moral aphorisms which [she] apparently imagined were constantly at the beck and call of a great writer'.[117] She simply wanted, by extracting Chekhov's soul's secrets from him, to feel convinced of her closeness to him. One letter of hers to Chekhov, hitherto unpublished, makes this quite clear. Olga wrote in 1903: 'You never say or hint at what you're feeling, and sometimes I so much want you to talk intimately, intimately with me, as you've never talked with anyone. Then I shall feel altogether close to you.'[118]

Chekhov's riposte (as published in the same number of *Oktyabr'*, p. 196) of 12 November 1903: 'I squeeze your hoof and stroke your little tail' stands; but ' . . . I stroke your little tail' is omitted, and without indication of the omission, in *Works*, 1944–51.

Hence, throughout her marriage to Chekhov, Olga tried, with hints, demands and reproaches, to make him communicate with her at a deeper level in his letters; and Chekhov persistently failed to oblige her.

'Write about absolutely everything, don't be afraid, I understand everything,'[119] Olga wrote. And: 'Do you know me? Or do you only love me, without knowing me?'[120]—signing herself 'Olya' instead of by some pet-name—a possible indication of the gravity of her mood. A few weeks later: '. . . be frank with me about everything. I am not a doll, after all, but a human being. You know, you hurt me a little with this attitude of yours.'[121] Chekhov finally reacted: 'You ask why I keep you at a distance from myself. What silliness, child!'[122]

Olga was not reassured. 'I'm afraid that you . . . will regard me as a sort of unnecessary ballast in your life,' she said plaintively;[123] and later, more bitterly: 'I don't know what goes on in your head, what you're thinking about, I feel distant from everything, a stranger to everything. You never share things with me, and then you call me your friend.'[124] She had complained that Chekhov would not write to her about the play that was occupying him; and for once, Chekhov countered the accusation specifically, pointing out that he would write rubbish and become bored with the play if he put his thoughts in a letter; that he would talk to her about it, if that were only possible. He tried to reason her out of her depression, saying, 'Your life is full enough as it is.'[125]

But still he had not grasped, or would not grasp, the point that Olga wanted to know something of his intellectual life. She wrote a day or two later, with a touch of her latent resentment of Masha, that there was no letter from him: 'Masha says you don't know what to write to me about . . .'. Did he realize that he need not have facts to write to her about?[126] He made no comment on this.

Over a year later he was apparently still as reticent. 'Have you finished your story? What is it called?' wrote Olga. 'I'm terribly hurt that you keep stubbornly silent on this topic in your letters, I feel that I'm a stranger to you at those times.'[127]

One can sympathize with Chekhov, who in the years of his marriage was already so ill as to find creative writing a strain, when he resisted Olga's invitations to expatiate on his mental processes. It is moreover doubtful whether these were always as involved as Olga seemed to suspect, especially where matters verging on the philosophical were concerned. 'What is life? I don't understand . . .' she asked him once.[128] His answer: 'You ask what life is? That's like asking: what is a carrot? A carrot is a carrot, and that's all we know about it'[129] is the sort of reply he might have put in the mouth of one of his fictional characters. In this case, as no doubt in many others, when Chekhov was brief it was because he had nothing more to say.

But in this case, and no doubt in others, he was really failing to respond to an urgent need in Olga—the need for close spiritual contact with him. When she asked him 'what life was' it was in a fit of acute depression: 'I'm terribly dismal and low', she had written in the same letter. Chekhov's answer to this—the main burden of her letter—was a brisk couple of lines: 'Keep well, don't pine and mope, you'll see your husband soon. I embrace you and tug your foot.'[130]

Olga was inclined to be neurotic, and no doubt as a doctor Chekhov had been hardened to tales of woe; but there is nevertheless something slightly disingenuous in the manner in which he consistently seemed to evade those issues in her letters to him which mattered to her, even if he himself judged them unimportant. His cheerful exhortations and repeated assurances of love must often, under these circumstances, have irritated Olga further.

Thus, though Chekhov meant well by his wife, he hurt her by letting her feel that he was denying her access to some part of his mind: how much of a secret inner life he actually had being less relevant in this connection than the fact that she retained the impression that she was being excluded from something.

Besides keeping Olga out of a part of his private life, Chekhov also, it seems, kept himself out of a part of their mutual affairs. When she was trying to settle the question of when they would marry, Olga wrote to him: 'I know you hate any kind of "serious" discussion . . .';[131] in a later letter she began to analyse their relationship: 'I am "something to you" all the same, aren't I?'; but stopped abruptly, adding: 'I'm sorry, I know you dislike and don't understand these problems.'[132] Chekhov's attitude here —common enough among husbands perhaps—again illustrates his facility for not learning what he did not want to know.

He loved his wife: but one suspects that he perhaps wished to keep the emotion he felt unalloyed by the difficulties of a personal relationship, the difficulty being in his case the effort of sharing himself with another person. Did he resent that attitude of Olga's which caused her once to remark: 'I need to know every little detail of your life'?[133] Chekhov had once written to Suvorin: '. . . give me a wife who, like the moon, would not appear in my sky every day'.[134] Chekhov's attitude to his sister and to Lika Mizinova suggests that he tended to view with indifference the emotional difficulties even of persons for whom he felt great affection. When he fell in love, did he want the satisfaction of experiencing the emotion of love without the responsibilities of taking upon himself another's emotional burden? Tolstoy once wrote: 'Perhaps the whole delight consists in standing on the threshold of love.'[135] Did Chekhov find it so, because he instinctively feared too deep an involvement with another person? The cynical heroes for whom Chekhov betrayed sympathy reject the romantic heroine plainly on account of some such more or less conscious fear. Having found love with Olga Knipper, Chekhov was clearly happy in the role of lover: but did his instinctive reserve make it impossible for him fully to accept the role of husband, with its implicit obligation to live with a creature of flesh and blood rather than with a romantic dream? We now examine Chekhov's attitude to the institution of marriage.

7 *Marriage*

Chekhov once wrote to a friend: 'Alas, I am not capable of such a complex, involved business as marriage. And the role of husband alarms me: it has an element of harshness, like the role of general.'[1]

What Chekhov would seem to be implying—that love-affairs are simpler than marriage, and that husbands have to adopt an air of command in a regimented home-life—is a justification of bachelor existence which might seem natural enough in a young man leading an unsettled existence and chiefly interested in the sexual side of relationships with women. But, as the confession of a man of thirty-eight, leading a relatively static existence, and by his own admission no longer interested in mistresses, it only emphasizes again how persistently Chekhov clung to his vision of love as something transcendental, an experience in connection with which the trammels of domesticity and the idea of the slow passage of time and the evolution of a relationship seemed irrelevant and tiresome details. 'I don't want to marry,' Chekhov had written to Suvorin in 1892, 'not that there is anyone. The hell with it. I'd find it a bore having a wife to deal with.'[2]

And yet his attitude to marriage was ambivalent. On the one hand, by continually making a point of denying rumours that he was about to marry, or—alternatively—speaking with obvious insincerity of his intention to do so, Chekhov built up over the years the image of himself as a permanent bachelor. Remarks such as, 'I am above marriage!'[3]—to Mariya Kiseleva, and: 'Oh, what good fortune it is to be still unmarried!'[4]—to Elena Shavrova—were clearly intended to fortify the façade and to discourage his women-friends from regarding him as a prospective bridegroom. To his sister Masha, for whom, as we have seen, the fact of his being a bachelor was even more important, he would write in the same vein of ponderous humour: 'I'll begin with a piece of news. Good and unexpected news. Don't think that I want to marry and have proposed . . .'.[5]

Such remarks however also indicate how often the question of marriage was in his mind. Likewise, the very relish with which he seemed to envisage his celibate future ('I don't intend to marry. I should like now to be a bald little old man and sit behind a big desk in a nice study'[6]) suggests that he must often have thought about the alternative.

Shortly before his thirtieth birthday he commented: 'Hail, lonely old age, burn out, useless life!'[7] This would seem to show that, at this comparatively early age, he was resigned to not marrying. But, in spite of the facetious tone, there is a trace in the remark, if not of bitterness, at least of vague dissatisfaction.

It would seem to be such a feeling of dissatisfaction, rather than any clearly defined desire to marry, that lay at the root of the obverse of Chekhov's bachelor-pose: the man who appeared to envy his friends when they married. 'Congratulations on your intention of entering into lawful matrimony,' he wrote to Shekhtel in 1887, 'I approve, and would be only too glad to emulate you, if a suitable bride were available.'[8] The following year he had this to say to Leikin on the impending marriages of their friends Ezhov and Lazarev: 'Let them marry! It's a good idea. Better badly-off married than well-off idling around. (*Luchshe plokhoi brak chem khoroshee shematonstvo.*) I myself would gladly bind myself with Hymen's knots, but, alas, circumstances have control of me, not vice-versa.'[9]

These circumstances were the facts that Chekhov was the family breadwinner and was responsible for the well-being of a large number of persons. 'I am tied hand and foot. You have a *wife*, who'll forgive you if you have no money, I have a *household* that will collapse if I don't earn a certain number of roubles a month,'[10] he had told Leontiev a month or two previously. There were eight people living in his house at the time.

Chekhov's financial situation was subject to ups and downs throughout his life, and his sense of responsibility was such that this was for him an important argument against keeping a wife.

However, the idea had its attractions. A few days after writing the letter to Leikin quoted above, he wrote a letter of congratulation to Lazarev, and added a footnote: 'I regret not being married, or at least not having any children.'[11] As his correspondence with Olga Knipper was later to make plain, Chekhov wanted a child very much indeed.[12]

The possibility of having a child was not, however, the only factor which drew Chekhov to contemplate marriage—although it was perhaps the only positive factor. In so far as one can judge from his letters, Chekhov's thoughts turned towards marriage particularly at times when his spirits were at a very low ebb; it was a possibility, but one viewed apathetically, when life was tedious, or unsatisfactory in some way.

'Shall I get married?' he suggested in a letter to Suvorin in 1889. 'Or shall I go off as a ship's doctor with the volunteer fleet?'[13] The sudden proposal of two such different courses of action was explained by his mood, which he described a week or so later: 'My soul is in a sort of stagnant state. I account for this by the stagnant state my personal life is in. I'm not disillusioned, not overtired, not moping, but all at once I've simply lost interest in things.'[14] In the course of the same month he wrote to Leikin the letter previously quoted in which he talked of 'living like a human being' when he had a 'place of his own and his own wife, not someone else's'.[15] Six years later Chekhov wrote a letter, also previously quoted, in which, while claiming to be afraid of a wife and family routine, he spoke with distaste of 'tossing in the sea of life' and 'bobbing about in the frail bark of profligacy'.[16] And we note that these sentiments coincided with a period of ill-health: in his letter Chekhov prefaced these remarks with: ' . . . my palpitations have become more frequent, I'm late in getting to sleep, and in general feel bad . . .'.[17]

Significant in this connection is the point previously made that Chekhov, years after he had lost interest in amorous adventures for their own sake, would talk of having love-affairs, and miss the society of women, when he was abroad and at other times when he felt bored and lonely. The desire for marriage almost always appears to have been motivated by similar circumstances. While one part of Chekhov feared the intrusion of a woman into the recesses of his soul, he seemed intermittently to have need of a relationship with a woman that was less demanding, more prosaic and—one might almost say—cosier than the passionate love of which he perhaps also dreamed.

Whether he consciously desired such a relationship is not so certain. However, it is possible that he was aware in himself of a proclivity towards something of the sort: we recall his comment to Suvorin: 'Silk night gowns only spell pleasure to me in that they are soft to the touch. Comfort appeals to me, but debauchery has no allure for me . . .'.[18]

The significance of this desire for 'comfort' might conceivably be of interest to a psychologist. But what is relevant to this study is that this desire, and this desire only, seems to be what invested marriage as such—as opposed to the begetting of children—with what limited appeal it had for Chekhov. And this desire was generated by unhappiness.

The casual reader of Chekhov's letters might well imagine that Chekhov's life-history could be summed up in Gogol's celebrated conclusion to one of his short stories: 'It's a depressing world, gentlemen!' (*Skuchno na etom svete, gospoda!*).[19] For as one leafs through the correspondence one is struck by the continual recurrence of the word *skuka* and its derivatives—words which no single English term can translate completely, since their meaning embraces a wide range of feelings from trivial boredom through depression to anguished yearning.

It should be pointed out that Chekhov's life was by no means an unbroken expanse of tedium, and indeed the prevalence of this mood in his correspondence is to some extent explained simply by the fact that when Chekhov was doing the things that most absorbed him—seeing friends, gadding about Moscow, working, and so forth—he was not writing letters. Complaints of the boredom that dogged his day-to-day existence do not become a dominant feature of his letters to family and friends until the latter 1890s. But by this time he did have much cause for complaint: he was compelled to spend first the winters and, subsequently, most of the year abroad, far from Moscow where his interests lay; and his activities were severely restricted by ill-health.

However, Chekhov's letters show that he was subject to fits of gloom long before the onset of his tubercular troubles. These moods were provoked by many and complex causes: his depression at the end of the 1880s, for instance, was due partly to the death of his brother Nikolai, and partly to dissatisfaction with his work. Later, however, it seems that the real trouble lay in his personal life. The apathy to which he confessed at the time was one side of it. But one suspects that there was more to it than that.

Chekhov's was a withdrawn and even cold nature, but he was also, almost certainly, a very lonely man.

One might suppose that in either physical or spiritual isolation from his fellow-men a man like Chekhov would have found solace in his own company and in the world of his imagination. But if he found such solace, it can only have been to a very limited extent. Chekhov was not a self-sufficient man. He needed novelty and diversion in his life, and above all he needed other people.

To ascertain how great a part loneliness played in Chekhov's life is not easy. Chekhov was not the sort of man who would talk of such a personal matter to all and sundry; the conclusions one reaches are dependent less upon concrete evidence than upon the overall impression produced by the documentary sources.

However, the evidence that exists is telling. There is a letter to Chekhov from his brother Aleksandr of September 1887 which contains the comment: 'You write that you are lonely, have no one to talk to or to write to . . .'.[20] Unfortunately, there is nothing in Chekhov's extant letters to his brother at this time to which this could be a reply: but it is noteworthy that he had spent the months previous to September in travelling and visiting: so that the loneliness to which he referred seems unlikely to have been a superficial feeling engendered of temporary boredom.

Chekhov wore on his watch-chain a pendant that had belonged to his father with the rather trite inscription: 'For the lonely man the desert is everywhere.'[21] There is a jotting in one of his note-books: 'As I shall lie alone in the grave, so in actual fact do I live alone.'[22] Much more revealing than any of these things, however, are two comments Chekhov made to one of his very few intimate friends, Suvorin. In 1889 he wrote: 'I simply can't live without guests. When I'm by myself, for some reason I feel frightened.'[23] And, nearly a decade later: 'I find living alone boring and depressing.'[24] The significance of these admissions in connection with Chekhov's attitude to marriage is considerable.

Masha Chekhova, in her solicitude, would not have failed to recognize such a need of companionship in her brother; and this would go far to explain the sacrifices she made in order not to desert him. But the company of her and her parents was not enough to keep Chekhov happy. The delights of country life, which had lured him from Moscow to Melikhovo, turned sour on him during the long winter evenings there. Aleksandr

Chekhov in a letter to Anton candidly described the latter's home-life as 'foul' (*pakostnoe*); he referred to their mother's ignorance and the complete lack of understanding between Anton and the rest of the family; also to their constant worrying about his health.[25]

When Chekhov was bored, and even more especially when he really was ill, it can well be imagined that he wanted something more exhilarating in the way of feminine company than this. It seems more than probable that this was what attracted Chekhov in the first place to Lika Mizinova, and made him continue to value her friendship. Lika's exuberance made the whole household gay; she was in her way as devoted to him as was Masha, but her devotion was more flattering. She was attractive to look at, sang extremely well, and her vacillating moods made her an amusingly unpredictable companion: particularly since Chekhov was not much moved by her more serious emotional crises. For him it was a comfortable and comforting relationship.

Lika knew this, just as she also knew in her most realistic moments that he felt no deeper involvement with her. She wrote to him in 1893: 'You need people for when there's a spell of bad weather, and the nights are drawing in, when there's nothing to do and it's too early to go to bed, so that you can have someone beside you to relieve your boredom, but as soon as the moment passes you don't give a thought to that person.'[26]

Certainly it might be argued that Lika's assessments of Chekhov's character were not disinterested. And yet these words would seem to comprise, by accident as it were, the most perceptive of comments on the dilemma of Chekhov's private life; in that they recognize both that basic indifference to others which was a barrier to Chekhov's forming relationships, and the value that contact with others had for him notwithstanding. While Chekhov dreamed of romantic love, perhaps he involuntarily pined for prosaic domesticity, because he could not bear to be alone.

2

In Chekhov's work we find persuasive evidence of his loneliness: in his perceptive and sympathetic treatment of the theme of human isolation, and in the fact that this theme dominates

Olga Knipper

Chekhov with Olga Knipper

Chekhov's presentation of human relationships in the years of his literary maturity.

Chekhov approached this theme at every point on the social scale and it is the subject of some of his simplest and some of his most complex works. In 'Sorrow' (*Toska*, 1886) he makes a brief, rather sentimental appeal to the reader's pity: an old cabman who has lost his son and who can find no one to talk to about his misery is reduced to telling his horse. How much less straight-forward is the presentation of isolation in *Ivanov*: on the surface of it it seems impossible to sympathize with the hero, whose behaviour to his wife alone marks him out for odium. And yet he is not unsympathetic, maintaining in his isolation the pathos and the dignity of the misunderstood: 'No, doctor,' he tells Lvov, the principal critic of his behaviour, 'every one of us has too many wheels, screws, and valves for us to be able to judge one another on first impressions or by one or two outward distinguishing marks.' These words are not perhaps a totally convincing justification of Ivanov's behaviour, but they serve their purpose of making one pause before condemning him.

Likewise, the principal character in 'A Dreary History' is seen to be, as Chekhov intended, in many ways unattractive: Nikolai Stepanovich at times seems simply a peevish and disgruntled old reactionary, a no longer competent lecturer who ought to, but will not, make way for a younger man. And yet there is perhaps nothing so moving in all Chekhov's writing as the old man's sense of isolation in the face of his approaching death:

In the midst of my lecture a lump comes into my throat, my eyes start to prick, and I am conscious of a passionate, hysterical desire to stretch out my hands and make a loud protest. I want to cry out loud that fate has condemned me, a famous man, to death and that in six months or so another man will hold sway here in the lecture-hall. . . . And on these occasions my predicament seems so appalling that I want my entire audience to feel appalled, to leap from their seats and rush for the exit in panic and terror, wailing in despair.

It is hard to get through moments like those.

'A Dreary History' is probably the most important of certain of Chekhov's stories which have become known by Elton's term as the 'clinical studies'.[27] They include 'Typhus' (*Tif*, 1887), 'The Party' and 'Nervous Breakdown'. Each of these stories is concerned with the analysis of a mood, and because the analysis is done painstakingly, with attention to detail, Elton states that in them Chekhov gives, and feels, 'less the pleasure of a work of art than of a perfect surgical operation.'[28] The term 'clinical' however is perhaps subject to misinterpretation, for as the extract from 'A Dreary History' quoted above demonstrates, such a story is not necessarily devoid of emotion. Hingley has come closer to defining the mood of these stories when he writes that, together with *Ivanov*, they have 'one thing in common—they convey *with almost unbearable vividness* a condition of mental or physical ill-health'.[29] (My italics.) It is precisely the unbearably vivid quality in the writing of these stories which indicates that the author's involvement was much greater than that of a diagnostician; and the dry, restrained language in which they are, for the most part, told does not imply indifference, but a conscious attempt on Chekhov's part to increase their effect by understatement.

It is no coincidence that these stories deal in one form or another with the situation of the isolated human being, because this was the theme that touched him most nearly.

In many treatments of this theme, and even in the 'clinical studies', Chekhov did not show the principal protagonist's mental or physical state to be the exclusive cause of his sense of isolation. Part of the sympathy we feel for Ivanov and Nikolai Stepanovich is of course engendered by the fact that they are surrounded by *poshlyaki*. The party scene in *Ivanov* is strongly reminiscent of the similar party in Griboedov's *Woe from Wit*, where Chatsky is driven distraught by the pettiness and stupidity of his fellow-men. Such a situation is frequently used by Chekhov in his portrayals of isolation. In the story actually called 'The Party', the false behaviour and forms of entertainment that social intercourse demands emphasize the misery of the hostess, alone with her private problems. The heroine of 'Home' is driven to desperation by the company of no one save her unenlightened aunt and grandfather, and a young doctor, Neshchapov, who wants to marry her but cannot find a word to say for himself. The young girl who owns a factory in 'A Doctor's Visit' is similarly afflicted by a life of seclusion shared only by her un-educated mother and pretentious governess.

In 'A Dreary History' the professor's sense of being surrounded by an atmosphere of Philistinism (*poshlost'*) is shared by his ward, Katya. For him, however, this is the more bitter in that it is his own family who make him feel this: his fussy wife and affected daughter, and her suitor, a young man who reminds the professor of a crayfish.

It is incomprehensible to him how his own daughter can love such a man, and this is one facet of the professor's real problem: he used to feel close to his wife and daughter, but 'their inner life has long since escaped' him. He can no longer communicate with them. When he is called upon to help his daughter overcome a fit of depression, all he can say is: 'I am unhappy myself.' The worst aspect of his isolation is that he cannot communicate with Katya whom he loves and who loves him, but who eventually lapses into a state of isolation similar to his own. Throughout the story these two are on the point of admitting what they mean to one another, but never do: he feels unable to accept her offers of money and a room in her flat to work in, and criticizes her way of life, although her company is a necessity to him, just as she criticizes him for not looking after his health, rather than own that it worries her. Finally, when she comes in desperation to ask for his help, all that he can suggest is that they have lunch, and he evades talking of her problems by reminding her of his own: 'I haven't long to live, Katya.' Katya gives him her hand without looking at him and departs.

The moment in a relationship where communication was possible but which is allowed to slip past irretrievably recurs frequently in Chekhov's work. In 'Rothschild's Violin' (*Skripka Rotshil'da*, 1894) a coffin-maker measures his wife's length as she lies dying: only after the funeral does he feel 'deep sorrow' and realize that he lived with her for fifty-two years without knowing her. Anna Akimovna, the factory owner in 'A Woman's King-dom' (*Bab'e Tsarstvo*, 1894) is attracted by the idea of marrying one of the workers, Pimenov. After the workers' communal visit on Christmas morning she shakes Pimenov's hand and wants to tell him to come and see her one day: ' . . . but she could not: her tongue simply refused to obey her; and lest it be thought that she was attracted to Pimenov, she shook hands with his com-panions too'. When in *The Cherry Orchard*, Varya and Lopakhin, another couple separated by class, are supposed to become engaged, the opportunity slides away while they make embar-rassed small-talk.

'The Party' concerns Olga Mikhailovna's estrangement not

only from her guests but also from her husband. Here, however, the lapse in communication is brief. For the course of a day she considers that he is behaving unlike his real self, flippant and debonair when she knows him to be worried and depressed. Her husband for his part is irritated by her hysterical criticisms of him. However, at the end of the day, when she goes into premature labour, she realizes how great her love for him is after all. The description of this sticky patch in their marriage—caused, is the implication, by the pregnant woman's hypersensitive state—provides a fair picture of the trivia which go to make a crisis of this kind; it is only a pity that the story is for some reason not very moving—even when the baby is stillborn: perhaps because by the time that the long-drawn-out account of the day and the woman's impressions has come to an end (it takes Chekhov over a page to make a point about the husband's pomposity) we feel as tired and apathetic as the heroine herself.

'My Wife' (*Zhena*, 1892) offers no explanation, clinical or otherwise, for the estrangement of a married couple. Ostensibly based on a sociological theme, the plot concerns the futile efforts of a landowner, Asorin, and his wife to organize famine relief. In fact the interest of the story lies in the barrier that exists between husband and wife. She hates him and has lived in another part of the house for years; given her feelings towards him, it is difficult to see why she married him. He, while acknowledging the complete estrangement, will not give her a passport to go away and pesters her by interfering in her charitable work. At the climax of the story there is a ridiculous episode between them. He goes to tell her that he is leaving home: a scene ensues, with her first threatening to leave, and then ordering him to go. He sets off, but soon returns, and his wife greets him with a shriek of hysteria—but then life continues much as usual.

Elsewhere Chekhov is more explicit concerning the reasons why relationships break up. In 'The Duel', the love-affair between Laevsky and Nadezhda Fedorovna—in the course of which they came to the Black Sea with the aim of starting a new life—has lost its charm for both of them. As in 'My Wife', the end of the affair is characterized by the cessation of squabbling: Laevsky and his mistress are polite to one another like strangers; they no longer refer to the 'new life', since both are idling the time away in more or less disreputable ways, Laevsky with cards and drink,

Nadezhda Fedorovna with brief, squalid liaisons. How wide the gap between them has grown is indicated by the fact that neither is aware that the other feels guilty about the situation and wishes to separate. The difficulties are exacerbated by the minor irritations which combine to inspire physical aversion: Laevsky's slipper-shuffling and nail-biting, the sickroom smell of his mistress's room, the noise of her sipping milk. Such details, zealously amassed by Chekhov, give an overwhelming impression of the unpoetic aspects of cohabitation.

The theme of absence of communication is presented more graphically and yet perhaps with greater subtlety in 'Three Years', where it forms the basis of the plot-structure. Laptev and his wife Yuliya are seen to embody diametrically opposed concepts and qualities. Laptev is ugly, rich, hard-working, and not religious. Yuliya is beautiful, relatively poor, idle, and religious. None of these particular factors is intended to make one seem better than the other: they simply suggest from the start of the story that their relationship will be fraught with difficulties. And so it proves, but as the action develops, the gap between them is indicated no longer simply by the revelation of conflicting attributes, but by certain incidents: in Laptev's impression that Yuliya walks unsteadily on the foot he has kissed in a moment of unreturned passion: in Yuliya's pleasure when she believes she understands a certain painting, and depression when she realizes that Laptev does not; in the fact that she weeps at a friend's house, not at home, after the death of their baby. Ironically, the moment when they are closest is in the moving scene at the end of chapter sixteen when both are simultaneously aware of their unhappiness. The very mechanics of the plot are based on a principle of lack of communication: in time Yuliya comes to love Laptev, but by that time he has fallen out of love with her.

When he chooses to concentrate on the isolation of people one from another, Chekhov provides us with his most convincing and artistically accomplished portrayals of unhappy relations between men and women. Such portrayals lack the bias of, say, 'Ariadna'—where woman appears as a monster of sensuality—and the flatness of 'My Life', in which Masha Poloznev seems constricted in the strait-jacket of her sociological significance. Those female characters who are lonely and isolated are the most sympathetic and convincing in Chekhov's work, because he understood their problems: and in the context of this problem he seemed to see them not as women, either poeticized, feared, or despised, but as individuals.

His studies of such women are, however, not especially profound: he gains the reader's sympathy for them through several straightforward literary devices. Firstly, through pathos—which is not necessarily sentimentality. Yuliya, at the stage where Laptev still thinks of her in romantic terms, is presented to the reader as an ordinary, fallible girl, in a dilemma that touches us because it is so natural. She is not at all attracted to Laptev, is horrified at his proposal of marriage, and at first refuses him. But she is afraid of becoming an old maid, afraid of hurting him, and—most important—she has no one to tell her that she has done right in refusing him. Chiefly as a result of this last fortuitous circumstance, her resolution is worn away by indecision and she takes the disastrous step of marrying a man whom she does not love.

The same atmosphere of pathos without sentimentality surrounds certain of Chekhov's stage heroines. The isolation of human beings is more than a theme in Chekhov's major plays—it is a fundamental part of his stage-technique, since much of the text is composed of brief soliloquies to which none of the other characters are listening. 'I would love my husband', Olga Prozorova remarks wistfully in *Three Sisters*, but her grievance against fate is drowned in the noisy entrance of Tuzenbakh and Soleny. In *Uncle Vanya* Sonya has this splendid interchange with Elena:

SONYA: I'm not beautiful.
ELENA ANDREEVNA: You have beautiful hair.
SONYA: No! (*Looks round to see herself in the mirror*) No! When a woman isn't beautiful, people tell her, 'You have beautiful eyes, you have beautiful hair.'

That glance at the mirror, hopeful in spite of her comment, makes Sonya more sympathetic than do all her *ingénue* speeches put together.

Occasionally the pathos is even more direct. In 'A Doctor's Visit' it is expressed in the following incident. The doctor, Korolev, cannot find anything organically wrong with the girl to whom he has been urgently summoned: 'At that moment someone brought a lamp into the bedroom. The patient screwed up her eyes at the light, and suddenly, clutching her head in her hands, burst into tears. And all at once she ceased to seem plain and wretched, and Korolev was no longer conscious of the small eyes or the coarse lower half of her face: he saw her face take on an expression of meek suffering, so wise and touching that she seemed to him altogether refined, feminine and straightforward, and he wanted to soothe her not with drugs or advice, but simply with a kindly word or two.' Here, this most unpoetic of heroines is for a brief moment poeticized; nor does this seem sentimental, because the moment is brief, and because the doctor is a down-to-earth character.

In *The Cherry Orchard* Chekhov makes two lonely women, Varya and Sharlotta, into comic figures: but they are not absurd. The audience may not consider Varya's fate a tragedy, but Ranevskaya is there to feel for her; just as Dr. Dorn is there to comfort Masha in *The Seagull*, taking for the moment this drooping figure, who always wears black 'in mourning for her life' as seriously as she takes herself.

Another method of presentation relies not on pathos but on honesty of approach. In 'A Woman's Kingdom' Chekhov gains our sympathy for the heroine, Anna Akimovna, simply by putting himself—and the reader—into her place and recounting her thoughts, impressions, and activities during the course of one day. Anna Akimovna is seen to have comfortably trivial feminine failings, such as vanity, and to enjoy simple pleasures—the anticipation of Christmas day, the feel of a new dress. There is something touching in her awkward attempts at philanthropy, undertaken principally out of boredom. But the most engaging thing about her is the frankness with which she admits to her friends that she would like to marry: her isolated position seems unnatural and

. . . she felt she would give half a lifetime and all her wealth to know that there was somebody upstairs who was nearer to her than anyone on earth, that he loved her dearly and pined for her. And her heart stirred at the thought of this delightful intimacy, such that no words could describe it. And the false, flattering instinct of youth and health told her that the real poetry of life was yet to come, and she believed it . . .

She has more clear-sighted moments, however, and 'as always on a feast-day, she was depressed by loneliness and the thought that her beauty, health, and riches were pointless, since the world could get along without her, nobody needed her and nobody loved her'.

In 'In the Cart' Chekhov uses substantially the same method of presentation: again we have a *tranche de vie* illuminated by insight into the heroine's thoughts. In this very short story the method is seen at its most refined. A spinster schoolmistress on a journey has a brief fantasy of home life inspired by idle reflections about a handsome bachelor landowner whom she encounters and by a glimpse of a woman on a passing train who reminds her of her dead mother. The contrast between her musings on her dreary present existence and the background of the damp muddy landscape, and the exalted, lyrical mood provoked in her by her memories of warm family-life is strikingly effective. The economy of the artistic method makes the story superior, for instance, to 'The Party', and for this reason the schoolmistress appears more sympathetic than the heroine of 'The Party'.

In 'The Duel' Chekhov resorts to various methods in order to make Nadezhda Fedorovna, Laevsky's mistress, a likeable character. She behaves with dignity in the face of Laevsky's peevish, irritable criticisms; and although a 'fallen woman' she seems much more decent than her respectable but hypocritical 'friend', Mariya Konstantinovna, who harangues her for not marrying for form's sake, and whose homily on womanly virtue in chapter ten is one of the finest satirical pieces Chekhov ever wrote.

Also, as in his treatment of Anna Akimovna and the schoolmistress, there is charm in Chekhov's description of Nadezhda Fedorovna's impulses and moods, particularly on the occasion of the picnic, when she 'was in a cheerful, mischievous mood'. 'She wanted to skip about, to laugh and shout, to tease and flirt. In her inexpensive cotton dress . . . she felt simple and petite, light and airy as a butterfly.' On this occasion her coquettish mood is merely part of a feeling of childlike *joie de vivre*: 'she felt pure in heart' and is actually displeased when one of her lovers approaches her; and thus our sympathy is aroused when Laevsky accuses her of behaving 'like a tart': it seems to her at this moment unjust, and it is a measure of Chekhov's artistry that, at this moment, so it seems to us.

What is unexpected in Chekhov's attempt to depict Nadezhda

Fedorovna with sympathy is that she in many respects comes close to the type of the Chekhovian anti-heroine. Laevsky has a point: although at the picnic she experiences a sort of spiritual exaltation and feels ethereal, the truth is that she is fat and tipsy. Moreover, there is more than a touch of irony, familiar from Chekhov's critical portraits of women, in his description of the naïve, rather vulgar thoughts that run through Nadezhda Fedorovna's head: 'She fancied she was ever so sweet' (*ona kazalas' sebe ochen' milen'koi*); 'She reflected happily that there was nothing terrible in her infidelity. Her heart played no part in her infidelity . . .'. Worse still, we are told that she was possessed by desire: 'like a madwoman, day and night she thought of nothing else.' Her behaviour gives Laevsky reason to assert that 'for women the most important thing is the bedroom'.

Laevsky is of course meant to be exaggerating, but none the less it is impossible to see Nadezhda Fedorovna as invested with any of the poetry, let alone the purity, of the romantic heroine, even when at the end of the story she is living with Laevsky as his lawful wife. Laevsky comes to believe that he is to blame for her corruption; but still there clings to her what seems like the stigma of an inferior breed. Her vulgar flirtatiousness cannot but remind us that in much of Chekhov's work a continual battle between the sexes appears to be the *status quo*. Olga Mikhailovna's outburst of hysteria in 'The Party' also reminds us of this. Where a woman is isolated not within a relationship with a man, but because she has no relationship with any man, Chekhov apparently found it easier to portray her with total sympathy: and he seems to feel nothing but sympathy for the desire of such women to marry—to enter into a relationship that in the world of his fiction so often proves injurious to the man.

And that he should treat them with such sympathy is particularly remarkable in view of the fact that these women are set apart from the romantic heroine on an issue that is fundamental to all relationships with the opposite sex. Whereas Chekhov's image of the romantic heroine is connected with the concept of an idealized, poetic love, these women seem connected with a concept of love which comes closer to that more prosaic companionship which Chekhov himself seemed to need.

For the lonely men whom Chekhov depicted, companionship is certainly necessary: witness in 'A Dreary History' the old professor's need to sit with Katya, his longing that the student who comes to him on formal business would talk informally about himself; witness in 'My Wife' Asorin's intense desire to see and talk to his wife, which amounts to an obsession.* Both these men, however, married not for companionship, but for love. And this is true of Chekhov's men in general, with the exception of the occasional one who has been forced into marriage for one reason or another.

There is no theme in Chekhov's work of men voluntarily seeking marriage for the sake of being married. But Vera, heroine of 'Home', eventually marries the unprepossessing Dr. Neshchapov—admittedly as a last resort, yet she does it. In *Three Sisters* Olga confesses to Irina—the romantic heroine of that moment, who balks at marrying Tuzenbakh without love—that she herself would do so—that she would marry anyone, even an old man, provided only he were respectable.

Of course, in Chekhov's day it was very much more important for a woman that she should marry than it was for a man, and Chekhov, in those cases where a woman's loneliness seems uppermost in his mind (rather than some man's fear of being trapped) does not condemn such women for wanting marriage. What is significant is their prosaic approach to the subject, and the consequent fact that through the stories in which they figure the question arises of what the desire for marriage involves—and whether a marriage that involves companionship rather than love is necessarily second-best.

In 'A Doctor's Visit' the thought that flashes through Korolev's head when he is confronted with his patient's misery is: 'It's time she married.' This very reasonable man sees not love, but marriage as the solution: that is simply what women need.

---

* 'My Wife' contains the following passage: 'Anyone who has lived in the country in winter and knows those long dull evenings, when even the dogs are too bored to bark and the clocks seem to be tired of ticking, whose awakening conscience has troubled him on such evenings and who has paced about uneasily, trying to suppress, and then to examine it, will understand what a diversion and delight it was to me to hear a woman's voice resounding in the cosy little room and telling me that I was a bad man.' These lines, written in late 1891, are interesting in view of Lika's accusation, in her letters of 1892 and 1893 (see above, p. 186 and note 26 to that passage), that Chekhov used other people as a diversion; especially as Lika's company no doubt entailed as much criticism of Chekhov as did her letters to him.

Anna Akimovna in 'A Woman's Kingdom' dreams of being loved, of a 'delightful intimacy'. But she suddenly begins to contemplate marrying Pimenov, simply because he is there; subsequently she gives up the idea of marrying him simply because her social position makes her feel that it is impossible. It is the past, when she was not isolated, that she really longs for: '. . . when as a small girl she slept under one quilt with her mother, and close by in the next room the lodger, a laundress, did her washing, and through the thin walls you could hear people laughing and scolding in the neighbouring flats, and children crying, and the whir of lathes and sewing machines . . .'. In the closing lines of the story it is again on this gregarious childhood that she broods, while conscious that she will never make a new life for herself.

Similarly, in 'In the Cart', the thought of marrying Khanov, the landowner, comes to the schoolmistress as an idle reflection: it seems stupid that he should live on his huge estate alone, and she alone in the schoolhouse, when they two are the only educated people for miles around. But the thoughts which fill her with joy and enthusiasm are remembrances of her erstwhile family life:

. . . vividly, with an amazing clarity, for the first time in all these thirteen years she had a vision of her mother, her father and brother, the Moscow flat and the aquarium with its little fishes, and all this down to the last detail: she suddenly heard the sound of the piano, her father's voice, and felt that she was as she had been in those days —young, beautiful, and elegant, in a bright warm room in the circle of her family. A sense of joy and happiness suddenly overwhelmed her, and she pressed her palms to her temples in delight and cried out in a tender imploring voice: 'Mother!'.

In both 'In the Cart' and 'A Woman's Kingdom' marriage, as a solution to boredom and loneliness, is seen not in terms of falling in love, but of companionship; and in the terms of these stories it seems natural, even agreeable, to think of it in this way. Homely companionship in fact is invested with the desirability of romantic love. In Chekhov's fiction romantic love seldom survives. Is happiness then to be found in this companionship? This is the question that Chekhov seems to pose in 'The Duel' and 'Three Years', his most honest and profound analyses of relationships between man and woman.

3

In 'The Duel', which concerns two conflicts—that between Laevsky and his mistress, and that between Laevsky and a zoologist, von Koren, Chekhov delves into a murky backwater of human relationships, dealing with petty irritations and irrational dislike amongst this far from admirable trio of central characters.

Von Koren's view of love is, to say the least, idealistic. He asserts that, 'everyone of us is dimly aware of a need for purity in love', and that were it not for this 'obscure force . . . the human race would degenerate within two years'. Consequently he deplores sexual relationships outside of marriage, and in particular that between Laevsky and Nadezhda Fedorovna. However, even if his ideas made sense, it would still be impossible to take von Koren seriously, because he has obviously had no experience of love in any form.

More impressive, on account of his experience, is Laevsky's cynicism, summed up in his comment: 'Beautiful, poetic, sacred love—all that's roses, meant to cover up the rot underneath.' Nevertheless Laevsky in his confused way seems to believe that some sort of desirable love exists: to marry without love, he states at one point, is as base as celebrating mass without being a believer. However, he has a theory that no love can survive cohabitation with any woman: he regards his home with his mistress as a prison. Only lack of money prevents him from leaving the region.

This *impasse* is resolved in a rather sudden and not entirely satisfactory fashion. Laevsky receives two shocks: after a quarrel von Koren challenges him to a duel, and he accepts; the same night he discovers that Nadezhda Fedorovna is with another man. He spends an unpleasant night of self-examination in the anticipation of death. As he is about to leave the house at dawn, he comes across an equally abject Nadezhda Fedorovna. The reconciliation follows swiftly:

He embraced her impetuously and tightly and covered her arms and knees with kisses. And then she murmured something, shuddering as she remembered, and he stroked her hair, and looking into her face realized that this wretched, immoral woman was the only being close to him, the only being whom nobody could replace.

When he . . . got into the carriage he wanted to come back alive.

Thus communication is re-established. The moment is credible, if a little melodramatic. But hereafter Chekhov taxes our credibility. Are we to believe that this reunion, which in spite of the kisses is provoked not by passion, but by pity and a desire for closeness, will bring in its wake a renewal of the passion Laevsky once felt for Nadezhda Fedorovna? It seems scarcely likely. By a mere chance Laevsky does return from the duel alive, and the experience of being nearly killed is the final prod which makes him change his ways. In the last chapter clearly some sort of regeneration is in progress: he walks about 'with a new expression on his face', has become hard-working and has married Nadezhda Fedorovna. Then, if Laevsky is faithful to his tenets, he must love his wife. But can he have become reconciled to the horrors of life with this woman, which he enumerated as 'the smell of ironing, powder, and medicines, the same old curling papers every morning?' Will the bedroom be cleared of 'the underclothes scattered everywhere', of Nadezhda Fedorovna's 'various rubber things . . . hanging on the walls' of the 'basins standing about'? Alternatively, are we to suppose that Laevsky has stopped biting his nails? Presumably, but it is hard to believe it. Laevsky and Nadezhda Fedorovna are a prosaic couple and it would seem that they are doomed to settle for a prosaic companionship. Did Chekhov see virtue in this companionship? If so, he fails in this instance to convince the reader of its charms. Or did he envisage their future in other terms, in terms of poetic love? If so, he fails to convince the reader of the likelihood of this happening. The unconvincing conclusion of 'The Duel' suggests that Chekhov was unsure whether happiness could be found either in the poetry or in the prose of life.

In 'Three Years' the same question is raised, but Chekhov's standpoint seems much more clearly defined. The story begins with Laptev waiting for Yuliya, the girl whom he wishes to marry. He has frequented circles in Moscow in which it has been mooted that it is possible to live without love; that passionate love is a mental disease; that love only denotes physical attraction; and Laptev 'was thinking wistfully that if someone asked him now what love was, he would not know how to reply'.

In fact it soon becomes apparent that Laptev's love for Yuliya undoubtedly contains a strong element of sexual desire, but his idea of love is still rooted in a youthful idealism: Yuliya 'had a faint, scarcely perceptible smell of incense, and this reminded him of the days when he too believed in God . . . and was always dreaming of pure, poetic love. And because this girl did not love him, he now felt that any possibility of finding that happiness of which he had then dreamt was lost for ever.' Yuliya, seen through his eyes, has the attractions of the romantic heroine: purity, youth, innocence. She is invested with all the poetry of the one-and-only, the unattainable.

However, although he expects to be refused, Laptev is unable to resist proposing marriage. And at this juncture both make a false move. Yuliya, for the reasons previously described, accepts Laptev although she does not love him: and he accepts her acceptance, although he knows that she does not love him.

Even in spite of the fact that he imagines—wrongly—that Yuliya is marrying him for his money, Laptev's romantic pre-conception of her is dominant: 'His love grew more intense every day, and Yuliya seemed to him poetic and exalted . . .'. And yet he acknowledges to himself that they are making a terrible mistake: for 'all the same, there was no mutual love between them'. There follows the wretched period of their estrangement when both suffer for their mistake. As time passes, however, Yuliya's attitude towards her marriage changes, as she explains in the following excerpts from her conversation with her friend Ivan Yartsev:

' . . . You know, I didn't marry Aleksei for love. I used to be silly, so unhappy, always thinking I had ruined both his life and mine, but now I see that love isn't at all important, that that's all nonsense.'

'But if it's not love, what feeling does bind you to your husband? Why do you live with him?'

'I don't know—I suppose it must be habit. I respect him, and I'm bored when he's away for a long time, but that isn't love. He's an intelligent, decent person, and that's enough for me to be happy . . .'

. . . 'Tea-time!' said Yuliya Sergeevna, getting to her feet. She had filled out recently, and already her walk was that of a woman, rather indolent.

'All the same, it's no good without love,' said Yartsev, following her. 'We keep on only talking and reading about love, and don't do enough loving ourselves, and really it's no good.'

'That's a lot of nonsense, Ivan Gavrilych,' said Yuliya. 'That's not what happiness is about.'

Thus Yuliya has accepted the prose of marriage instead of the poetry. She has even, like Tolstoy's Natasha, lost some of the physical attributes of the romantic heroine. By the end of three years she is ready to offer Laptev her affection as love. In the last scene of the story, in contrast to the opening scene, it is she who, at a *dacha*, is waiting for Laptev. He comes from town to visit her:

'Why haven't you been for so long?' she asked, keeping hold of his hand. 'I've been sitting here for days and days watching for your arrival. I miss you when you're not here!'

She stood up and ran her hand over his hair, and examined his face, his shoulders, his hat with interest.

'I love you, you know,' she said, blushing. 'You're dear to me. Now you're here, I can look at you and I can't tell you how happy I am. Well, let's talk. Tell me about things.'

She had told him that she loved him, but he had the feeling that he had been married to her for ten years already, and he wanted to have lunch. She had put her arm around his neck and the silk of her dress tickled his cheek: he cautiously removed her arm, got up and without a word walked away towards the house. . . .

For Laptev the opportunity of happiness, the poetry of love has been irretrievably lost, and what Yuliya can give him now is no substitute. The story ends as Laptev idly muses on what the future will bring: 'And he thought: "Life will go on, and we shall see." ' The conclusion of 'The Duel' also looked towards the future, on an unconvincing note of hope. But the open conclusion to 'Three Years' is merely a stylistic device: Laptev's melancholy resignation is the true and totally convincing conclusion.

Since Chekhov's compassionate treatment of women in isolation sprang from his emotional identification with this particular problem, and since he did not appear to identify, let alone sympathize, with women in so many other aspects of their experience, Chekhov's lonely female characters are not paragons. Chekhov seems not to have had, for example, the experience of being highly sexed: when in 'The Duel' the plot demands that he delineate a woman both isolated and highly sexed, Chekhov's prejudices against this type of woman inevitably colour his presentation of her.

However, the reader who does not share Chekhov's prejudices in these matters will probably find Nadezhda Fedorovna the more human for her failings. The most attractive quality of Chekhov's 'isolated women' who seek marriage, or companionship within marriage, is their very ordinariness, by virtue of which they seem to inhabit a real world, in contrast to the distorted spheres in which alone the romantic heroine and the anti-heroine can exist. These isolated women have, then, an important place in Chekhov's work, for precisely their down-to-earth quality makes them persuasive in what they would appear to suggest: that there is a level in heterosexual relationships somewhere between poetic, spiritual love and purely carnal, sordid cohabitation. In 'The Duel' and 'Three Years' Chekhov seems to attempt to show that there are indeed shades and degrees of happiness in such relationships. But even in these works he is, from an artistic point of view, most impressive and convincing when he depicts the absence of communication and the loss of poetry. A relationship in which both these desirables are present would seem to be the ideal love: whether expressly or not, 'Three Years' and 'The Duel' suggest that companionship is no substitute for it.

4

That after so many years of writing about ill-fated love and wretched marriage, Chekhov should finally have found a woman whom he loved, who loved him and who was free to marry him seems more than he could have expected—it is tempting to add, more than he deserved. Certainly it appears that Chekhov did not expect the happiness his marriage brought him. 'You were always saying that you never thought marriage could be so good,'[30] Olga Knipper reminisced in one of the letters that she wrote to Chekhov after his death.

It is also the case that some months elapsed before Chekhov took the decisive step. But it is absurd to suggest, as Rachmanowa has done, in the chapter of her book entitled '*Olga Leonardowna*

Knipper will die Heirat erzwingen',[31] that Olga forced the marriage on Chekhov against his will. It has been mentioned that early in 1901, which was when Olga was beginning to be impatient, Chekhov talked of his being capable of a lasting love.[32] He jokingly referred to 'divorcing'[33] her, and the tone of his letters in general suggests that he was well aware that they would marry sooner or later, and was by no means unwilling to do so. Indeed, on 22 April 1901 he wrote to Olga: 'At the beginning of May, in the first few days, I shall come to Moscow, we'll marry, if possible, and go off down the Volga, or first we'll go down the Volga and then marry, whatever suits you best. . . . My cough takes away all my energy, I can't think of the future except with apathy. . . . You think of the future, and cope with things for me, I'll do as you say, or else we shan't live, it'll be like sipping life by the tablespoonful once an hour.'[34] This letter makes nonsense of any suggestion that Olga coerced Chekhov into marriage.

They had had a battle of wills about rather a different matter, which Chekhov in fact in his quiet way had won. In January of 1901 Olga had inaugurated a campaign to settle a date for the wedding. Chekhov had agreed in February to come to Moscow at Easter,[35] but subsequently shifted his ground and suggested that she come to Yalta. He became quite insistent about this. Olga however was anxious not to do so, for reasons she made clear in her letters: 'You, with your sensibility, invite me to come!'[36] she wrote, and, enlarging on her objection in a subsequent letter: 'Concealment all over again, and your mother being upset again, playing hide-and-seek . . .'; why should they have to keep the fact that they were lovers an embarrassing secret? 'I can't stand the absence of a clear-cut situation. Well, have you understood me, do you agree?'[37]

Olga's objections seem reasonable enough; one can imagine how trying it must have been for her to meet what she later described as Masha's 'look of bewilderment',[38] and it argues a certain insensitivity in Chekhov not to have thought of this. Only now, when faced with these objections did he admit that he was 'terribly anxious not to leave Yalta',[39] and make it clear that his health was not up to it. None the less, he said, he would come to Moscow.

Now Olga was in a quandary, realizing that he ought not to

come, and yet feeling herself no less justified in refusing to go. At the last moment she did in fact go; and perhaps gained something by climbing down, for Chekhov's gratitude probably made him eager to oblige her wishes in connection with the marriage ceremony by fixing the date for this as soon as possible.

The point at issue, therefore, when Chekhov met his ideal woman was not whether he would marry her, but simply when and where, and this depended entirely on factors other than their feelings for one another. As Chekhov put it in the autumn of 1900: 'If at present we're not together, it's not my fault or yours, but the fault of the demon who has filled me with bacilli and you with love for your art.'[40]

If Olga appeared somewhat desperate in her attempts to fix on a date for the marriage, this was because Chekhov was slow to make clear to her, in the months before this event, exactly how far his actions were dictated by his health. Some personal scruple made him dislike the image of himself as an invalid as much as he disliked that of the conventional bridegroom, 'smiling vaguely' over a glass of champagne as he received congratulations.[41] (For which reason his own wedding was to be a quiet affair.)

It has been suggested that Chekhov regarded his state of health as an argument against marriage. Simmons writes: 'The terrible, overriding obstacle was to consign his diseased, wasting body to a healthy young woman! He had given himself six years. . . . In his evasive way he had tried to tell her this, but it made no difference.'[42] What is meant by this seems somewhat obscure. Chekhov's body—if we take the meaning literally—was already consigned to Olga Knipper. It is true that Chekhov had no illusions concerning his possible life-span. Friends testify to his saying that he would not live long.[43] And indeed he wrote jokingly to Olga a few weeks before their marriage, apropos of her friendship with the actor Vishnevsky: 'Evidently he's counting on your being widowed soon, but tell him that to spite him I'm going to leave a will forbidding you to marry.'[44]

The point was that, despite an increasing debility, Chekhov himself was anxious to make light of his troubles. When at the close of the year Olga telegraphed for news of his health he replied with evident irritation and embarrassment, 'I got your telegram today and it took me some time to decide what to reply. Should I have answered: "Strong as an ox"? I'd be ashamed to. But how about

your health?' And in the following spring when his health broke
down severely, far from trying 'evasively' to impress this fact on
Olga, he appears rather to be reassuring himself that his health
was good. 'I'm well—word of honour,' he wrote;[45] and: 'I'm
alive, and it seems, well, though I still have a frightful cough.'[46]
After making plain his objections to travelling to Moscow, he
himself seemed to feel he was pessimistic, and hastily dismissed
them as 'nonsense'[47]—although Olga took them seriously enough
to consider it out of the question for him to come. When he
wrote, a few days later, ' . . . my health is evidently becoming
that of an old man—so that incidentally you are going to acquire
in my person not a husband but a grandfather . . .', and in the
same paragraph talked of when he would marry her,[48] he appeared
to be voicing a fear in order to overcome it, not suggesting that
the marriage should not take place.

Simmons refers to 'the accursed formalities' of life, and says
that Chekhov preferred to drift along enjoying his happiness
without these.[49] It is doubtless true that Chekhov found the idea
of the documentation involved in getting married tiresome: Olga
saw to that side of the matter. But there is no real evidence that
he found the prospect of marriage *per se* unattractive. It was the
prospect of the invalid life ahead of him that he found unattractive. 'Drifting along' was surely exactly the sort of existence
he had in mind when he talked of 'sipping life by the tablespoonful
once an hour'. As this remark shows, with Olga firmly incorpor-
ated into his existence he hoped for a better life.

Very possibly the prospect of death within a few years
strengthened Chekhov's desire for a child—a desire which would
appear to constitute a conclusive argument against any theory
that Chekhov had to be bludgeoned into marriage.

Their correspondence shows that, as soon as Chekhov and
Olga were married, the hope of Olga's becoming pregnant was
uppermost in their minds. As one might expect, the non-existent
child was given nicknames: 'the little half-German' and 'Pamfil',
and there were repeated references to it. Chekhov was anxious
that the gay life Olga led with her troupe should not prejudice
her chances of bearing him a child. 'I've nothing against your
becoming famous and making 25–40 thousand, only, first of all,
try for Pamfil,'[50] he wrote to her in March 1902. The miscarriage
that Olga suffered within days of receiving this encouragement

was a bitter disappointment to Chekhov,* as is shown by his remark to Olga, quoted previously, that she might do as she liked once they had a child.[51] Perhaps Olga did not take offence at this because she understood and shared his disappointment. The thought of the child possibly played its part in healing the breach between them in August 1902.

Chekhov was to become obsessed by a consciousness of the passage of time. 'You and I have only a short while left to live,' he wrote to Olga at the beginning of 1903, 'youth (if you can call it that) will pass in 2–3 years' time, so we must make haste and harness all our know-how, that something may come of it.'[52] This 'something' was surely a child. But Chekhov's wish was not fulfilled, and by the end of that year he must have suspected that it never would be. However, he and Olga still talked of their hopes. 'So you want a baby? Darling, I want one too. I'll try, I promise you,' wrote Olga in March of 1904.[53] But within four months Chekhov was dead, and there was no child. A few days before his death, he and Olga talked of the little girl that would be born to them: so Olga noted in one of the letters she wrote to Chekhov in the months following his death. 'How it grieves my heart that no child remains . . . how you would have loved it!'[54] To the last then, it seems, Chekhov had not given up hope— or else, as he had been accustomed to advise Olga to do, he had concealed what he really felt in order to appear cheerful.

That there was no child was almost certainly the most bitter disappointment of Chekhov's married life. In other respects he considered himself fortunate. Love was mutual, and in spite of her difficulties with Masha, Olga was made happy by the legitimization of their relationship. Chekhov was satisfied that he had not made a mistake. On 25 August Chekhov wrote to his wife: 'Today, darling, it's exactly three months since we were married. I've been happy, thank you, my joy, a thousand kisses.'[55] Again

* The assertion of Rachmanowa (p. 378) that Chekhov was tortured by the 'certainty' that Olga knew she was pregnant, and did nothing to take care of herself, appears to be a gratuitous slander on Olga. Those passages deleted by the editors of Olga's letters to Chekhov which deal with this intimate matter make it clear that Olga had reason to believe she was not pregnant, and that she probably could not have prevented the miscarriage even if she had known. Olga wrote moreover on 31 March 1902 to Chekhov: 'the doctors say now that I could become pregnant right away—do you understand? I'm rushing to Yalta.' (See *Otd. ruk.* 331.76.21–5.)

in November he assured her how glad he was to be married to her.[56] Nearly two years later, in October 1903, he wrote: 'How glad I am I married you, funny face, now I have everything, I feel your presence night and day.'[57]

But of course his merely being able to 'feel his wife's presence' meant that Chekhov did not have everything. And he was perfectly aware of this. The bachelor who had talked breezily of having a wife who would 'not appear in his sky every day' found himself hoist by his own petard: for the fact that he and Olga were separated so many times during their few years together proved a source of great unhappiness to him—an unhappiness which, if perhaps less acute than his disappointment over the child, did more to spoil his marriage in being the more prolonged.

It might be thought, as Chekhov perhaps had thought, that in a marriage in which the partners did not see too much of one another the poetry might be preserved; and perhaps this did prove to be the case in Chekhov's marriage: but only to a certain extent. There was another side to the coin. In one of Chekhov's note-books, amidst notes that deal with *The Cherry Orchard* and other works that were written during the years of his marriage, we find the following statement: 'Love. Either it is the remains of something that was once colossal and has degenerated, or else it is part of something which in the future will develop into something colossal, but at the present it is not satisfying, gives much less than you expect.'[58] As is the case with all notes in Chekhov's papers, we cannot be certain that this note is a comment on Chekhov's personal experience. And yet it very possibly does reflect some sense of disillusionment that Chekhov was conscious of, when he discovered that the sensation of being in love was not equivalent to living with the woman one loved. Communication by letter was a pale substitute for living together, and it brought its own irritations. Olga suspected that Chekhov was withholding some part of himself. Chekhov seemed to entertain no such suspicions regarding her, but the degree of frustration he felt at being unable to be with her shows itself in the very triviality of the things that irritated him. He grumbled for days when Olga was slow to send him the exact type of writing paper he wanted;[59] he complained peevishly when she ordered him a new fur coat of what he considered to be inferior quality;[60] he criticized the ink she used, which made the pages of her letters stick together;[61] when letters failed to arrive he would send urgent, anxious telegrams. Worst of all were the occasions when Olga moved from one flat to another and he was in temporary ignorance of her address. This happened in November 1901 and again in March 1903. On the second occasion Chekhov became thoroughly upset—partly, it is clear, because Olga believed that she had sent the address, and thought that he was fussing unnecessarily. 'I just knew I'd be the one to be at fault,' Chekhov wrote. 'I've got all your letters intact and I'll show you them . . . I've been so offended this last fortnight over this address business that I still can't calm down.'[62]

Never until these years of his marriage do Chekhov's letters contain such undertones of genuine bad-temper. This fault—which he himself readily acknowledged—was a symptom of deep unhappiness: the unhappiness of loneliness made now so much more acute by the absence of the woman he loved.

Chekhov had disliked Yalta at the best of times. 'He spoke of Moscow like a schoolboy talking of his home town where he goes for the holidays,' commented a contemporary who knew Chekhov in Yalta.[63] It can be maintained without casting any slight on Olga Knipper that her attractiveness for Chekhov was connected with the attractions of Moscow and the life of the theatre there. 'I miss Moscow, and I miss you, my dear actress,' he wrote to Olga in 1899.[64] In Yalta he felt as if he were 'in prison',[65] 'in exile'.[66] Moscow and Olga lent one another glamour, and her pleasures there struck home to him the tedium of his own existence. 'What a gay life you lead, and what a dreary life I lead here', he commented sadly on hearing of her doings;[67] and Olga, encouraged by him to be cheerful, would innocently make remarks that seemed the height of tactlessness, such as 'What scope and beauty life has, Anton, hasn't it?'[68]

As time passed, however, the absence of Olga gradually became the true focus of Chekhov's discontent. 'It's devilish dull without you,' Chekhov once wrote to Olga when she was his mistress.[69] That was his situation in a nutshell. But how much more forcibly its pathos strikes us in a letter that he wrote to Olga two years later: 'I feel that if I spent as much as half a night with my nose tucked into your shoulder I'd feel better and stop fretting. I can't do without you . . .'.[70]

It is difficult to believe that parts of Chekhov's letters to his wife, especially in the last two years of his life, were written by the man whose correspondence with women was, in general, characterized by superficiality, by condescension, or at best by a jocular amiability which did not wholly conceal an underlying reserve, even hardness. To Olga he could be unashamedly sentimental: once he quoted in full a poem he admitted to be bad; but he 'liked very much' its concluding couplet, which ran:

I have lain my head upon my arms, and have lapsed into a deep
Sad reverie of thee. But thou . . . thou art so far away![71]

There is nothing unusual in a lover's predilection for such sentiments; and this is perhaps why Chekhov's letters to Olga Knipper have disappointed at least one critic.[72] Another critic professes himself delighted with what he tentatively describes as the 'frisky quality' of Chekhov's relationship with his wife, as made manifest in his love-letters:[73] having in mind, it seems, the playful, bantering tone which Chekhov never completely abandoned.

This tone can, in fact, be oddly moving when used to express sentiments that are banal but none the less sincere. In Chekhov's last letter to his wife, written just before he joined her in Moscow to begin the visit to Germany during which he died, he wrote: 'Doggie, doggie, I've missed you so much!'[74] As the last word on Chekhov's marriage, the words have this claim to dignity, that they express quite appropriately in the simplest sentimentality, the essential pathos of a very ordinary but very unfortunate situation.

'You and I have one fault in common—that we married one another too late':[75] the sanguine tone of Chekhov's comment on his marriage belies what he must have felt in the face of the fact that fate had given him love when he had only a few years left to live; and—what was perhaps more bitter—when it was too late to enjoy it to the full. Chekhov wrote to his sister shortly after his wedding: 'I don't think my taking this step will change my life in any way at all, nor the circumstances in which I have lived hitherto.'[76] The words were written casually, as a reassurance rather than as a prophecy. But, in the fact that Chekhov's marriage did not change his life or his circumstances as much as he would have wished lay the deep irony of his fate.

5

Chekhov's ambivalent attitude to love and cohabitation was the basis of all he wrote about relationships between men and women. On the one hand, his concept of an ideal love led to an apotheosis of the romantic heroine and denigration of sensuality. The profound emotion with which Chekhov clearly adhered to this concept, and with which he expressed it, is the source of the 'poetry' in his love-stories, a quality which many would consider to be their principal charm. Yet another result of this emotion was the sentimentalization of many romantic heroines, and that lack of finesse characteristic of the depiction of the anti-heroine. Misyus is the antithesis of Ariadna—but both are stereotypes in their relationship to men. This is because Chekhov was writing about an idea and not about relationships of which he himself had had any experience to speak of.

Since the romantic heroine is really love—an abstract—Chekhov is not entirely comfortable with her human face, and thus he is motivated to reject her. The cynical hero reflects that fear of intrusion into his inner sanctum which those women closest to Chekhov detected sometimes in his indifference to the difficulties of others. It is a fear engendered, perhaps, of devotion to the abstract ideal of love, but it drives a cold blast between the rantings of Shamokhin and the ravings of Misyus's artist, and is thus, in the present writer's view, wholly salutary.

Chekhov's artistic technique depended heavily upon inspiring in the reader or audience an emotional identification with his theme. His studies of women do not rely for their effect on dispassionate observation or psychological profundities—they rely upon the successful transmission of feeling. Chekhov has to produce a vivid awareness of shared emotional experience.

It is for this reason that the most wholly satisfying of his works tend to be those in which Chekhov describes human isolation. For whereas, as seems clear, Chekhov's feelings about love-affairs, sex, and cohabitation derived largely from ideals and not from personal experience, his involvement in the theme of isolation derived from the actual predicament of his day-to-day life: Chekhov tried to evade what he considered to be the sordid reality of love, and yet the concept of conjugal devotion was indispensable to him: his characters desire passionately to be both devoted and devotee. They are not faceless antagonists in the battle of the sexes, but individuals, and their predicament is arresting for that reason.

But most interesting of all, and arguably most perfect as works of art, are those stories in which the theme of isolation is depicted in conjunction with the love versus companionship problem. In 'Three Years', 'The Duel', and other of the later love-stories, man or woman is confronted with what was for Chekhov the ultimate riddle—how to reconcile with a need for companionship the desire to preserve an ideal of love. These stories are profoundly moving because the contrast between dream and reality is sharply pointed up. The humdrum, the prosaic difficulties are there, and so also is the possibility of the ideal. There is a striking sense of pain in these stories, a restless sense of perpetual seeking that makes them disturbing to read and hard to forget. Here Chekhov describes his deepest feelings most sincerely and most successfully, because he is caught on the horns of his own dilemma.

8 The Lady with the Dog

It will by now be apparent that Anna Sergeevna, the lady with the dog, can be considered symbolic of the ideal love that Chekhov could envisage but not embrace—that remained, so to speak, behind a pane of glass, as in Heifitz's film. But the significance of the whole story is much greater than that comprised in Anna Sergeevna alone.

No other single work of Chekhov's fiction constitutes a more meaningful comment on Chekhov's attitude to women and to love than does 'The Lady with the Dog'. So many threads of Chekhov's thought and experience appear to have been woven together into this succinct story that it may be regarded as something in the nature of a summary of the entire topic.

Gurov, the hero of the story, may at first appear no more closely identifiable with Chekhov himself than are many other sympathetic male characters in Chekhov's fiction: he has a post in a bank and is a married man with three children. It is because he has this wife and family that his love-affair with Anna Sergeevna leads him into an *impasse*. And the affair itself, involving Gurov's desperate trip to Anna's home town, has no obvious feature in common with anything we know of Chekhov's amorous liaisons.

And yet Chekhov's own attitudes and experience have clearly shaped Gurov's character and fate. The reader is told that Gurov 'was not yet forty': Chekhov was thirty-nine when he wrote 'The Lady with the Dog'. Gurov 'was married young' (*ego zhenili rano*): there is a faint implication in the phrase that an element of coercion played some part in his taking this step—a step which Chekhov, when he was young, managed to avoid. As in general with early marriages in Chekhov's fiction, Gurov's has not proved a success. His wife seems 'much older than he' and imagines herself to be an intellectual: familiar danger-signals. She is summed-up in three words: 'stiff, pompous, dignified' (*pryamaya, vazhnaya, solidnaya*) which epitomize a type of woman (and man) that Chekhov heartily disliked.

Gurov's wife treats sex as something more complicated than it is, and spoils it for him; and it is also spoilt for him by those mistresses of whom he soon tires: beautiful, cold women with a 'predatory' expression who are determined to snatch what they can from life. 'When Gurov grew cold to them, their beauty aroused hatred in him and the lace on their linen reminded him of scales.' It would seem that exactly some such sentiment inspired Chekhov when he depicted Ariadna, Nyuta, and the other anti-heroines.

Gurov has had, however, liaisons that were, for him, enjoyable —and these we note, were brief: as was Chekhov's liaison with Yavorskaya and indeed, so far as we know, all the sexual relationships that he had before he met Olga Knipper.

'Frequent experience and indeed bitter experience had long since taught [Gurov] that every liaison which to begin with makes such a pleasant change . . . inevitably evolves into a real and extremely complex problem, and the situation eventually becomes a burden.' That his friendships with, for instance, Lika and Avilova should evolve into a situation of this kind seems to have been exactly what Chekhov himself feared: he backed out of these friendships as soon as there appeared to be a danger of close involvement.

Gurov cannot do without the company of women, and yet he describes them as an 'inferior breed': his experience of intimacy with women is limited to casual affairs and an unsatisfactory marriage. Chekhov also enjoyed the company of women and had many female friends and admirers: but he failed, or was unwilling, to involve himself deeply or lastingly with them. That in his work he should suggest that women are an inferior breed can be to some extent explained by the limited knowledge of women his self-contained attitude brought him—and perhaps, to some extent, by a sense of guilt concerning his inability to feel involved.

Gurov's behaviour to Anna Sergeevna at the beginning of their love-affair is characterized by an absence of emotional involvement, just such as appears in Chekhov's attitude towards certain women. There is a scene in 'The Lady with the Dog'

where, after they have been to bed together, Gurov eats a water-
melon while Anna Sergeevna weeps over her corruption. It is not
difficult to imagine Chekhov doing something similarly prosaic
—weeding his garden, perhaps—while Lika poured out her
emotional troubles to him.

Gurov's egocentricity is dispelled, however, by the potent
influence of love, because Anna Sergeevna turns out to be the
ideal type of woman: pitiable, defenceless, childlike, capable of
offering Gurov an unquestioning love. Love is seen to operate as
a force for good: under its influence Gurov feels revulsion for the
philistinism of his normal life and associates. Soviet interpreters
have made much of the theme of regeneration,* of the idea
implicit in the story that 'a profound love experienced by ordinary
people has become an enormous moral force'.† In fact, although
some idea of this sort is certainly implicit in the story, Chekhov

---

* B. S. Meilakh in his article 'Dva resheniya odnoi temy' (see bibliography)
states that in 'The Lady with the Dog' Chekhov was seeking to present in
terms of everyday people (i.e. not the nobility) the problem Tolstoy had
posed in *Anna Karenina*: how can there be happiness in the false society that
has made it possible for two such dissimilar people as Anna and Karenin
to be united? Meilakh writes: Anna Karenina 'perishes as the victim of the
cruel mores which constituted the norm of existence for a person of her
milieu'. Chekhov, he holds, was showing his lovers to be in virtually the
same predicament; but by not resolving the problem in death, Chekhov was
suggesting that the more the situation seems impossible, the more one
should intensify the search for an exit. In fact, Tolstoy was if anything more
concerned with doing away with the evils of the old order than Chekhov:
in 'The Lady with the Dog' the lovers blame fate, not society, for their
predicament, and the way in which they confront their situation probably
only means that Chekhov preferred less dramatic effects and positive statements than Tolstoy, and did not wish to copy the latter too closely. For a
discussion of the similarities between *Anna Karenina* and 'The Lady with
the Dog', and an interesting analysis of the artistic methods used in 'The
Lady with the Dog', see Winner, pp. 216–25.

† K. M. Vinogradova, 'Stranitsa iz chernovoi rukopisi rasskaza "Dama
s sobachkoi"' (see bibliography): Vinogradova maintains that Chekhov's
alterations to the first-published text of 'The Lady with the Dog' were made
to underline the theme of Gurov's regeneration. However, the changes she
adduces seem rather to have been dictated by artistic considerations, and
with the aim of making both lovers appear more ordinary, less wholly good,
less wholly bad. Chekhov cuts out, for example, a series of coarse rejoinders
that Gurov makes to Anna Sergeevna in the bedroom scene: which would
have been better left in, had Chekhov wished to point up the change in
Gurov's character to the utmost.

is surely attempting above all to evoke what love meant to his protagonists as they themselves saw their situation. Chekhov originally wrote in the conclusion of 'The Lady with the Dog' that the love of Gurov and Anna Sergeevna had 'made them both better'. He altered this subsequently to 'changed them both for the better'; but still dissatisfied, finally he altered this once more to 'had changed them both', and thus avoided any overt suggestion of pointing a moral.[1]

The point is that we are not seeing the lovers changed in relation to society, but in relation to their own inner lives. Gurov is shaken out of his romantic dreaming by a sudden recognition of the grossness of others in his stratum of society: but he does not give up his job or abandon his social life. Instead, he leads a double existence, and imagines that every man's 'real, most interesting life' goes on in secret. It is this life that Chekhov is interested in, not in Gurov as a representative of his class or his time.

That Gurov and Anna Sergeevna are alone amongst their fellow-men does not point a moral: but it is where the pathos of their initial situation lies. We are not impressed by their moral superiority, but moved by their loneliness. Love is the answer to this loneliness, and there is no need to bring morality into it. Chekhov, where love was concerned, wrote from the heart, not the head.

Chekhov wrote 'The Lady with the Dog' in Yalta in the autumn of 1899, not long after he and Olga were there together (although they were not, as yet, lovers) and had made the trip back to Moscow together. In the Kokkoz valley, it will be remembered, they apparently agreed to marry: and so by then, we may presume, Chekhov knew what it was to love.

How do Gurov and Anna Sergeevna love one another? Not unnaturally, Chekhov describes the affair from the man's point of view. As one might expect, Gurov's love for Anna Sergeevna has its romantic side. It is associated with the beauty of nature, for it is helped into existence by the view of the sea at Oreanda. When, back in Moscow, Gurov thinks of Anna, he poeticizes her: the whole affair becomes the subject of a daydream, and ultimately an obsession. So, perhaps, did Chekhov's thoughts dwell on Olga Knipper when she was in Moscow and he recalled their time in Yalta and journey through an area of great natural beauty.

Olga Knipper, however, was no dream. And Anna Sergeevna is not seen solely in terms of 'poetry', even by Gurov. Forced to seek Anna out in her home town, from this point Gurov is back in reality. At the theatre he—and the reader—see her as a 'small woman who was in no way remarkable, with a cheap-looking lorgnette in her hand'. But this does not detract from her appeal for him (and it enhances her appeal for the reader). The romantic heroine has become a creature of flesh and blood, and Gurov still loves her: 'she . . . now filled his whole life, she was his joy and his grief, the sole happiness that he now desired; and to the sound of the bad orchestra, the wretched philistine violins, he mused on how fine she was. He mused and dreamed dreams.'

Gurov dreams—but dreaming is not enough for him. He has tasted happiness: the affair in Yalta was happy, in spite of Anna's sense of guilt. His love there developed from when, after Anna's self-recrimination and his irritation, they suddenly laughed together. This laugh denotes the beginning of communication: the tension relaxes and they behave normally, and find enjoyment in each other's company as well as in 'love'. Love, in fact, has come down to earth. Sex, communication, and simple companionship all play their part in it, in addition to 'poetry'.

And there the problem lies: the love-affair being rooted in reality, Anna and Gurov have to face the world's problems. Gurov, unlike Laevsky and Laptev, has found romantic love: but he also wants the companionship that Laevsky and Laptev had, and because he and Anna Sergeevna are already married, he cannot have it.

The situation, indeed the entire plot of 'The Lady with the Dog', is obvious, even banal, and its merit as a work of art lies in the artistry with which Chekhov has preserved in the story a balance between the poetic and the prosaic, and in the careful characterization, dependent upon the use of half-tones. Soviet critics have a valid point when they regard Gurov as a sort of Everyman; 'The Lady with the Dog' is an essentially simple exposition of a commonplace theme. Unlike in 'The Duel' and 'Three Years', in 'The Lady with the Dog' Chekhov has made no attempt to investigate the problems of love: the conclusion of 'The Lady with the Dog' is left really and truly open: there is no suggestion, nor have we any inkling, of what the future may bring: 'And it seemed that in a very little while an answer would be found, and a new and beautiful life would begin. And to both it was evident that the end was far, far away, and that the hardest, most complicated part was only just beginning.'

There can be no doubt but that the policy of expounding questions without presuming to answer them—that policy which Chekhov had declared to be the writer's task*—suited his style best. A full appreciation of Chekhov's work requires of the reader a certain degree of involvement, a response intellectual, or, as in the case of his love-stories, emotional, that Chekhov invites rather than commandeers. Ultimately, all depends on how Chekhov is read; but much depends on his striking the delicate balance between sentimentality and flatness.

All must surely agree that the right balance has been achieved in the final scene of 'The Lady with the Dog', which is as direct an appeal to the heart as can be found in Chekhov's fiction:

His hair was already beginning to turn grey. And it struck him as strange that he had aged so in the last few years, and lost his good looks. Her shoulders, on which he had lain his hands, were warm and shook slightly. He felt a pang of compassion for this life that was still warm and beautiful, but which would probably soon begin to fade and wither, like his own life. Why did she love him so? He had always appeared to women as something which he was not, and they had loved in him not him himself, but a creature of their own imagination, which they had sought again and again in their own lives; and then, when they perceived their mistake, they loved him all the same. And not one of them had been happy with him. Time passed, he would strike up an acquaintance, have an affair, and part, but never once had he loved; he had had everything he might wish for, only not love.

And only now, when his hair had gone grey, he had fallen in love properly, genuinely—for the first time in his life.

This passage, read in the light of what we know of the author, gains a new dimension of pathos. The history of Gurov's relationships with women is a transmutation of Chekhov's history, and the essential point of the fiction was reality for him: true love had come too late, and complete happiness—poetry and communication and companionship—was impossible.

* See letter to A. S. Suvorin, 27 October 1888, where Chekhov wrote: ' . . . you are confusing two things: solving the problem and the correct exposition of the problem. In *Anna Karenina* and [*Evgeny*] *Onegin* not a single problem is solved, but they are wholly satisfying, just because all the problems in them are correctly set out.'

Chekhov wrote that Gurov and Anna Sergeevna 'loved one another . . . as husband and wife'. But how are we to explain the incongruity of this bland phrase 'as husband and wife' in the context of Chekhov's entire *œuvre*, in which the love of husband and wife is thwarted and cheapened—virtually never, in fact, seen to exist? Gurov and Anna are, after all, husband and wife, and he does not love his wife, nor she her husband. The irony here, whether conscious or unconscious, finds its origin in Chekhov's apparently unshakeable belief that an ideal love somewhere, somehow could exist.

2

It seems then cruel indeed that he should see fate cheat him of the chance of such love. His happiness was incomplete; and it is difficult not to regard Chekhov's situation as tragic. And yet one question remains. Could Chekhov, so happy as he stood on the threshold of love, ever have crossed that threshold, even in more fortunate circumstances? Could he have lived with love instead of dreaming about it? There is of course no evidence to suggest that his feelings for Olga Knipper would have altered with the passage of time, had she stayed constantly by his side. But evidence there is that, to the last, love as Chekhov conceived it retained its distant, intangible quality.

Konstantin Stanislavsky wrote of Chekhov's last years: 'He dreamed of a new play . . . two friends, both young men, love one and the same woman. Their relationship with one another is complicated by their common love and jealousy. It ends with both of them setting off on a trip to the North Pole. The set for the last act consists of a huge ship wedged in the ice-floes. In the final scene of the play the two friends see a white phantom gliding across the ice. It is clear this is the shade of the soul of the beloved who has died far away in their country.'[2]

Despite the original visual effects this would have entailed—reminiscent of similarly unusual sound-effects in the plays that were realized—the ostensibly prosaic provincial world of those plays seems a far cry from this fantasy, and it is easy to comprehend Stanislavsky's comment that the plot was 'somehow un-Chekhovian'.

And yet it is truly, deeply, Chekhovian. This sketch of a plot shows clearly that, where love was the issue, a dissociation from facts and retreat into a dream world was for Chekhov a continuing process: that the romantic heroine could only be such in apotheosis. In the real world she provokes complications—but her shade is mysterious, beautiful, and fascinating.

And thus before we regard Chekhov's life as tragic, there is an important factor to bear in mind: the possibility that Chekhov, never to experience the reality of a normal marriage, was perhaps by this very misfortune preserved from a disillusionment in his ideal of love which might have proved more bitter than any irony of destiny. Thus the very significance—the supreme significance —which love as an ideal had for Chekhov provides us with an alternative view of his fate. It is not a tragedy: there is no victim. And Chekhov, whose dislike of self-dramatization was one of his most attractive qualities, would surely have preferred this latter view.

Q

Notes and References

Preliminary Pages

1 See, e.g. I. M. Geizer's *Chekhov i meditsina*, M., 1954.
2 There are indications that this attitude no longer prevails. In November 1965 the Vakhtangov Theatre in Moscow produced a play by L. A. Malyugin entitled *Nasmeshlivoe moe schast'e* (translated into English by Olga Franklin under the title: *How Comical my Happiness*), which portrays, on a somewhat superficial level, Chekhov's relationship to L. S. Mizinova. Shortly before his death the celebrated critic Leonid Grossman also wrote on the same subject a long article: 'Roman Niny Zarechnoi' ('The Romance of Nina Zarechnaya': see bibliography).
3 Triolet, p. 79.
4 Zaitsev, p. 160.
5 Abramovich, p. 3.
6 Middleton Murry, p. 300.
7 Yu. Sobolev used archive material relevant to this topic in his excellent: *Chekhov*, M., 1930. Grossman tells us, however, that Sobolev was obliged to use inaccurate copies of the letters which he cited. (See Grossman, p. 289.)
8 Laffitte, p. 198.
9 Letter to A. S. Suvorin, 26 December 1888.
10 Bates, p. 84.
11 Letter to A. S. Suvorin, 30 August 1891.
12 Jacoby, p. 29.
13 Bunin, 'Iz nezakonchennoi knigi o Chekhove', p. 674.
14 Excerpts from Mizinova's letters are to be found in the works of Malyugin, Grossman, and Sobolev cited above.
15 Where, in the case of certain of Chekhov's plays, two dates of publication are given, the reader is referred to *Works*, 1944–51, vol. 11, p. 630.
16 An exception to this rule has been made in the case of E. J. Simmons: references throughout to 'Simmons' refer to his biography of Chekhov and not to his biography of Tolstoy.

Chapter 1   Introductory

1 Gorky, *Izbrannye . . . stat'i*, p. 153.

2 Potapenko, p. 330.
3 See Bunin, 'Chekhov', p. 524.
4 Charques, p. 794.
5 Korolenko, p. 139.
6 I. S. Turgenev, letter to E. E. Lambert, 27 March 1859.
7 Letter to M. V. Kiseleva, 14 January 1887.
8 Letter to A. S. Suvorin, 30 May 1888.
9 Letter to Al. P. Chekhov, *c.* 20 February 1883.
10 Erenburg, p. 38.
11 Bates, p. 91.
12 Gerhardi, p. 54.
13 Abramovich, pp. 17–18.
14 Letter to L. A. Avilova, 29 April 1892. The story to which Chekhov referred was 'Ward no. 6' (*Palata no. 6*, 1892).

Chapter 2 Misogyny

1 From *Anna Karenina*.
2 Toumanova-Andronikova, p. 150.
3 Laffitte, p. 198.
4 Nevedomsky, p. 64.
5 'Oh, my Teeth!' (*Akh, zuby!* 1886.)
6 See also 'Concerning Women' (*O zhenshchinakh*, 1886).
7 'A Trivial Incident' (*Zhitei-skaya meloch*', 1886).
8 Hingley, *The Oxford Chekhov*, vol. 6, p. 9.
9 See 'Ariadna' and 'His Wife' respectively.
10 'The Pink-Stocking' (*Rosovy chulok*, 1886).
11 Satina, p. 84.
12 Letter to Al. P. Chekhov, 17 or 18 April 1883.
13 Notes, sheet 14, notes 4 and 5. The sheet was numbered by the Central State Archive of Literature and Art (*TsGALI*). There is no indication as to its date.
14 Letter to A. S. Suvorin, 8 January 1900.
15 Letter to A. S. Suvorin, 11 September 1888.
16 *Novoe vremya* was generally recognized as a reactionary right-wing paper. Chekhov, however, did not appear to let this affect his friendly feelings for Suvorin until 1898, when *Novoe vremya* ran an anti-Semitic campaign against Dreyfus, whose defence had just become a *cause célèbre* in Russia.
17 Letter to I. L. Leontiev (Shcheglov), 20 December 1888.
18 Letter to M. P. Chekhova, 22 July 1888.
19 Ibid.
20 See Winner, pp. 69–80.
21 Ibid., p. 75.
22 Toumanova-Andronikova, p. 150.
23 Notebook I, p. 50, notes 1 and 2.
24 Abramovich, pp. 19–20.
25 Hingley, *The Oxford Chekhov*, vol. 8, p. 9.
26 Shchepkina-Kupernik describes in her memoirs (p. 316) how Chekhov mimicked in disgust a woman he had heard say, as Ariadna does in the

narrator's hearing, '*Jean*, your chickie's been seasick'.

27 The italics are mine.

28 Erenburg, p. 51.

Chapter 3   Sexual Relationships

1 The 'Theatre-Manager under the Sofa' (*Antreprener pod divanom*, 1885).

2 The 'schoolmaster's wife' is a capricious young woman named Ariadna.

3 'A Living Chattel' (*Zhivoi tovar*, 1882).

4 See 'Anyuta' (1886). Sections of the text of the second part of this story were omitted from the version published in the collected works of 1900. In the earlier version, published in *Motley Stories* (*Pestrye rasskaz y*, 1886), the degradation of Anyuta is more vividly brought out.

5 Letter to A. S. Suvorin, 24 February 1893.

6 See Winner, pp. 59–60, for comments on the relationship between 'Misfortune' and *Anna Karenina*.

7 Letter to A. S. Suvorin, 11 November 1888.

8 Letter to M. P. Chekhov, between 6 and 8 April 1879.

9 Letter to N. P. Chekhov, March 1886. The editors' bowdlerization of this passage is typical of their procedure throughout editions of Chekhov's letters.

10 Letter to N. P. Chekhov, March 1886.

11 Simmons, *Tolstoy*, p. 49.

12 Gorky, *Izbrannye . . . stat'i*, p. 115.

13 Letter to A. S. Suvorin, 17 December 1890.

14 Letter to A. S. Suvorin, 27 March 1894.

15 Letter to V. A. Tikhonov, 22 February 1892.

16 M. P. Chekhov, *Vokrug Chekhova*, p. 68.

17 See, e.g., letter to A. P. Chekhov, 4–5 March 1899. (Al. P. Chekhov, *Pis'ma A. P. Chekhovu*, p. 387.)

18 Letter to V. V. Bilibin, 4 April 1886. (*LN*, p. 172.) 'Assertain': Chekhov used in jest the word *konstantirovat'*, a common misrendering of *konstatirovat'*, to assert, to establish.

19 Letter to N. A. Leikin, June 1886.

20 Letter to F. O. Shekhtel, 11 April 1887.

21 Letter to N. A. Leikin, 4 June 1887.

22 Letter to I. L. Leontiev (Shcheglov), 10 January 1888.

23 Nemirovich-Danchenko, 'Chekhov', p. 429.

24 Letter to M. P. Chekhova, 14 July 1888.

25 Nemirovich-Danchenko, 'Chekhov', p. 429.

26 For references to Chekhov's female admirers, see, e.g.: Lazarev-Gruzinsky, p. 186; M. P. Chekhova, *Iz dalekogo proshlogo*, p. 32; Altshuller, 'O

Chekhove: (Iz vospominanii)'
p. 472.

27 See above, Ch. 1, note 2.

28 Letter to A. P. Chekhov, 1891.
(Levitan, p. 98.)

29 Veresaev, p. 675.

30 Letter to N. A. Leikin, 13
August 1889.

31 Letter to A. N. Pleshcheev,
15 February 1890.

32 Letter to A. S. Suvorin, 17
March 1890.

33 Letter to A. S. Suvorin, 20
May 1890.

34 Letter to A. S. Suvorin, 9
December 1890. See also in
this connection: Simmons, p.
233, footnote pertaining to
this letter.

35 Letters to L. S. Mizinova and
A. I. Suvorina of 18 September 1897 and 10 November
1897 respectively.

36 Letter to A. S. Suvorin, 27
January 1898.

37 Letter to Al. P. Chekhov, *c.* 20
February 1883.

38 Letters to V. A. Tikhonov and
G. I. Rossolimo respectively
of 5 January 1899 and 11
October 1899.

39 Letter to M. Gorky, 15 February 1900.

40 Letter to L. A. Avilova, 23
March 1899.

41 Letter to A. N. Pleshcheev,
15 February 1890.

42 'At the Lighthouse' (*Na mayake*) was published in *Novoe
vremya*, no. 4102, 1 August
1887, p. 2.

43 Third letter to A. P. Chekhov
of December 1893 (dated by

Chekhov) (*Otd. ruk.* 331.64.34).

44 Letter to A. P. Chekhov of 17
October 1894 (*Otd. ruk.* 331.64.
34). The italics are mine.

45 Letter to A. P. Chekhov, 1
January 1895 (*Otd. ruk.* 331.64.
34). 'St. Tatyana' was an
allusion to Tanya Shchepkina-
Kupernik.

46 Second letter to A. P. Chekhov of January 1895 (*Otd. ruk.*
331.64.34).

47 Shchepkina-Kupernik, *Dni
moei zhizni*, p. 298.

48 Shchepkina-Kupernik, ibid.

49 It was probably written shortly
before 2 March 1895, for
Chekhov refers to 'a letter in
verse from Yavorskaya' in a
letter to M. P. Chekhova of
that date. Both Yavorskaya's
letters in verse seem to be
written at about the same
period (*Otd. ruk.* 331.64.34).

50 Letter to A. P. Chekhov of
March 1895 (*Otd. ruk.* 331.64.
34).

51 Letter to A. S. Suvorin, 10
January 1895.

52 Letter to A. S. Suvorin, 30
March 1895.

53 Suvorin, p. 128.

54 Letter to A. S. Suvorin, 13
April 1895.

55 Letter to A. S. Suvorin, 18
April 1895.

56 Letter to A. P. Chekhov, 23
March 1894 (*Otd. ruk.* 331.64.
34).

57 For contemporary references
to these rumours see Lazarev-
Gruzinsky, pp. 177–8; and
Avilova, p. 243.

58 See Wilczkowski, p. 322; Laffitte, p. 192.

59 M. P. Chekhov, *Vokrug Chekhova*, pp. 207–9.

60 Bunin, 'Chekhov', p. 517.

61 Letter to O. L. Knipper, 7 March 1901.

62 Letter to A. S. Suvorin, 10 November 1895 (see M. P. Chekhova, *Pis'ma A. P. Chekhova*, vol. IV, p. 417). The editors of *Works*, 1944–51, omitted the last clause in this quotation.

63 Letter to A. P. Chekhov, 15 April 1893 (Al. P. Chekhov, *Pis'ma A. P. Chekhovu*, p. 275).

64 Jacoby, pp. 29–30.

65 Letter to O. L. Knipper, 12 December 1900.

66 Letter to O. L. Knipper, 7 January 1902.

67 Letter to O. L. Knipper, 18 December 1901 (*Perepiska*, vol. 2, p. 160).

68 Letter to Al. P. Chekhov, 2 January 1889.

69 See above, p. 49.

70 Gorky, 'A. P. Chekhov', p. 509.

71 Sobolev, p. 28.

72 M. P. Chekhova, 'Moya podruga Lika', p. 214.

73 M. P. Chekhov, *Anton Chekhov i ego syuzhety*, p. 124.

74 Letter to A. S. Suvorin, 26 April 1893.

75 Letter to A. S. Suvorin, 6 December 1895. It would seem unlikely, in view of Chekhov's feelings on the subject, that he had subscribed to rumours concerning Yavorskaya and lesbianism, which she wrote to him about in March 1894, i.e. before they became intimate. The facts that we know of Yavorskaya's life—including those culled from her letters to Chekhov— make the rumours seem scarcely credible.

76 Letter to A. S. Suvorin, 11 November 1893.

77 Letter to A. S. Suvorin, 24 August 1893.

78 Letter to A. S. Suvorin, 11 November 1893.

79 Letter to Al. P. Chekhov, 2 January 1889.

80 Not however in her extant letters to Chekhov of this period.

81 Letter to E. M. Shavrova, 16 September 1891.

Chapter 4   The Romantic Heroine

1 Simmons, p. 362.

2 See Zaitsev, pp. 200–3.

3 Letter to M. P. Chekhova, 29 or 30 March 1891.

4 Letter to M. P. Chekhova, 22 July 1888.

5 Letter to M. P. Chekhova, 18 July 1889.

6 Letter to A. S. Suvorin, 7 December 1889.

7 Chizhevsky (pp. 55–6) has stated that Chekhov 'read precisely ... those plays [of Maeterlinck] ... which depict

the intrusion of blind, ruthless forces into human lives.'

8 See Triolet, p. 139.

9 Letter to E. M. Shavrova, 26 November 1895.

10 Letter to A. P. Chekhov, December 1895 (*Otd. ruk.* 331.63.4b).

11 Letter to V. V. Bilibin, 18 January 1886.

12 Letter to Bilibin, 1 February 1886 (*LN*, p. 164).

13 Letter to Bilibin, 14 February 1886 (*LN*, p. 166).

14 Letter to Bilibin, 28 February 1886 (*LN*, p. 168).

15 Letter to Bilibin, 11 March 1886 (*LN*, p. 170). By the rather clumsy use of *nec plus ultra* (preceded in Russian by the preposition *do*) Chekhov presumably meant 'for good'.

16 Letter to A. P. Chekhov, 4 November 1887 (*Otd. ruk.* 331.47.48a).

17 Letter to A. P. Chekhov, 27 June 1886 (*Otd. ruk.* 331.64.20).

18 Letter to A. P. Chekhov, 31 July–2 August 1882 (Al. P. Chekhov, *Pis'ma A. P. Chekhovu*, p. 63).

19 M. P. Chekhov, *Anton Chekhov i ego syuzhety*, p. 22.

20 M. P. Chekhov, *Vokrug Chekhova*, p. 67.

21 Lazarev-Gruzinsky, p. 185.

22 Letter to person unknown, 11 December 1888 (*LN*, p. 178).

23 Wilczkowski, p. 318.

24 L. A. Avilova, 'A. P. Chekhov v moei zhizni', *Chvvs*, pp. 200–93. All references in the present study to Avilova's

account refer to this, the only unabridged version. A shorter version of her memoirs was published in the editions of *Chekhov v vospominaniyakh sovremennikov* of 1947, 1952, and 1954. For details of the previous publications of Avilova's short memoirs (which mention no romance) see *Chvvs*, p. 724.

25 Avilova, p. 204.

26 Avilova, pp. 229–30.

27 Avilova, p. 259.

28 Letter to L. A. Avilova, 10 July 1898.

29 Letter to L. A. Avilova, 14 February 1904.

30 Avilova, pp. 212–13. See also note to p. 213, *Chvvs*, p. 727.

31 Rachmanowa, pp. 304, 336.

32 Bunin, 'O Chekhove', p. 135.

33 Magarshack translated an English edition of Avilova's memoirs entitled: *Chekhov in My Life: a Love Story* (L, 1950).

34 Letter to N. M. Lintvareva, 11 February 1889.

35 Magarshack cites as evidence for his case, *inter alia*, Chekhov's references in his correspondence, shortly before his departure for Sakhalin, to 'running away'. On 28 January 1890 in a letter to his friend M. V. Kiseleva he joked about running away from his 'future spouse'—her small daughter. Magarshack continues (p. 192): 'only a week before starting on his journey he wrote to Suvorin that he had dreamt he was running away from a wolf. The point is not the particular

dream he had (though that, too, is not without some significance), but that it should have impressed him sufficiently for him to write about it to Suvorin.' If such *minutiae* are to be cited as evidence, it may as well be pointed out that what Chekhov actually said was: 'I dreamt a wolf was chasing after me'. (*Vo sne za mnoyu gonyalsya volk*): which, in view of Chekhov's proposed trip across Siberia seems a most natural dream to have had: and the comment is typical of the sort of wry joke that Chekhov liked to make.

36 Magarshack, p. 188.

37 Ibid., p. 244. What Magarshack actually says is, Chekhov's 'excitement is well conveyed in Lidiya's description of the dinner, and that is something that she could not possibly have invented'. Presumably he means that the other diners could give the lie to Avilova's description, were it false. But since the description is virtually a transcription of Chekhov's private conversation with her, she could have invented it with impunity, though this is not to say that she did.

38 For example, Wilczkowski's theory demands that Chekhov should have actually fallen in love with Avilova at their second meeting, in 1892. Yet Chekhov's declaration as given by Avilova makes it clear (in passages missing from Wilczkowski's version of the declaration) that he loved her from their *first* meeting.

39 For example, it is not true that Chekhov's third letter to Avilova was the 'first to contain a personal note' (Simmons, p. 256). His first letter (cited above, p. 98) did so.

40 Letter to L. A. Avilova, 19 March 1892.

41 Letter to L. A. Avilova, 3 March 1892.

42 Letter to A. S. Suvorin, 7 March 1892.

43 Letter to A. S. Suvorin, 8 April 1892.

44 Simmons, pp. 285–6.

45 Avilova, p. 222.

46 See *Works*, 1944–51, vol. 16, p. 537, and the letter to L. S. Mizinova of October 1896 to which the comments on that page refer. See also the unpublished letter to Chekhov from V. F. Kommissarzhevskaya of early 1897 (date illegible) (*Otd. ruk.* 331.48.7).

47 Leikin, see 'Iz dnevnika N. A. Leikina', entry for 9 March 1895.

48 See Simmons, p. 355; and Gitovich, p. 409.

49 Avilova, p. 240.

50 Ibid., p. 250.

51 See Gitovich, pp. 432–60.

52 Leikin, p. 506.

53 Simmons, p. 388.

54 Letter to L. A. Avilova, 30 August 1898.

55 Letter to L. A. Avilova, 5 February 1899.

56 See Avilova, pp. 282–5.

57 Ibid., p. 286.

58 Letter to L. A. Avilova, 29 October 1900.

59 Letter to L. A. Avilova, 14 February 1904.

60 Avilova, p. 293.

61 See M. P. Chekhova, *Iz dalekogo proshlogo*, pp. 167–70.

62 Simmons, p. 387, fn. 6 to p. 386.

63 See *Works*, 1944–51, vol. 20, p. 332.

64 The extant correspondence dates from January 1891; earlier letters may have been lost.

65 Letter to L. S. Mizinova, 11 January 1891.

66 Letter to L. S. Mizinova, 17 May 1891.

67 K. I. Mamuna was the countess to whom Misha Chekhov was briefly engaged.

68 Letter to M. P. Chekhova, 16 January 1891.

69 Letter to A. P. Chekhov, 13 January 1891 (*Otd. ruk.* 331.52.2a).

70 Letters to L. S. Mizinova of 17 May 1891; June–July 1891; November 1892. 'Guniyadi-Yanos' was the name of a brand of mineral water.

71 Letter to A. P. Chekhov, 26 June 1892 (*Otd. ruk.* 331.52.2a).

72 Letter to A. P. Chekhov, 13 January 1891 (*Otd. ruk.* 331.52.2a).

73 Letter to L. S. Mizinova, 12 June 1891.

74 Letter to A. P. Chekhov, 17 June 1891 (*Otd. ruk.* 331.52.2a).

75 Letter to A. P. Chekhov, 2 July 1892 (*Otd. ruk.* 331.52.2a).

76 Letter to L. S. Mizinova, June–July 1891.

77 Letter to A. P. Chekhov, 21 January 1892 (*Otd. ruk.* 331.52.2a).

78 Letter to A. P. Chekhov, 17 June 1891 (*Otd. ruk.* 331.52.2a).

79 Letter to A. P. Chekhov, 9 January 1891 (*Otd. ruk.* 331.52.2a).

80 M. P. Chekhova, *Iz dalekogo proshlogo*, p. 143.

81 Shchepkina-Kupernik, *Dni moei zhizni*, pp. 272, 279.

82 M. P. Chekhov, *Vokrug Chekhova*, p. 196.

83 M. P. Chekhov, 'Anton Chekhov na kanikulakh', p. 95.

84 Rachmanowa, p. 299.

85 Letter to A. P. Chekhov, 18 June 1892 (*Otd. ruk.* 331.52.2a).

86 See Grossman, p. 232.

87 Letter to L. S. Mizinova, 23 June 1892.

88 Letter to A. P. Chekhov, 13 July 1892 (*Otd. ruk.* 331.52.2a).

89 Letter to L. S. Mizinova, 29 March 1892. Chekhov called Lika (occasionally) 'Melita', Levitan 'Phaon' and Kuvshinnikova 'Sappho' after the characters in Grillparzer's *Sappho*, since Levitan was attracted to Lika as well as to his mistress.

90 Letter to L. S. Mizinova, 27 March 1892.

91 Letter to L. S. Mizinova, 28 June 1892. Chekhov called Lika 'Canteloupe' because she wore a melon-coloured hat.

92 Letter to L. S. Mizinova, 14

January 1893. This letter does not suggest that Chekhov was interested in Avilova at this time (see above, p. 103).

93 Letter to A. P. Chekhov, 13 July 1892 (*Otd. ruk.* 331.52.2a).

94 Letter to A. P. Chekhov, 29 September 1892 (*Otd. ruk.* 331.52.2a).

95 Letter to A. P. Chekhov, 26 November 1892 (*Otd. ruk.* 331.52.2a).

96 Letter to A. P. Chekhov, 21 July 1893 (*Otd. ruk.* 331.52.2b).

97 Letter to A. P. Chekhov, 28 July 1893 (*Otd. ruk.* 331.52.2b).

98 Letter to A. P. Chekhov, 22 August 1893 (*Otd. ruk.* 331.52.2b).

99 Letter to A. P. Chekhov, 2 November 1893 (*Otd. ruk.* 331.52.2b).

100 Letter to L. S. Mizinova, 19 December 1893.

101 Letter to A. P. Chekhov, May 1894 (*Otd. ruk.* 331.50.11).

102 Letter to A. P. Chekhov, 23 May 1894 (*Otd. ruk.* 331.50.11).

103 See Drozdova, p. 217.

104 Letter to A. P. Chekhov, 4 October 1897 (*Otd. ruk.* 331.52.2g).

105 Letter to A. P. Chekhov, 20 February 1898 (*Otd. ruk.* 331.52.2d).

106 Letter to A. P. Chekhov, 23 October 1898 (*Otd. ruk.* 331.52.2d).

107 Wilczkowski (see pp. 315–19) uses the Lika–Nina connection as evidence for Chekhov's having loved Avilova. His theory is that, whereas Che-

khov, judging by his fiction, seemed guiltily obsessed with the theme of masculine egoism in the years 1887–8, when, later, he came to write *The Seagull* he glossed over his true part in the affair—'*un rôle peu reluisant*'—i.e. his shameful act of abandoning Lika to Potapenko. Wilczkowski concludes that only an absorbing passion —that is, Avilova—could have permitted Chekhov thus to expose a friend's wretchedness with apparent abnegation of responsibility. The flaw in this theory is the assumption that Chekhov had an obligation towards Lika and that he ought to have felt especially guilty (see above, p. 161).

108 Nemirovich-Danchenko, 'Chekhov', p. 593.

109 Letter to A. P. Chekhov, 1 November 1896 (*Otd. ruk.* 331.52.2v).

110 Grossman, p. 220.

111 Ibid., p. 243.

112 Letter to L. S. Mizinova, 18 September 1894.

113 Grossman, p. 243.

114 M. P. Chekhova, *Pis'ma k bratu*, p. 26.

115 Drozdova (p. 217) writes that she remembers Lika as always having had a cigarette in her mouth.

116 Letter to A. P. Chekhov, 22 December 1901 (*Perepiska*, vol. 1, pp. 169–70).

117 Letter to L. S. Mizinova, 23 July 1893.

118 Letter to A. P. Chekhov, 28

July 1893 (*Otd. ruk.* 331.52.2b).

119 Letter to A. P. Chekhov, 1 August 1897 (*Otd. ruk.* 331. 52.2g).

120 Letter to M. P. Chekhov, 26 October 1898.

121 See above, p. xv.

122 Lika in fact suffered from ill-health—principally, a cough—in the 1890s, as her letters to Chekhov reveal. However, she lived on, an émigrée in France, till 1937, i.e. until her latter sixties.

123 Shchepkina-Kupernik, *Dni moei zhizni*, pp. 272, 279.

124 Letter to M. P. Chekhova, 7–19 April 1887.

125 Letter to A. P. Chekhov, October 1898 (*Otd. ruk.* 331. 48.7).

126 Letter to V. F. Kommissar-zhevskaya, 2 November 1898.

127 Letter to V. F. Kommissar-zhevskaya, 27 January 1903.

128 Letter to A. P. Chekhov, January 1903 (*Otd. ruk.* 331. 48.7).

129 Letter to A. P. Chekhov, August 1900 (*Otd. ruk.* 331. 48.7).

130 Brisson, p. 50. In this book the importance of the supposed liaison is emphasized by the fact that Brisson mentions none of the other women in Chekhov's life save his wife.

131 Letter to L. S. Mizinova, 29 January 1900.

132 M. P. Chekhova, *Iz dalekogo proshlogo*, p. 142.

133 Letter to A. S. Suvorin, 30 May 1888.

134 Letter to Al. P. Chekhov, 25 December 1887.

135 Letter to A. S. Suvorin, 18 November 1888.

136 There are indications however that Olga Knipper may have had a childlike sense of fun: see above, p. 131.

137 Simmons, p. 280.

138 Letter to M. P. Chekhova, 8 June 1904.

Chapter 5 Love

1 Letter to A. S. Suvorin, 18 October 1892.

2 Letter to E. M. Shavrova, 2 December 1896.

3 Suvorin, p. 165.

4 See above, p. 120.

5 Letter to Al. P. Chekhov, 28 August 1888.

6 Wilczkowski, p. 313.

7 Abramovich, p. 5.

8 Letter to A. S. Suvorin, 23 October 1889.

9 Collins, pp. 40–1.

10 Letter to A. S. Suvorin, 8 October 1898.

11 Letter to O. L. Knipper, 17 June 1899 (*LN*, p. 225).

12 Letter to A. P. Chekhov, 19–28 January 1900 (*Perepiska*, vol. 1, p. 122).

13 Letter to O. L. Knipper, 9 September 1899.

14 Letter to O. L. Knipper, 2 January 1901.

15 Telegram to O. L. Knipper, 19 February 1901.

16 Letter to O. L. Knipper, 29 October 1901.

17 Letter to O. L. Knipper, 14 December 1902.

18 Letter to O. L. Knipper, 17 February 1904.

19 Collins, p. 41.

20 See above, p. 100.

21 Altshuller, 'Eshche o Chekhove', p. 684.

22 Bunin, 'Iz nezakonchennoi knigi o Chekhove', p. 653.

23 Altshuller, 'Eshche o Chekhove', p. 694.

24 Letter to A. P. Chekhov, 16 August 1900.

25 Letter to O. L. Knipper, 20 September 1902.

26 Rachmanowa (p. 338) suggests that Chekhov intended Lidiya Avilova to 'recognize herself' in the character of Masha. The parallel would, however, seem considerably weaker even than that between Avilova and Luganovich in 'About Love'; moreover, Chekhov had not seen Avilova for over a year when he wrote *Three Sisters*, while his love-affair with Knipper was then at its zenith. It seems scarcely credible that he should write a part for her, and simultaneously have the image of Avilova in his mind.

27 Letter to O. L. Knipper, 28 September 1900.

28 Letter to O. L. Knipper, 21 January 1901.

29 Ibid.

30 Notebook I, p. 39, note 1.

31 Bayley, p. 232.

32 See Shestov, *passim*.

33 The theory is that of Dr. Dorn in *The Seagull*.

Chapter 6   The Cynical Hero

1 Letter to N. A. Leikin, 2 September 1887.

2 See Serebrov (Tikhonov), p. 655.

3 See above, p. 69.

4 See above, p. 8.

5 Letter to M. V. Kiseleva, 14 January 1887.

6 Wilczkowski, p. 314.

7 Shestov, p. 31.

8 Letter to A. S. Suvorin, 23 December 1888.

9 Letter to A. S. Suvorin, 26 December 1888.

10 Letter to A. S. Suvorin, 30 December 1888.

11 See 'A Nasty Story' (*Skvernaya istoriya*, 1882) and 'A Joker' (*Komik*, 1884).

12 'The Last of the Female Mohicans' (*Poslednyaya mogikansha*, 1885).

13 'The Turkey-Cock' (*Indeisky petukh*, 1885).

14 Except, perhaps, when she crosses the darkened stage with a candle in Act 3, 'à la Lady Macbeth', as Chekhov put it (see letter to K. S. Stanislavsky, 2 January 1901).

15 A *kulak* was a rich peasant who wielded economic power over other peasants.

16 Notebook I, p. 132, note 14.

17 Letter to M. V. Kiseleva, 21 February 1887.

18 Letter to A. P. Chekhov, 4 November 1887 (*Otd. ruk.* 331.47.48a).

19 Letter to Vl. I. Nemirovich-Danchenko, 26 November 1896. P. A. Sergeenko was a writer and knew Chekhov since their schooldays together in Taganrog.

20 Derman, *Anton Pavlovich Chekhov: kritiko-biografichesky ocherk*, p. 32.

21 O. L. Knipper, 'The Last Years', p. 698.

22 Kachalov, p. 446.

23 Chukovsky, p. 34.

24 Kovalevsky, p. 447.

25 Shchukin, p. 455.

26 Letter to A. P. Chekhov, 18 February 1888. (Al. P. Chekhov, *Pis'ma A. P. Chekhovu*, p. 196).

27 Letter to A. P. Chekhov, 18 December 1889 (see Toumanova, p. 171).

28 Potapenko, p. 307.

29 Nemirovich-Danchenko, 'Chekhov', p. 425.

30 Potapenko, p. 310.

31 See Bunin, 'O Chekhove', p. 73.

32 Suvorin, p. 118. See also Leontiev (Shcheglov), p. 484.

33 Zaitsev, p. 198.

34 Letter to A. P. Chekhov, December 1895 (*Otd. ruk.* 331.63.46).

35 Kuprin, p. 560.

36 Letter to M. V. Kiseleva, 5 April 1888.

37 Letter to E. M. Shavrova, 18 or 19 April 1896.

38 Letter to E. M. Shavrova, 2 March 1897.

39 Letter to T. L. Shchepkina-Kupernik, end of September 1895.

40 Letter to T. L. Shchepkina-Kupernik, 30 January 1900.

41 Letter to A. A. Khotyaintseva, 26 November 1897.

42 Letter to A. M. Evreinova, 10 March 1889.

43 Letter to A. P. Chekhov, 20 September 1894 (*Otd. ruk.* 331.52.2b).

44 Ladyzhensky, p. 306.

45 Letter to A. P. Chekhov, 29 April 1892 (*Otd. ruk.* 331.52.2a).

46 Letter to A. P. Chekhov, 22 August 1893 (*Otd. ruk.* 331.52.2b).

47 See Wilczkowski, p. 316; Grossman, p. 246.

48 Letter to A. P. Chekhov, 15 December 1894 (*Otd. ruk.* 331.52.2b).

49 Letter to A. P. Chekhov, 3 October (new style) 1894 (*Otd. ruk.* 331.52.2b).

50 Letter to A. P. Chekhov, 9 October (new style) 1894 (*Otd. ruk.* 331.52.2b).

51 Letter to M. P. Chekhova, 2 October 1894.

52 Letter to A. P. Chekhov, 15 March 1894 (*Otd. ruk.* 331.52.2b). Masha Chekhova in her memoirs (*Iz dalekogo proshlogo*, p. 147) states that Lika wrote in this letter that she was 'twice rejected' by Chekhov. In the original of the letter the words '*Ne zabyvaite otvergnutuyu Vami*' (literally: 'Don't forget the [woman] rejected by you')

are followed by a virtually indecipherable scrawl which does not however appear to read either '*dva raza*' or '*dva-zhdy*' ('two times', 'twice'). Masha may therefore have been extrapolating from something Chekhov might have told her concerning himself and Lika.

53 Letter to L. S. Mizinova, 27 March 1894.

54 Letter to A. P. Chekhov, 7 October 1893 (*Otd. ruk.* 331.52.2b).

55 Letter to A. P. Chekhov, December 1893 (*Otd. ruk.* 331.52.2b).

56 Letter to A. P. Chekhov, 14 July 1894 (*Otd. ruk.* 331.52.2b).

57 Letter to A. P. Chekhov, 20 September 1894 (*Otd. ruk.* 331.52.2b).

58 Letter to A. P. Chekhov, December 1893 (*Otd. ruk.* 331.52.2b).

59 See letter to A. P. Chekhov, 3 April 1894 (*Otd. ruk.* 331.52.2b).

60 Letter to J. A. Legras, 19 May 1894.

61 See letters to A. P. Chekhov of 3 April and 14 August 1894 respectively (*Otd. ruk.* 331.52.2b). In the earlier letter Lika gave Chekhov her Paris address, including the words 'Mme. Mizinoff', and wrote: 'Here everyone thinks I'm married—Varya Eberle showed the landlady your picture, saying it was my husband. She insisted on

seeing him, so it had to be.'

62 Nemirovich-Danchenko, 'Chekhov', p. 426.

63 Bragin, p. 67.

64 Letter to A. P. Chekhov, before 15 June 1893 (Al. P. Chekhov, *Pis'ma A. P. Chekhovu*, p. 283).

65 Bragin, p. 5.

66 Aliger, pp. 34–5.

67 Bragin, p. 5.

68 Chekhova, *Iz dalekogo proshlogo*, pp. 34–5.

69 Paustovsky, pp. 41–2.

70 Chekhova, *Iz dalekogo proshlogo*, p. 44.

71 Ibid., p. 76.

72 Ibid., p. 43.

73 Letter to A. P. Chekhov, 24 May 1901 (*Pis'ma k bratu*, pp. 182–3). 'You will always be able to marry' may mean that Masha had in mind the possibility of Olga's becoming pregnant.

74 Letter to A. P. Chekhov, 28 May 1901 (*Iz dalekogo proshlogo*, p. 244).

75 Letter to O. L. Knipper, 30 May 1901 (Bragin, p. 139).

76 See letter to A. P. Chekhov, 5 February 1899 (*Pis'ma k bratu*, p. 103).

77 See letter to A. P. Chekhov, 16 June 1901 (*Pis'ma k bratu*, p. 187).

78 Letter to A. P. Chekhov, 19 August 1904 (*Otd. ruk.* 331.77.9).

79 Letter to M. P. Chekhova, 4 June 1901 (*LN*, p. 236).

80 Bunin, 'Iz nezakonchennoi knigi o Chekhove', p. 652.

81 Letter to A. S. Suvorin, 10 October 1888.

82 Letter to A. S. Suvorin, 11 April 1890.

83 Letter to A. S. Suvorin, 22 October 1896.

84 Letter to L. S. Mizinova, 18 September 1894.

85 Letter to A. S. Suvorin, 18 October 1892.

86 Rachmanowa, p. 422.

87 Letter to M. P. Chekhova, 28 June 1904.

88 Letter to A. P. Chekhov, 30 May 1903 (*Pis'ma k bratu*, p. 216).

89 Letter to M. P. Chekhova, 7 June 1903.

90 Letter to O. L. Knipper, 16 August 1948 (Bragin, p. 145). Masha died in 1957.

91 Fausset, p. 316.

92 The correspondence was published in Derman's editions, 1934 and 1936.

93 Letter to O. L. Knipper, 1 September 1902.

94 Letter to A. P. Chekhov, 13 February 1903 (*Otd. ruk.* 331. 76.31).

95 They are fully given in Simmons, pp. 573–5.

96 Letter to F. D. Batyushkov, 4 June 1902.

97 Letter to Vl. I. Nemirovich-Danchenko, 16 June 1902.

98 Letter to M. P. Chekhova, 17 June 1902.

99 Letter to O. L. Knipper, 18 June 1902.

100 Letter to M. Gorky, 24 June 1902.

101 Letter to O. L. Knipper, 17 August 1902.

102 Letter to O. L. Knipper, 27 August 1902.

103 Letter to O. L. Knipper, 1 September 1902.

104 Letter to O. L. Knipper, 27 August 1902.

105 Letter to A. P. Chekhov, 27 August 1902 (*Perepiska*, vol. 2, p. 468).

106 Letter to A. P. Chekhov, 22 August 1902 (*Perepiska*, vol. 2, pp. 454–5).

107 Letter to A. P. Chekhov, 28 August 1902 (*Perepiska*, vol. 2, pp. 470–1).

108 Letter to A. P. Chekhov, 29 August 1902 (*Perepiska*, vol. 2, p. 475).

109 Letter to O. L. Knipper, 1 September 1902.

110 Letter to A. P. Chekhov, 2 September 1902 (*Perepiska*, vol. 2, p. 483).

111 Letter to A. P. Chekhov, 7 September 1902 (*Perepiska*, vol. 2, p. 493).

112 Letter to A. P. Chekhov, 24 August 1900 (*Perepiska*, vol. 1, p. 172).

113 Letter to O. L. Knipper, 30 September 1899. Chekhov used the word *zmeenysh*, which as well as meaning 'little snake' has the figurative meaning that 'viper' has in English.

114 Letter to V. M. Sobolevsky, 9 June 1901.

115 Letter to O. L. Knipper, 2 January 1901.

116 Letter to O. L. Knipper, 7 November 1901.

117 Simmons, p. 553.
118 Letter to A. P. Chekhov, 15 January 1903 (*Otd. ruk.* 331. 76.29).
119 Letter to A. P. Chekhov, 26 October 1901 (*Perepiska*, vol. 2, p. 11).
120 Letter to A. P. Chekhov, 22 November 1901 (*Perepiska*, vol. 2, p. 90).
121 Letter to A. P. Chekhov, 8 December 1901 (*Perepiska*, vol. 2, p. 135).
122 Letter to O. L. Knipper, 12 December 1901.
123 Letter to A. P. Chekhov, 27 December 1901 (*Perepiska*, vol. 2, p. 185).
124 Letter to A. P. Chekhov, 14 January 1902 (*Perepiska*, vol. 2, p. 242).
125 Letter to O. L. Knipper, 20 January 1902.
126 Letter to A. P. Chekhov, 23 January 1902 (*Perepiska*, vol. 2, p. 266).
127 Letter to A. P. Chekhov, 24 February 1903 (*Otd. ruk.* 331. 76.31).
128 Letter to A. P. Chekhov, 15 April 1904 (*Otd. ruk.* 331.77.8).
129 Letter to O. L. Knipper, 20 April 1904.
130 Letter to O. L. Knipper, 20 April 1904.
131 Letter to A. P. Chekhov, 17 April 1901 (*Perepiska*, vol. 1, p. 380).
132 Letter to A. P. Chekhov, 18 January 1902 (*Perepiska*, vol. 2, p. 251).
133 Letter to A. P. Chekhov, 23

October 1903 (*Oktyabr'*, no. 7, 1939, p. 180).
134 Letter to A. S. Suvorin, 23 March 1895.
135 Simmons, *Tolstoy*, p. 146.

Chapter 7   *Marriage*

1 Letter to M. M. Kovalevsky, 10 February (new style) 1898 (*LN*, p. 218).
2 Letter to A. S. Suvorin, 18 October 1892.
3 Letter to M. V. Kiseleva, 21 September 1886.
4 Letter to E. M. Shavrova, 29 October 1897.
5 Letter to M. P. Chekhova, 8 December 1898.
6 Letter to A. S. Suvorin, 10 May 1891.
7 Letter to A. S. Suvorin, 7 December 1889.
8 Letter to F. O. Shekhtel, 17 May 1887.
9 Letter to N. A. Leikin, 21 June 1888.
10 Letter to I. L. Leontiev (Shcheglov), 18 April, 1888.
11 Letter to A. S. Lazarev-Gruzinsky, 26 June 1888.
12 Ronald Bryden in an article entitled 'Chekhov: secret of *The Seagull*' has tentatively put forward the hypothesis that Chekhov had an illegitimate daughter. The source of Bryden's speculations is the presence in *The Seagull*, *Three Sisters*, and *The Cherry Orchard*

of a young girl who seeks comfort in vain from an older man. Bryden suggests that this recurring theme reflects Chekhov's guilt at having a child whom he did not acknowledge. While his hypothesis is at least as plausible as much that has been written about Chekhov with less diffidence, there is, as Bryden virtually admits, no evidence at all to support it.

13 Letter to A. S. Suvorin, 17 April 1889.

14 Letter to A. S. Suvorin, 4 May 1889.

15 Letter to N. A. Leikin, 22 May 1889 (see above, p. 99).

16 Letter to A. S. Suvorin, 10 November 1895 (see above, p. 62).

17 Ibid.

18 Letter to A. S. Suvorin, 21 January 1895.

19 'The tale of how Ivan Ivanovich quarrelled with Ivan Nikiforovich.'

20 Letter to A. P. Chekhov, 5–6 September 1887 (*Pis'ma A. P. Chekhovu*, p. 171).

21 Simmons, p. 310.

22 Notebook I, p. 121, note 14.

23 Letter to A. S. Suvorin, 9 June 1889.

24 Letter to A. S. Suvorin, 16 December 1897.

25 Letter to A. P. Chekhov, before 15 June 1893 (*Pis'ma A. P. Chekhovu*, p. 283).

26 Letter to A. P. Chekhov, 22 August 1893 (*Otd. ruk.* 331.52.2b). On an earlier occasion Lika had written virtually the same thing: 'You need people only as long as they can divert you in your boredom, but when you're not bored you forget about them completely . . .' (letter to A. P. Chekhov of 3 August 1892 [*Otd. ruk.* 331.52.2a]).

27 Elton, p. 20.

28 Ibid.

29 Hingley, *Chekhov*, p. 99.

30 Letter to A. P. Chekhov, 11 September 1904 (*Otd. ruk.* 331.77.9).

31 See Rachmanowa, Chapter XVII.

32 See above, p. 129.

33 Letter to O. L. Knipper, 14 January 1901.

34 Letter to O. L. Knipper, 22 April 1901.

35 Letter to O. L. Knipper, 20 February 1901.

36 Letter to A. P. Chekhov, 20 January 1901 (*Perepiska*, vol. 1, p. 344).

37 Letter to A. P. Chekhov, 9 March 1901 (*Perepiska*, vol. 1, pp. 353–4).

38 Letter to A. P. Chekhov, 21 March 1901 (*Perepiska*, vol. 1, p. 370).

39 Letter to O. L. Knipper, 11 March 1901.

40 Letter to O. L. Knipper, 27 September 1900.

41 Letter to O. L. Knipper, 26 April 1901.

42 Simmons, p. 529.

43 See, e.g., Yakovlev, p. 601, and Kovalevsky, p. 450.

44 Letter to O. L. Knipper, 2 May 1901.

R

45 Letter to O. L. Knipper, 1 March 1901.

46 Letter to O. L. Knipper, 7 March 1901.

47 Letter to O. L. Knipper, 11 March 1901.

48 Letter to O. L. Knipper, 16 March 1901.

49 Simmons, p. 529.

50 Letter to O. L. Knipper, 17 March 1902.

51 See above, p. 175.

52 Letter to O. L. Knipper, 24 January 1903.

53 Letter to A. P. Chekhov, 26 March 1904 (*Otd. ruk.* 331.77.7).

54 Letter to A. P. Chekhov, 11 September 1904 (*Otd. ruk.* 331.77.9).

55 Letter to O. L. Knipper, 25 August 1901.

56 Letter to O. L. Knipper, 30 November 1901.

57 Letter to O. L. Knipper, 2 October 1903.

58 Notebook I, p. 111, note 11.

59 See letter to O. L. Knipper, 12 November 1903.

60 See letter to O. L. Knipper, 17 November 1903.

61 See letter to O. L. Knipper, 15 March 1904.

62 Letter to O. L. Knipper, 21 March 1903.

63 Veresaev, p. 675.

64 Letter to O. L. Knipper, 9 September 1899.

65 Letter to O. L. Knipper, 30 October 1899.

66 Letter to O. L. Knipper, 21 October 1903.

67 Letter to O. L. Knipper, 31 January 1902.

68 Letter to A. P. Chekhov, 8 November 1901 (*Perepiska*, vol. 2, p. 51).

69 Letter to O. L. Knipper, 20 August 1900.

70 Letter to O. L. Knipper, 25 December 1902.

71 Letter to O. L. Knipper, 17 December 1902. The lines run in Russian:
   Vot golovu sklonil ya na ruki.
   Gluboko
   Vzgrustnilos' o tebe. A ty
   . . . ty tak daleko!
   (Poem by A. M. Fedorov)

72 See Sherman, p. 134.

73 Fausset, p. 315.

74 Letter to O. L. Knipper, 22 April 1904.

75 Letter to O. L. Knipper, 15 December 1902.

76 Letter to M. P. Chekhova, 2 June 1901.

Chapter 8   *The Lady with the Dog*

1 Vinogradova, p. 140.

2 Stanislavsky, p. 415.

Bibliography

The following bibliography is in no sense a comprehensive bibliography of works concerning Chekhov. The number of books and articles on Chekhov is enormous, and in the West it increases on the occasion of almost every new production of a Chekhov play. The present list is confined to books, articles, and archive material cited in the text of this study, and to those that were of use, or of especial interest, in connection with the topic under consideration. Several bibliographies, which between them cover a very wide range of material on most aspects of Chekhov's life and work, are cited in Section I below.

Titles in Sections I and IV are listed according to the name of the author or editor, in alphabetical order. A few works, the editors of which are not named, are listed separately in Section IV (ii). Dates are those of the editions consulted.

Many of the articles cited in the text constitute part of a collection of articles, or of articles and other material, which proved useful *in toto*. Such collections are listed under the name of the editor—with one exception, in Section IV (ii). However, to facilitate reference, it has seemed desirable also to list the articles in question individually, under the name of the author. This has inevitably involved the reiteration of certain titles, but not, it is hoped, to any undue extent. Use has been made, where appropriate, of the abbreviated titles used throughout the text. (See above, p. xxi.) All translations are from the Russian unless otherwise indicated.

I.   Bibliographies and Archive Guides

Aleksandrov, B. I.: *Seminarii po Chekhovu*, M, 1957, pp. 53–65.

Elizarova, M. E.: *Tvorchestvo Chekhova i voprosy realizma kontsa XIX veka*, M, 1958, pp. 195–9.

Heifetz, A.: *Chekhov in English: a list of works by and about him*, N.Y., 1949.

Klensky, M. P.: 'Bibliografiya', *A. P. Chekhov: zateryannye proizvedeniya, neizdannye pis'ma, vospominaniya*, ed. by M. D. Belyaev and A. S. Dolinin, LG, 1925, pp. 253–301.

Laffitte, S.: 'Chekhov vo Frantsii', *LN*, pp. 743–6.

Leitnekker, E. E.: *Rukopisi A. P. Chekhova: opisanie*, M, 1938.

—— *Arkhiv A. P. Chekhova: annotirovannoe opisanie pisem k A. P. Chekhovu;* vol. 1, M, 1939; vol. 2, M, 1941.

Masanova, I. F.: *Chekhoviana*, vol. 1, M, 1929.

Malova, M. M.: *Rukopisi Chekhova v sobranii Instituty Literatury (Pushkinskogo doma)*, M, 1947.

Nechaev, V. P. (ed., with Yu. M. Murkina): *A. P. Chekhov: rukopisi, pis'ma, biograficheskie dokumenty. Opisanie materialov Tsentralnogo Gosudarstvennogo Archiva literatury i iskusstva*, M, 1960.

Polotskaya, E. A.: *Anton Pavlovich Chekhov: rekomendatel'ny ukazatel' literatury*, M, 1955.

—— 'Bibliografiya vospominanii o Chekhove', *LN*, pp. 881–928.

Sakharova, E. M.: *Anton Pavlovich Chekhov: 1860–1904*, M, 1954.

Shereshevskaya, M. A.: 'Angliiskie pisateli i kritiki o Chekhove', *LN*, see pp. 804–32.*

Sobolev, Yu.: *Chekhov: stat'i, materialy, bibliografiya*, M, 1930, pp. 307–39.

Winner, T.: 'Chekhov v Soedinennykh Shtatakh Ameriki', *LN*, see pp. 796–800.*

Yachnin, R.: *The Chekhov Centennial. Chekhov in English: a selective list by and about him, 1949–1960*, N.Y., 1960.

II.   Archive Material

Use was made of the following material from the Chekhov archive (*fond* 331) in the *Otdel rukopisei* of the Lenin Library, Moscow: Letters to A. P. Chekhov from: E. I. Efros; M. V. Kiseleva; O. L. Knipper; V. F. Kommissarzhevskaya; I. L. Leontiev (Shcheglov); A. A. Lesova; L. S. Mizinova; A. A. Pokhlebina; T. L. Shchepkina-Kupernik; E. M. Shavrova; L. B. Yavorskaya.

III.   Works and Letters of A. P. Chekhov

Polnoe sobranie sochinenii i pisem A. P. Chekhova, ed. by S. D. Balukhaty, V. P. Potemkin, N.

---

* Although these pages do not constitute a formal bibliography, details of many titles are given.

S. Tikhonov, A. M. Egolin, vols. 1–20, M, 1944–51.

Pis'ma A. P. Chekhova, ed. by M. P. Chekhova, vols. 1–6, M, 1912–16.

Perepiska A. P. Chekhova i O. L. Knipper, ed. by A. B. Derman, vol. 1, M, 1934; vol. 2, M, 1936.

'Perepiska A. P. Chekhova i O. L. Knipper: 1903–1904' (incomplete), ed. by A. B. Derman, *Novy mir*, 1938, no. 10, pp. 271–85; no. 11, pp. 232–59; no. 12, pp. 257–70. *Oktyabr'*, M, 1938, no. 7, pp. 171–207. *Teatr*, M, 1960, no. 1, pp. 152–6.

IV. Biography, Memoirs, Criticism, etc.

Abramovich, N. Ya.: 'Chelovechesky put' ', *Yubileiny chekhovsky sbornik*, M, 1910, pp. 1–28.

Aldanov, M.: 'Reflections on Chekhov', trans. by I. Estrin, *Russian Review*, N.Y., 1955, vol. 14, pp. 83–92.

Aliger, M.: 'V gostyakh u Marii Pavlovny', *Khozyaika chekhovskogo doma*, ed. by S. G. Bragin, Simferopol', 1965, pp. 30–9.

Altshuller, I. N.: 'O Chekhove (Iz vospominanii)', *Sovremennye zapiski*, Paris, 1930, pp. 470–85. —— 'Eshche o Chekhove', *LN*, pp. 681–702.

Arseniev, K.: 'Belletristy poslednogo vremeni', *Vestnik Evropy*, SPB, 1887, vol. 12, pp. 766–76.

Avilova, L. A.: 'A. P. Chekhov v moei zhizni', *Chvvs*, pp. 200–93.

Balukhaty, S. D.: *Chekhov dramaturg*, LG, 1936.

Bates, H. E.: *The Modern Short Story: a critical survey*, Chapter 4: 'Tchehov and Maupassant', L, 1941, pp. 72–94.

Bayley, J.: *Tolstoy and the Novel*, L, 1966.

Belyaev, Yu. D.: *L. B. Yavorskaya: kritiko-biografichesky etyud*. SPB, 1900.

Berdnikov, G. P.: *Chekhov dramaturg*, M, 1957. —— *A. P. Chekhov: ideinye i tvorcheskie iskaniya*, LG, 1970.

Bicilli, P. M.: *Anton P. Čechov: das Werk und sein Stil*, trans. by V. Sieveking, Munich, 1966.

Bragin, S. G. (ed.): *Khozyaika chekhovskogo doma*, Simferopol', 1965.

Brewster, D.: *East–West Passage: a study in literary relationships*, L, 1954.

Brisson, P.: *Tchékov et sa vie*, Paris, 1955.

Bruford, W. H.: *Chekhov and his Russia: a sociological study*, L, 1948. —— *Anton Chekhov*, L. 1957.

Bryden, R.: 'Chekhov: secret of *The Seagull*', *Observer Magazine*, L, 1970, 31 May, pp. 10–20.

Bulgakov, S. N.: *Chekhov kak myslitel'*, Kiev, 1905.

Bunin, I. A.: *O Chekhove: nezakonchennaya rukopis'*, N.Y., 1955. —— 'Chekhov', *Chvvs*, pp. 512–38. —— 'Iz nezakonchennoi knigi o Chekhove', *LN*, pp. 639–80.

Carr, E. H.: 'Chekhov: twenty-five years after', *The Spectator*, L, 1929, vol. 143, pp. 72–3.

Charques, R. D.: 'Books and Writers', *The Spectator*, L, 1950, vol. 184, p. 744.

Chekhov, Al. P.: *Pis'ma A. P. Chekhovu ego brata Aleksandra Chekhova*, ed. by I. S. Ezhov, M, 1939.

—— 'Na mayake', *Novoe vremya*, SPB, 1 Aug. 1887, no. 4102, p. 2.

Chekhov, M. P.: *Anton Chekhov i ego syuzhety*, M, 1923.

—— *Vokrug Chekhova*, M, 1959.

—— 'Anton Chekhov na kanikulakh', *Chvvs*, pp. 75–97.

Chekhova, M. P.: *Pis'ma k bratu A. P. Chekhovu*, M, 1954.

—— 'Moya podruga Lika', *Moskva*, M, 1958, no. 6, pp. 211–21.

—— *Iz dalekogo proshlogo*, M, 1960.

Chizhevsky, D.: 'Chekhov in the Development of Russian literature', *Chekhov: a collection of critical essays*, ed. by R. L. Jackson, New Jersey, 1967, pp. 49–56.

Chukovsky, K. I.: *Chekhov the Man*, trans. by P. Rose, L, 1945.

Collins, H. P.: 'Chekhov: the last phase', *Contemporary Review*, L, 1954, vol. 186, pp. 37–41.

Derman, A. B.: *Tvorchesky portret Chekhova*, M, 1929.

—— *Anton Pavlovich Chekhov: kritiko-biografichesky ocherk*, M, 1939.

—— (ed.): *A. P. Chekhov: sbornik dokumentov i materialov*, M, 1947.

Drozdova, M. T.: 'Iz vospominanii ob A. P. Chekhove', *Novy mir*, M, 1954, no. 7, pp. 211–22.

Eekman, T. (ed.): *Anton Čechov: 1860–1960*, Leiden, 1960.

Elpatevsky, S. Ya.: 'Anton Pavlovich Chekhov', *Chvvs*, pp. 570–82.

Elton, O.: *Chekhov* (the Taylorian lecture), Oxford, 1929.

Erenburg, I.: 'On re-reading Chekhov', *Chekhov, Stendhal and other essays*, trans. by A. Bostock in collaboration with Y. Kapp, L, 1962.

Ermilov, V. V.: *Dramaturgiya A. P. Chekhova*, M, 1954.

—— *A. P. Chekhov: 1860–1904*, M, 1959.

Fausset, H. l'A.: 'Tchehov as Lover', *The Bookman*, L, 1926, vol. 69, pp. 315–16.

Feider, V. (ed.): *A. P. Chekhov: literaturny byt i tvorchestvo po memuarnym materialam*, LG, 1928.

Fridkes, L. M.: *Opisanie memuarov o Chekhove*, M, 1930.

Garnett, E.: *Chekhov and his Art*, L, 1929.

Geizer, I. M.: *Chekhov i meditsina*, M, 1954.

Gerhardi, W.: *Anton Chekhov: a critical study*, N.Y., 1923.

Gillès, D.: *Tchékhov: ou le spectateur désenchanté*, Paris, 1967.

Gilyarovsky, V. A.: 'Zhizneradostnye lyudi', *Moskva i Moskvichi*, M, 1959, pp. 347–73.

Gitovich, N. I.: *Letopis' zhizni i tvorchestva A. P. Chekhova*, M, 1955.

Golubkov, V. V.: *Masterstvo A. P. Chekhova*, M, 1958.

Golubov, S. N. (ed., with others): *A. P. Chekhov v vospominaniyakh sovremennikov*, M, 1960.

Gorky, M.: *Reminiscences of Tolstoy, Chekhov and Andreyev*, trans. by K. Mansfield, S. S. Koteliansky, L. Woolf, L, 1934.

—— 'A. P. Chekhov', *Chvvs*, pp. 493–511.

Gorky, M.: *Izbrannye Literaturno-kriticheskie Stat'i*, M, 1941.

Gromov, L.: *Realizm A. P. Chekhova vtoroi poloviny 80-kh godov*, Rostov-na-Donu, 1958.

—— 'Rasskaz Chekhova "Ogni" i ego mesto v tvorcheskoi biografii pisatelya', *A. P. Chekhov: sbornik*, Rostov-na-Donu, 1954, pp. 100–30.

Grossman, L.: 'Roman Niny Zarechnoi', *Prometei*, M, 1967, no. 2, pp. 218–89.

Gushchin, M.: *Tvorchestvo A. P. Chekhova*, Khar'kov, 1954.

Hingley, R. F.: *Chekhov: a biographical and critical study*, L, 1950.

—— *The Oxford Chekhov*, vols. 1–3, 5, 6, 8, L, 1964–.

Izmailov, A. A.: *Chekhov 1860–1904: biograficheský nabrosok*, M, 1916.

Jackson, R. L. (ed.): *Chekhov: a collection of critical essays*, New Jersey, 1967.

Jacoby, J.: 'Tchékhov et les Femmes', *Les Œuvres Libres*, Paris, 1960, pp. 21–36.

Kachalov, V. I.: ('Vospominaniya'), *Chvvs*, pp. 443–6.

Katzer, J. (ed.): *A. P. Chekhov: 1860–1960*, trans. by Foreign Languages Publishing House, M, 1960.

Knipper, O. L.: 'The Last Years', *A. P. Chekhov: 1860–1960*, ed. by J. Katzer, M, 1960, pp. 31–55.

—— 'ob A. P. Chekhove', *Chvvs*, pp. 680–702.

Korolenko, V. G.: 'Anton Pavlovich Chekhov', *Chvvs*, pp. 135–48.

Kovalevsky, M. M.: 'Ob A. P.

Chekhove', *Chvvs*, pp. 447–52.

Krolenko, Ya. A. (ed.): *Chekhovsky sbornik: naidennye stat'i i pis'ma; vospominaniya, kritika, bibliografiya*, M, 1929.

Kuprin, A. I.: 'Pamyati Chekhova', *Chvvs*, pp. 539–69.

Kurdyumov, M.: *Serdtse smyatennoe: o tvorchestve A. P. Chekhova*, Paris, 1934.

Ladyzhensky, V. N.: 'V sumerki: iz vospominanii ob A. P. Chekhove', *Chvvs*, pp. 294–306.

Laffitte, S.: *Tchékhov: 1860–1904*, Paris, 1963.

Lakshin, V. A.: *Iskusstvo psikhologicheskoi dramy Chekhova i Tolstogo*, M, 1958.

Lavrin, J.: 'Chekhov and Maupassant', *Slavonic Review*, L, 1926, vol. 5, pp. 1–24.

Lazarev-Gruzinsky, A. S.: 'A. P. Chekhov', *Chvvs*, pp. 151–88.

Leikin, N. A.: 'Iz dnevnika N. A. Leikina', *LN*, pp. 499–510.

Leontiev (Shcheglov), I. L.: 'Iz dnevnika I. L. Shcheglova (Leontieva)', *LN*, pp. 479–98.

Levitan, I. I.: *Vospominaniya i pis'ma*, M, 1950.

Lykiardopoulos, M.: *New Statesman*, L, 1919, vol. 13, pp. 238–9.

Lyskov, I. P.: *Chekhov v ponimanii kritiki*, M, 1905.

Magarshack, D.: *Chekhov: a life*, L, 1952.

—— *Chekhov the Dramatist*, L, 1952.

Malyugin, L. A.: *Nasmeshlivoe moe schast'e*, M, 1965.

Meilakh, B. S.: 'Dva resheniya odnoi temy', *Neva*, LG, 1956, no. 9, pp. 184–8.

Middleton Murry, J.: 'The Humanity of Chekhov', *The Athenaeum*, L, 1920, vol. 152, pp. 299–301.

Nemirovich-Danchenko, Vl. I.: *Iz proshlogo*, M, 1938.

—— 'Chekhov', *Chvvs*, pp. 419–38.

Némirovsky, I.: *A Life of Chekhov*, trans. from the French by E. de Mauny, L, 1950.

Noyes, G. R.: 'Chekhov', *The Nation*, N.Y., 1918, vol. 107, pp. 406–8.

Nevedomsky, M.: 'Bez kryl'ev', *Yubileiny chekhovsky sbornik*, M, 1910, pp. 49–114.

Paperny, Z.: 'K 50-letiyu so dnya smerti A. P. Chekhova: "O lyubvi" ', *Znamya*, M, 1954, vol. 7, pp. 149–65.

—— *A. P. Chekhov: ocherk tvorchestva*, M, 1960.

Patrick, G. Z.: 'Chekhov's attitude towards life', *Slavonic and East European Review*, L, 1932, vol. 10, pp. 658–68.

Paustovsky, K. G.: 'Legkaya pamyat' ', *Khozyaika chekhovskogo doma*, ed. by S. G. Bragin, Simferopol', 1965, pp. 40–9.

Phelps, G.: *The Russian Novel in English Fiction*, L, 1956.

Pokrovsky, V. (ed.): *A. P. Chekhov: ego zhizn' i sochineniya*, M, 1907.

Potapenko, I. N.: 'Neskol'ko let s A. P. Chekhovym', *Chvvs*, pp. 307–63.

Rachmanowa, A.: *Ein Kurzer Tag: das Leben des Arztes und Schriftstellers Anton Pawlowitsch Tschechow*, trans. by Dr. A. von Hoyer, Frauenfeld, 1961.

Rostovstev, A.: *Pevets toski sumerek Anton Chekhov*, SPB, 1904.

Satina, S.: *Education of Women in Pre-Revolutionary Russia*, trans. by A. F. Poustchine, N.Y., 1966.

Saunders, B.: *Tchehov the Man*, L, 1960.

Semanova, M. L.: 'Turgenev i Chekhov', *Uchenye zapiski Leningradskogo pedagogicheskogo instituta imeni A. I. Gertsena*, LG, 1957, vol. 134, pp. 177–223.

—— *Chekhov i sovetskaya literatura*, M, 1966.

Serebrov (Tikhonov), A.: 'O Chekhove', *Chvvs*, pp. 643–57.

Shchepkina-Kupernik, T. L.: *Dni moei zhizni*, M, 1928.

—— 'V yunye gody', in Levitan, pp. 64–6.

Shchukin, S. N.: 'Iz vospominanii ob A. P. Chekhove', *Chvvs*, pp. 453–67.

Sherman, S. P.: *Critical Woodcuts*, N.Y., 1926.

Shestov, L.: *Anton Tchekov and other Essays*, trans. by S. S. Koteliansky and J. M. Murry, Dublin, 1916.

Shishkoff, P.: 'I knew Chekhov', *The Listener*, L, 1938, vol. 20, pp. 927–9.

Simmons, E. J.: *Leo Tolstoy*, L, 1949.

—— *Chekhov: a biography*, Boston, 1962.

Sleptsov, V. A.: *Trudnoe vremya*, M, 1922.

Sobolev, Yu.: *Chekhov*, M, 1930.

Stanislavsky, K. S.: *Moya zhizn' v iskusstve*, M, 1954.

—— 'Chekhov', *Chvvs*, pp. 371–418.

Struve, G.: 'Chekhov in Communist censorship', *Slavonic and East*

European Review, L, 1955, vol. 33, pp. 327–41.

Surkov, E. D. (ed.): *Chekhov i teatr*, M, 1961.

Teplinsky, M. V. (ed.): *A. P. Chekhov: sbornik statei*, Yuzhno-Sakhalinsk, 1959.

Toumanova-Andronikova, N.: *Anton Chekhov: The Voice of Twilight Russia*, L, 1937.

Triolet, E.: *L'Histoire d'Anton Tchékov*, Paris, 1954.

Turkin, M. M.: *A. P. Chekhov i nash krai*, Rostov-na-Donu, 1935.

Veresaev, V. V.: 'A. P. Chekhov', *Chvvs*, pp. 673–6.

Vinogradov, V. V. (ed., with others): *Literaturnoe nasledstvo: Chekhov*, (vol. 68), M, 1960.

Vinogradova, K. M.: 'Stranitsa iz chernovoi rukopisi rasskaza "Dama s sobachkoi"', *LN*, pp. 133–40.

Wilczkowski, C.: 'Un amour de Čechov', *Anton Čechov: 1860–1960*, ed. by T. Eekman, Leiden, 1960, pp. 311–24.

Winner, T.: *Chekhov and his Prose*, N.Y., 1966.

Woolf, L. S. S.: *New Statesman*, L, 1917, vol. 9, pp. 446–8.

Woolf, V.: 'The Russian Point of View', *The Common Reader*, L, 1925, pp. 222–5.

Yakovlev, A. S.: 'A. P. Chekhov: vospominaniya', *LN*, pp. 597–604.

Yavorskaya, L. B.: 'Artisty o Chekhove', *Novosti*, SPB, 31 Aug. 1904, p. 2.

Zaitsev, B.: *Chekhov: literaturnaya biografiya*, N.Y., 1954.

Zankovetskaya, M. K.: 'Iz vospominanii', *LN*, pp. 592–3.

Zola, E.: *Le Docteur Pascal, Œuvres complètes*, Paris, 1927–9, vol. 9.

Zundelovich, Ya. O.: ' "Nevesta" ,' *Trudy uzbekskogo gosudarstvennogo universiteta*, Samarkand, 1957, no. 72, pp. 3–17.

ii. *A. P. Chekhov: sbornik statei*, M, 1910.

Yubileiny chekhovsky sbornik, M, 1910.

Iz arkhiva A. P. Chekhova, M, 1960.

Index

The Notes and References are not included. A few frequently mentioned fictional characters have been listed separately, but page references for them are given under the story or play in which they figure.

LIBRARY
FLORISSANT VALLEY COMMUNITY COLLEGE
ST. LOUIS, MO.

COMPLETED

INVENTORY 1983